3⁰⁰

Art
Objects

Art Objects

THEIR CARE AND PRESERVATION

A HANDBOOK FOR MUSEUMS AND COLLECTORS

Frieda Kay Fall

LAURENCE McGILVERY / LA JOLLA, CALIFORNIA

1973

Originally published 1971 by Boston Book & Art,
Publisher. New material (pages 309-32) added to
this edition.

Library of Congress Catalog Card Number 72-148177
ISBN 0-910938-55-5   trade cloth binding
ISBN 0-910938-56-3   library binding

Manufactured in the United States of America

Contents

CONTENTS

Preface

Museums and private collectors often take the responsibility for the care of a work of art too casually and do not realize the gradual deterioration to a physical object caused by the environment in which we live. Hundreds of years can be removed from its life by neglect and its beauty destroyed by the careless handling of untrained personnel. The author has created this book as a primer for the care and handling of a work of art and has suggested *what not to do*, a feature which distinguishes it from similar published books on the subject.

A private collector or a museum curator is only the custodian of a work of art, and their objective should be to conserve the objects entrusted to them in as static a state as possible in order to be handed down to future generations. In this book, the emphasis has been placed on the consultation and the guidance of a trained conservator for the preservation of an object.

This book should be most useful to private collectors as well as to newcomers in museums. The author's experience as Registrar in a museum has been reflected in many common-sense precautions.

William J. Young, Conservator
Museum of Fine Arts, Boston

Art
Objects

Introduction

From the earliest days of recorded time, man has been a collector. At first he accumulated and stored only those items essential to his existence—food, clothing and weapons. Later, as civilization grew more complex, he began collecting objects which pleased him and those which other men coveted, and those which made his life more comfortable, safe or enviable—jewels, gold, silks, tapestries, arms and armor, sculpture and paintings. Collections became a reflection of culture, refinement, interest, prestige and individual taste. Later, such treasures were exchanged with political and marital alliances or through the fortunes of war.

In time, wealthy collectors found they had collected too many objects and did not have enough space to accommodate them. Their possessions demanded an ever-increasing amount of care. Moved by a spirit of generosity, some private collectors began opening their collections for the public to see and admire. Out of this arose the necessity for buildings to house collections, and these houses became the first museums.

Museums sprang up in every country. Often they were under royal patronage. Soon nations were vying with each other in the elegance and size of their buildings to house treasures and also in impressive ways to display them.

ART OBJECTS

Today, museums exist in great numbers throughout the world. In every museum, regardless of the size or scope of its collections, the story of man and his environment is related through objects, paintings, displays. The responsibility of a museum, then, is to care for, maintain, preserve, study and exhibit those articles which have found their way from many civilizations to residence under one roof.

A museum's primary reason for existence is to protect and hold in trust works which are irreplaceable symbols of esthetic and historical importance. Museums are custodians of man's heritage. Their staff members are obliged to exercise constant care in the handling, storage and exhibition of works of art and to take every precaution to conserve the museum's holdings. Public custodians as well as private collectors are charged with a responsibility to prevent a progression of old damages, to prevent new damages, and to provide a healthy atmosphere for art objects. If this obligation is faithfully and continuously fulfilled, objects of art will continue in a reasonable state of preservation for the enjoyment and education of future generations.

When objects enter a museum, they are seldom in the same condition as when they were created. Through an active technical program, deterioration can be arrested and adverse conditions controlled. In some cases, objects can be restored to their original state. Today, in addition to technological advances, an exchange of knowledge and experience between museums and professional organizations has contributed to the preservation of collections.

Cultural objects must be protected against natural processes of destruction, physical and chemical, and against attacks by organisms. Whatever the condition, they must be handled, moved, stored, exhibited, packed and shipped in special ways, depending on the composition of the object. Generally, the components of art objects may be classified into three groups: 1: Organic material—material of animal or vegetable origin such as parchment, hides, leather, paper, ivory, bone, textiles, hair, fur, feathers, wood, tissues, dyes and basketry. 2. Inorganic

2

materials—metals and their alloys, such as gold, silver, tin, lead, copper, iron and steel; ceramics, bricks and glass. 3. Paintings, both easel and mural. Paintings include some organic substances such as some pigments and almost all binding media. Supports such as canvas, wood, and paper, are organic.

Objects of inorganic material may be regarded as relatively stable. They do not require as much protection as objects of organic origin. It must be emphasized, however, that all objects can suffer from adverse conditions and improper handling. While inorganic matter may be subject to rapid deterioration under improper care, it is organic substances that offer less resistance to decay.

Damage from decay cannot always be prevented, but if the basic construction of materials is understood, and if sources of possible deterioration are known, much can be accomplished to maintain art objects in a reasonably good state of preservation. The condition of an object changes because it breaks, becomes worn or damaged, or because it fades, rots or corrodes. Any of these changes, or any combination of them, can be directly traced to handling (including storage) or environmental climate, or both.

Humidity is responsible for most forms of decay. It provokes mechanical, chemical and biological reactions. Relative humidity (RH) expresses the relationship between the quantity of water present in a given volume of air at a given temperature and the maximum quantity of water which the same volume may contain at the same temperature. The close relation of humidity with surrounding temperature is an important consideration in relation to art objects.

Almost no form of chemical deterioration can take place without water. High relative humidity also creates an ideal situation for the growth of micro-organisms and insects. Objects of organic materials are essentially of a cellular structure. Cells become swollen by increased humidity causing an expansion of the material. Dryness causes the cells to lose their liquid content, making them contract. Water dissolves salts in some ob-

3

jects; in some it crystallizes them, increasing volume and causing increased dryness. Without the presence of water, oxidation of metals would be greatly reduced, as well as migration of soluble salts and discoloration of tissues.

There are differing specifications and a variance of opinions among professionals regarding the desired safe RH range for various types of objects and for the ideal overall building RH range. Plenderleith [1] maintains that picture galleries require a constant relative humidity of 58% at about 63 degrees F. Richard D. Buck has written, "Plenderleith's recommendation is so rigorous as to be almost unattainable in many American climates." Theoretically, most forms of deterioration would be slowed down by complete stabilization of the atmosphere. Many specialists recommend that museums should strive to maintain an RH of about 60% to 65%, based on a "mold formation point" fixed at 70% and the importance of never allowing the RH to be reduced to 50% or below.

Temperature itself is of no real concern except in regard to relative humidity. A rise in temperature reduces the relative humidity; lowering temperature increases relative humidity. The important consideration is to avoid changes, especially abrupt changes. For both hot or damp climates, air must be circulated, the building well ventilated to avoid a stagnation of air. Ideally, all museums should be air conditioned and be humidity controlled; art objects should live in pure, homogenous air. When air conditioning is not feasible, apparatus for measuring temperature and humidity should be provided to record the environment to which the objects are exposed.

An important consideration for the preservation of museum objects is light and its effects. Light is definitely the cause of deterioration of many objects. The intensity of direct sunlight is infinitely stronger than any artificial light. Organic substances are most affected by light. Any specimen composed of organic substances, in whole or in part, offers little resistance to the

1. Plenderleith, H. J., *The Conservation of Antiquities and Works of Art*, London, Oxford University Press, 1956.

damaging effects of light. Inorganic substances, metals and their alloys, are more stable.

Preservation and conservation, as distinguished from restoration, are broad terms referring to the action taken to prevent, arrest or retard deterioration. Restoration refers to the action taken to rehabilitate a damaged work of art and return it to a structurally and esthetically more stable condition. Restorations should be undertaken only by a professional conservator who has a thorough knowledge of the physical behavior and chemical properties of the raw materials; the technology which brought about their creation; all types of deterioration and the causes; and the equipment and techniques necessary for conservation and restoration. He must have acquired an advanced degree of manipulative, investigative and artistic skills, which can be attained only through intensive study and training in laboratory and studio practices. With it all, and above all, a professional art conservator possesses a deep respect for the work of art entrusted to him and for the artist or artisan who created it.

The advanced technical skill of conservators is not the subject of this volume. Repairs, restorations, and the cleaning of art objects should be referred to conservators, but a museum must protect its collections on two fronts. Art museum handlers—preparators, custodians, packers, as well as curators—should be required to keep abreast of developments which contribute to the safety and security of art objects. A general program of training should be required in every museum. There should be frequent appraisals of handling techniques for the re-education of experienced personnel and a program of orientation and conditioning for new personnel.

Conservators are experts on environmental control—humidity and temperature—but they can only be expected to act as advisors. They should be consulted by handlers and curators when a temperature or humidity extreme exists. They offer advice and recommendations so that artificial and natural light will not fade or rot works of art susceptible to the damaging effects of light. All technical questions and operations should be referred to him. He is the authority on all aspects of the care, handling, preservation and restoration of art objects.

Almost everyone has at some time picked up, held, handled, lifted, transferred or touched an object of art. Every home contains pieces which the owner regards with pride because of monetary value, esthetic quality or sentimental attachment, or a combination of them.

To avoid unhappy incidents and conditions which contribute to deterioration requires a knowledge of how objects should be handled and what causes them to deteriorate or change. There is a correct way to handle every art object; there are many incorrect ways.

Obviously, professional conservators cannot do everything. Others must engage in the auxiliary duties relative to works of art. It is for those others, as well as for collectors or any persons interested in preserving their possessions, that this review of handling rules and recommendations has been prepared. It has been generally conceded that even with ideal environment the greatest exposure of objects to damage occurs in the handling and movement of them on the premises.

Much of the contents of this volume will be information already known by experienced museum workers and serious private collectors. For them, as well as for new museum personnel and new collectors, this condensed review should be regarded as a handy reference. It is hoped that even the experienced professional will become more alert to the need of frequent checks of handling techniques and atmospheric environment.

There are certain general rules which apply to the movement and handling of all museum objects. Such rules should be enforced by every museum in combination with specific handling regulations and precautions.

Figure 1. Dr. Benjamin Johnson, head of the Conservation Department at the Los Angeles County Museum of Art, looks on as Dr. Thomas Cairns, chemist in the laboratory, operates a mass spectrograph (MS-702), an instrument used for examination of inorganic materials, such as ceramics, pigments, metals, and stones. It provides qualitative and quantitative analysis with specifically accurate results on trace analysis. *Courtesy, Conservation Department, Los Angeles County Museum of Art.*

Figure 2. Planned action, teamwork, and the part each person would play was outlined before this Tony Smith steel sculpture was installed in a reflecting pond. *Courtesy, Los Angeles County Museum of Art.*

GENERAL RULES FOR CARE
AND HANDLING

Each object in a museum's collection should be considered irre- *Regard all*
placeable. Those who are engaged in the movement, transfer, stor- *museum*
age, packing and installation of art objects should handle each one *objects as*
as if it were the most valuable possession of the museum. Handlers *irreplaceable*
should be made aware that Fine Arts insurance policies include a
clause which states that loss or damage caused by unskilled, unpro-
fessional handling is not covered by the policy. *Collecting from an*
insurance carrier only means payment in cash, not the replacement
of a valuable art object.

Hands should be thoroughly washed just before touching any *Wash hands*
art object, even when gloves are worn. Perspiration damages most
materials. Deposits of perspiration or natural oils from the skin when
combined with dirt or grime can cause damage long after the
deposit has been left. Soft, white cotton gloves are advisable for
handling and moving most museum objects. They must also be clean. *Gloves must*
Frequent changing of gloves is an inexpensive type of insurance. *be clean*

A *No Smoking* rule should be rigidly enforced while working *No smoking*
with museum objects or in the same room with them. Not only is
cigarette smoking a fire hazard but the fumes and smoke leave a
yellow, oily deposit.

Work areas and packing areas must be clean and uncluttered. *Keep work*
Dirt and litter should never be permitted wherever objects are *areas clean*
placed. Regardless of tight exhibition schedules or insufficient staff,
there is no excuse for working in dirty, unorganized areas which
expose valuable objects to danger.

Avoid haste in handling and moving objects. Avoid speed, par- *Avoid haste*
ticularly when moving museum objects on hand trucks or dollies. *and speed with*
No travel shock should be transmitted to museum objects by abrupt *hand trucks*
stops and starts with hand trucks. If rolling a hand truck up or
down an incline is necessary, one or two men should precede the
conveyance to control speed and effect a slow, even descent.

Before any object is moved, know the nature of the material *Know the*
used in its construction and be certain that each helper shares this *object before*
information. Discuss the structural composition of the piece, its *moving*

9

weak and strong elements. For example, when moving a large piece of sculpture or a heavy piece of furniture, one should determine in advance where stress and strain may be safely applied, where no stress should be placed, how the object will be placed on the dolly and exactly how each worker is to assist. Planned action insures safety. The danger in moving any type of valuable object increases with weight, size and unusual shape. Each item should be treated as an individual problem.

Coordinated action insures safety

Know where you are going to move an object and where you will deposit it before you touch it. This rule applies whether you are working alone or with others, whether the object is small or large. As the number of motions is reduced in moving an object, so is the risk of damage. Objects which cannot withstand the ordinary hazards involved in handling and movement should not be exposed to them.

Eliminate unnecessary movements

Always use both hands when carrying a museum object, regardless of size, even if it is to be moved no farther than a foot or two. Never overload or pack any container, carrying device, hand truck or dolly. Risks increase as the number of objects is increased.

Always use both hands

Do not overload carrying devices

Do not put lightweight and heavy objects together in a carrying box or on a hand truck or dolly. No carrying device should have a weight greater than two men can comfortably carry with safety. When more than one object is put into a carrying box, use separation battens, padding, and a shock absorbent material between the pieces.

Line carrying boxes

Boxes should be lined with some kind of cushioning material. The shapes of certain objects demand special cushioning to prevent movement within the box. All padding and cushioning should be resilient. Excelsior is not recommended, but if used, it must be fresh and clean so that its resilience is at a maximum. Do not allow excelsior to come in direct contact with objects; first wrap them with tissue paper.

Use resilient padding

All packing materials should be meticulously searched before discarding. Valuable, irreplaceable fragments have been lost in packing materials. If time does not permit searching through packing material at the time of unpacking, save the container and its packings for perusal later. If breakage should occur, carefully preserve all fragments, no matter how small. Successful reconstruction or

Search packing material

Preserve all fragments

10

restoration depends on the preservation of parts. Carefully check the structural integrity of an object before it is turned over to packers for shipment. *Check the structural integrity*

Do not allow any object to extend beyond the edges of a hand truck or dolly. If prevailing equipment does not permit this rule, adequate devices should be obtained. *Do not allow objects to protrude*

When in doubt about the handling or movement of an art object, consult a conservator-restorer. The life of an art object rests with those who handle it. The greatest exposure to possible damage from human handling occurs within the museum facility. *Consult a conservator when in doubt*

Periodic review of these rules and the specific rules contained in each chapter should be made by museum professionals, museum handlers and others concerned with the care and preservation of art objects.

1

Paintings on Canvas and Wood Panel

There are many kinds of paintings on many different materials. Painting has been done on stone, clay, wood, parchment, metal, leather, glass, ivory, textiles, and other supports. The prehistoric cave paintings at Lascaux, in the hills of southwestern France, were done on stone as long as 17,000 years ago. The paint was probably produced from oxidized minerals mixed with animal fat, water, blood serum, vegetable sugar, and perhaps egg whites.

For adhesion to any support, pigment must be mixed with a binding medium, such as glue, wax, egg, gum, oil, or resin. This discussion will concern mainly paintings on canvas and wood panel.

In the earliest days of recorded civilization, pictures were painted in a particular place for that place. They were not intended to be portable. There were no traveling exhibitions; one had to go to the painting to enjoy it. In those days almost nothing was known about the causes of the decay of picture materials. Today, these causes have multiplied to include modern heating systems; humidity; polluted atmosphere (including smog and smoke); rough, frequent handling; as well as the rigors of transportation by rail, motorized vehicles, airplanes and ships.

12

There is some evidence that until about the seventeenth century paintings were not intended to last indefinitely. They were expected to decay. The number of paintings that have survived are probably few in proportion to the number painted.

In the nineteenth century paintings began to be evaluated critically and concern over their conservation mounted. Methods of preserving art objects were given careful study and consideration. Until about 1850, it was assumed that the care of paintings was the proper responsibility of the artists who painted them. By the middle of the nineteenth century, the artist began to lose technical touch with his medium. No longer required to mix his own paints, he lost contact with the chemical components of paints and varnishes. Rapid technical advances in their manufacture by-passed the artist, leaving him improperly equipped to engage in the conservation of his own works. Indeed, many painter-restorers felt that the whole purpose of conservation was to make an old painting look new. How the artist went about this was not always in the interest of the survival of the painting.

By the end of the nineteenth century, efforts were made to improve methods of preserving paintings. Progress was spasmodic, but it did mark the beginning of what is now a very specialized science.

In 1930 a conference called by the International Museums Office (a division of the League of Nations) was held in Rome to discuss the examination and conservation of works of art. Among other things, the conference concluded that progress in conservation and preservation was being made through the application of scientific investigations, including infrared photography, spectroscopy, chemical and microchemical analyses.

The Rome Centre continues to carry on the work of keeping pace with technological developments. Organizations such as the International Institute for the Conservation of Historic and Artistic Works (IIC) meet regularly, providing leading conservators throughout the world with the opportunity to exchange ideas and report on their individual experiments. Their papers are later published to serve as valuable references.

Before the second quarter of this century, the emphasis was on *repairing* paintings; those engaged in the practice were known as restorers. Obviously, this often was after damages were incurred and had nothing to do with their prevention. Today the care of paintings is called conservation, a highly skilled and technical art. Conservators, who both conserve and restore paintings, are specialists with precise training and experience. They are knowledgeable in both the structural and chemical components of all kinds of works of art and experienced in the use of complex scientific laboratory instruments, which are their tools in the detective work necessary before treatment. Unfortunately, conservators are often kept busier repairing the work of earlier so-called restorers than they are with actual prevention of damage, decay or deterioration.

Painting techniques have changed through the centuries. New techniques are developed constantly. Regardless of technique, the structure of a painting is always a series of layers. Each has its own complexities and properties and is vulnerable to varying kinds of deterioration.

Every painting has a support, usually linen, cotton, or hemp canvas. In order to make the canvas nonabsorbent, first a coat of size is applied. During the Renaissance the Italian painters used gesso, a mixture of glue size and burnt gypsum as a priming for their wooden panels. When properly prepared, it becomes a hard smooth surface with just the right absorbency for paint. Many artists took advantage of this quality, using it as a foundation in preparing the ground for gold leaf.

Paint consists of pigment particles held together by a binding medium. Often a painting has a number of pigmented layers, one on top of the other. After the painting is completed, a layer of varnish (sometimes wax), is usually applied. Cennino Cennini describes this practice in his *Libro dell'Arte*, a famous handbook of the Middle Ages on painting and related arts written between 1397 and 1437. The varnish is intended to even out the reflections of light from the surface. This coating is also important to its protection from atmospheric contaminants.

Ordinary varnish, made of natural resin, conserves its original

14

properties under favorable conditions no longer than twenty to fifty years. Resin follows a slow but persistent course of chemical change, often becoming cloudy, dark and brittle with the passage of time. Dampness affects it so that it loses its elasticity, cracks and ceases to act as a protective layer on paint. When varnish begins to lose its elasticity, the physiochemical transformation may be recognized by a yellowing of the varnish surface. Although Rembrandt was a meticulous craftsman, some of his finest works, such as *The Night Watch*, have yellowed and darkened. Removal of old varnish (cleaning) and revarnishing should be attempted only by conservators.

The quality of the support is also of vital importance. Paintings on wood panel are more sensitive than paintings on canvas. This is particularly true if the panel is very large or composed of thin pieces and painted on one side only. Panel paintings are most easily damaged by careless lifting or moving, and by humidity changes. *Cradling* a panel painting gives it mechanical strength and confines movement during transportation, preventing warping. Cradling is a series of wooden strips rigidly fixed at precise intervals in the same direction along the grain of the wood panel. These strips have slots to accommodate another series of strips of wood in the opposite direction, movable and arranged at the same width intervals and at right angles to the grain of the wood. Many American conservators feel that cradling causes more damage than it prevents.

The advantages of a textile support for oil paintings began to be recognized in the fifteenth century. From the beginning of that century to the present day, canvas has been the principal form of support. Wood wedges (keys) in the corners of the stretcher allow the canvas to be tightened or loosened. A stretched canvas tightens on the frame when it is damp and expands when it is dry.

The older canvas is, the more easily it is torn or punctured. A blow to the back of a canvas can cause cracks in both the ground and the layers of pigment. When the entire canvas fabric becomes so weakened that it is no longer satisfactory as a support, it is sometimes backed with a fresh canvas. This

15

process is called *lining* the canvas or *relining* it. Relining is a repetition of lining, but with relining the first lining must be removed. This process is also a specialized one and should be attempted only by experienced conservators.

Chemists have developed synthetic paints over the past twenty years. They have proved to be so satisfactory that oil paints may become archaic as a medium. Many artists have switched to synthetic paints. In the late 1940's and early 1950's, Jackson Pollock was using synthetic Duco lacquers. The Dutch forger Hans van Meegeren, who painted "Vermeers" and copied other artists' works in the 1930's, mixed old pigments with a synthetic medium. With a simple laboratory test, a conservator can distinguish old oil paint from new, but van Meegeren used an artificial heat-setting, phenol-formaldehyde resin to avoid detection, and his forgeries successfully fooled the experts over a long period of years.

Synthetic paint, sometimes called plastic paint, is made from acrylic and vinyl resins consisting of emulsion polymers. With the evaporation of the water content, the polymers and pigments become a waterproof film. There are certain practical advantages of synthetic paints over oils. Water from the tap is used instead of turpentine or stand oil. It is odorless and non-toxic. It dries in minutes and colors change little in the drying process. When thoroughly dry, a synthetic paint, even with an impasto of up to three-quarters of an inch, can be bent or rolled up without cracking or buckling. These new paints are virtually fadeproof. Laboratory tests equivalent to forty-five years of direct sunlight have not caused any fading. Of all the technical developments and innovations in the long history of painting, perhaps synthetic paint will prove to be the most revolutionary in blazing new paths for artists to explore.

Meanwhile, old paintings and all nonsynthetic paintings must be preserved and cared for. If it were possible to keep them free of dirt, free from atmospheric changes and mold, and free from any handling or movement, they would experience little deterioration of organic or inorganic components.

16

RULES FOR CARE AND HANDLING

Never touch the surface of a painting for any reason. The "touch complex" is harmful to paintings and all other art objects. *Do not touch*

It is advisable to wear white cotton gloves while handling paintings and their frames. Even with gloves, hands should be thoroughly washed first. Perspiration can damage frames as well as paintings. The importance of wearing clean gloves cannot be too strongly stressed. Soiled gloves cause almost as much damage as soiled hands. *Wash hands and wear gloves*

The image (front) of a painting is obviously the most valuable side of the canvas, but it is also important that the back side of the canvas not be touched. Weakness in paint structure can develop into more serious conditions if pressure is exerted from the back side. This is especially true with thick impasto. All paintings on canvas should be protected with a heavy cardboard or beaverboard backing which should not be screwed tightly to the four sides. This would prevent expansion or contraction on a spring-loaded stretcher. Stretchers which are keyed at the corners also expand and contract, making it difficult to reinsert screws into earlier holes. *Avoid pressure on the back side of a canvas* *Do not screw backing tightly*

Examine a painting before assuming any responsibility for its movement. Examine its frame. Look for old and new damages. Look for conditions which may become progressive. Know what to look for. *Examine before moving*

Notations of conditions, old and new, should be written down, and the conditions should be brought to the attention of a conservator. Written condition inspection reports are extremely valuable. Photographic records of conditions are important but they should illustrate, not replace, written reports. *Record conditions*

Museum personnel involved in the handling and movement of paintings are not always trained in the procedures involved in making a professional condition inspection nor in recording findings with the professional nomenclature used to define and describe specific conditions. Nevertheless, a written record in any terms can aid a professional or conservator in thoroughly diagnosing conditions at a later time. It is important that any new or changing *Records aid diagnosis*

17

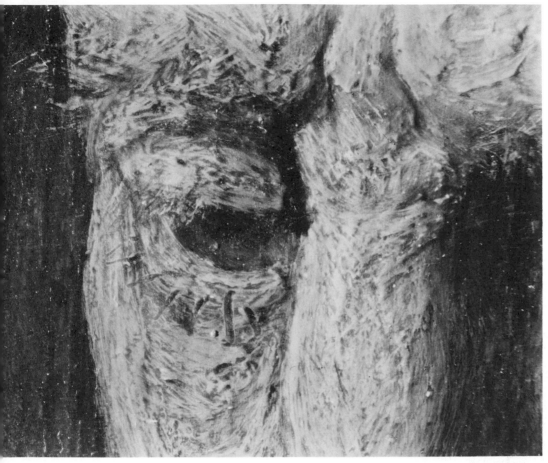

Figure 3. 1. PORTRAIT OF HIS FATHER. Rembrandt, Dutch, 1606-1669. Oil
on canvas. The dark film of old varnish, which obscures many paintings by this great master, has been removed from this portrait to
reveal Rembrandt's skillful handling of light and distinctive brush
strokes. 2. Raking light macrophotograph (magnification 6x) of eye
clarifies Rembrandt's technique of outlining the eyelashes in the wet
impasto with the end of his brush. *Courtesy, Research Laboratory,
Museum of Fine Arts, Boston.*

Figure 4.

Figure 5.

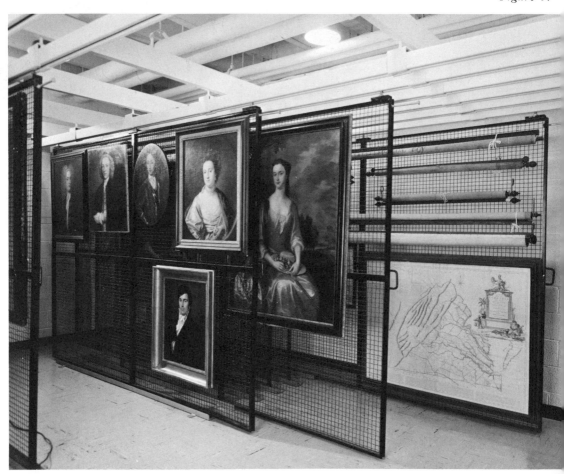

Figure 4. THE LAST SUPPER. Hans van Meegeren, Dutch, 1889-1947. Oil on canvas. The Dutch forger van Meegeren painted "Vermeers," such as this one, which fooled the experts by using an artificial heat-setting phenolformaldehyde resin. *Courtesy, Research Laboratory, Museum of Fine Arts, Boston.*

Figure 5. Storage Room for Paintings. Heavy gauge metal partitions on overhead tracks travel in floor channels. "S" hooks are used to hang paintings onto the wire partitions. Both sides of the partitions may be used. *Courtesy, Colonial Williamsburg Foundation.*

Figure 6. FRANCESCO D'ESTE. Rogier van der Weyden, Flemish, 1400-1464. Tempera and oil on wood. In this aloof portrait with reserved color and strange, cramped fingers, one sees to perfection the clarity and refinement of the Flemish technique, which lends itself so well to the depiction of minute detail. The fact that the modern process of oil painting developed out of this method of painting should be noted. *Courtesy, The Metropolitan Museum of Art.*

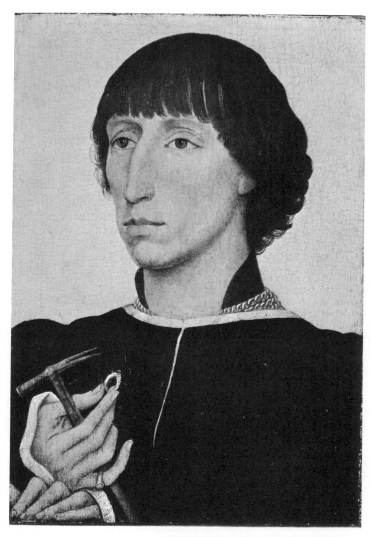

Figure 6.

Figure 7. 1. A shipping crate being equipped with inner bracings for shipment of a large painting; 2. Corner pads protect frames at their most vulnerable points, especially ornate frames; 3. Never use less than six metal straps if the painting is as large as 16″ x 20″. A painting, 17″ x 19″, was secured in this frame when it was shipped by only four straps. During transit one became detached from the frame. The liner at the top of the frame was broken, loosening the painting in the frame. Motion during transit and handling caused the other straps to loosen, endangering the painting. Excess wire left on the frame wound onto itself, creating another hazard. *Courtesy, Los Angeles County Museum of Art.*

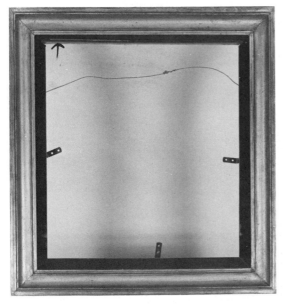

3.

2.

Figure 8.

Figure 9.

new
paint
film}

new
gesso}

old paint
and varnish
film}

old gesso}

1.
2.

3.

4.

Figure 10.

Figure 8. This portrait of a lady arrived at the Boston Museum purportedly as a fifteenth-century Florentine work. Spectro-chemical analysis proved portrait to be a forgery by presence of titanium white which was not known until 1920. *Figure 9.* Cross section of paint indicates painting was built up on an old panel. Note old and new layers of gesso. *Figure 10.* Cross section showing layers of paint in a fifteenth-century Florentine painting: 1. old varnish layer; 2. white lead and verdigris; 3. original ground; 4. original panel. *Courtesy, Research Laboratory, Museum of Fine Arts, Boston.*

1.

2.

3.

4.

5.

Figure 11. SIBYL. Ribera, Spanish, 1588-1656. Oil on canvas. Successive stages in the treatment of a seventeenth-century oil painting by the Conservation Center, Los Angeles County Museum appear in: 1. normal photograph before treatment; 2. ultraviolet photograph, showing darker area of late nineteenth-century overpainting in the lower-left corner, which is to be removed and retouched; 3. detail showing child's head hidden under repainted area; 4. normal photograph of stage after old varnish and retouching has been removed and painting relined, showing paint losses filled in, prior to repainting; 5. normal photograph of final stage with varnish and losses inpainted (cf. lighting of head and drapery of old woman with original state). The dramatic revelation of the child's head has aroused question as to the correct title. *Courtesy, San Diego Fine Arts Gallery.*

Figure 12. SCENES FROM THE LIFE OF ST. GEORGE. Triptych, School of Catalonia, late 14th century. Tempera on wood panel. 1. A ⅜″ paint loss, other small losses, and general cracking of paint surface due to the vertical warping of the wood panel. 2. Paint losses along bottom edge and a minute paint loss (on horse's leg) with surrounding lifting of paint, also caused by warping. *Courtesy, Los Angeles County Museum of Art.*

1.

2.

Figure 13.

Figure 14.

Figure 13. LE GIAOUR ET LE PACHA. Eugene Delacroix, French, 1798-1863. Oil on canvas. During the nineteenth century, there was a breakdown in the workshop tradition, and painters like Delacroix no longer ground their own pigments. He experimented with glazes and scrumbles which at first yield a brilliant, enamel-like effect but quickly darken and become brittle, producing a network of fine cracks through the bravura brushstrokes. *Courtesy, Fogg Art Museum, Harvard University.*

Figure 14. THE RAPE OF EUROPA. Titian, Venetian, 1488/90-1576. Oil on canvas.

The Venetian School excelled in the manipulation of various oils to make possible a freer expression, richer color, atmospheric effects, greater solidity, and more complex spatial organization. Direct oil is peculiarly adaptable, like clay with the sculptor, to spontaneous expression. Titian is perhaps the greatest exponent and in this superb work demonstrates his facility in handling pigment to create a magnificent surface. His loose, impressionistic, suggestive brushwork imparts a sparkle never before seen in painting. (Compare tempera technique in Paolo Uccello's *Lady of Fashion*.) *Courtesy, Isabella Stewart Gardner Museum.*

1.

2.

Figure 15. Museum technicians removing a large oil painting on canvas from a museum wall: 1. The painting is rolled for shipment; 2. The rolled, wrapped painting is being lifted into a shipping case. *Courtesy, Los Angeles County Museum of Art.*

condition of a painting be noted in writing and the report be dated. These notes later may become an important clue to other conditions which developed or progressed after the report was made.

Just to be aware of a condition of a painting or frame is not enough. To call attention to conditions verbally is not sufficient. Conditions must be recorded, dated and made a part of the record of a painting.

When inspecting frames, look for old breaks, scratches, gouges, points of weakness, open miters, repairs, gilt and gesso losses, abrasions and nicks.

Damages to frame

Never carry a frame by its top or by one side, even if it appears to be in good condition. Do not carry an unframed painting by the top or any one side of the stretcher. Always carry frames and stretchers with one hand at the bottom supporting it and one hand at a side. Handling a painting or frame in this way eliminates undue pressure and strain and balances the weight. If a painting is large enough to require two men to carry it, each man should have one hand at a bottom corner and the other hand at one side and towards a top corner.

Carry frames and stretchers with two hands

Before moving a painting, make sure it is secure in its frame. This should be determined when the painting and frame are inspected for conditions. A painting should not be moved until it has been secured in the frame.

Check security in frame

A painting should never be fastened into a frame with nails. Hammering nails moves the painting unnecessarily and usually causes damages to paint surface. Metal straps are recommended for securing paintings into frames. One end of a strap is screwed into the frame and the other end screwed to the stretcher or panel. The use of these straps is a simple but permanent method of securing a picture into a frame. Straps are a security measure for both painting and frame since the two are fastened together with screws. The use of screws eliminates the danger of hammer blows. Paintings and frames must never be subjected to the shock of a hammer.

Never use nails

Never hammer

The number of straps for maximum security and safety depends on the size of the frame and painting. Paintings no larger than 16"x20" require six straps, two each on the long sides and one each on the short sides. It is a good rule never to use less than six straps unless the painting is smaller than 8"x10". Metal straps are available in a number of sizes from most hardware and variety stores and

Use metal straps

31

Bend straps from art supply stores. These straps are easily bent so they can be adjusted to conform to stretcher and frame contours.

Check stretcher keys When inspecting the security of a stretcher in a frame, check the stretcher keys. See if any keys are loose. Check to see if any are missing. Only a professional or a conservator should key a painting. Keying is the adjustment of stretcher keys by tightening them or loosening them. Inserting and tightening keys must be done without shock to the painting. If keys are pushed in too far, the canvas becomes excessively taut which may be harmful to the painting; *Expansion-bolt or spring-loaded stretchers* if the canvas is too loose, the painting becomes damaged. Expansion-bolt or spring-loaded stretchers are recommended. Adjustment of the bolts accomplishes the same tightening or loosening of the canvas as keys but without the use of a hammer.

Remove screw eyes, hooks, and excess wire Screw eyes, wires and hooks can cause serious damage to paintings. If wire is used for hanging a picture, never allow excess lengths of the wire to remain. Winding an excess of wire onto itself is just as great a hazard as letting it hang loose. If there is too much wire, cut it off. A spool of picture wire is inexpensive. The repair of a scratched or punctured painting is not inexpensive. Screw eyes, wires and hooks should be removed from frames before paintings are stored, moved, packed or transported. Unless a painting is to be reinstalled almost immediately, screw eyes, wires and hooks should be removed as soon as the painting is removed from exhibition.

Stack paintings facing outward with separation boards Paintings actually should not be stacked. Lack of space compels most museums to stack at least a part of their paintings collections. When they are stacked, each painting should be separated with a sheet of corrugated board or similar material. The separation sheets should be several inches larger than the outermost frame projection. It is safer to stack paintings with the paint surface facing outward, provided separation sheets are used between each one. The last painting in the stack should have a separation sheet placed over it so that its surface is protected.

Stacking simple frames Very simple frames with flat projections and strip frames may be safely stacked alternating them back-to-back and face-to-face. Picture frame moldings with flat outer surfaces, made of raw wood, slightly painted wood, or wood which has been varnished or washed with a color, may sometimes be stacked against each other without protective dividers.

Paintings which are not hanging should rest on a cushioning

material unless the floor is carpeted. This applies to gallery areas, storage area floors, bins, hand trucks, dollies and the beds of motorized vehicles. Pieces of wood covered with scraps of carpeting have proved to be successful. Furniture pads or blankets can be used. Foam rubber provides good cushioning. Many museums have found that the quilted, rubberized padding manufactured as household rug and carpeting padding is reasonably inexpensive, provides the right resilience, and will not slip on the floor. Rubberized kneeling pads sold for household use are excellent for this purpose. *Paintings should rest on a cushioning material*

Foam rubber

Household kneeling pads

No matter how small, never move or carry more than one painting at a time. A large painting should always be carried by two men, regardless of its weight. Serious accidents have occurred because someone thought he could carry a large painting by himself and needed no help *Move one at a time*

Hand trucks for moving pictures should be at least two-thirds the height of the largest painting on the truck. No painting, including its frame, should be allowed to extend beyond the edges of the hand truck. Two men should always accompany a loaded hand truck, even if there is only one painting on it. This rule should be established in every museum and it should be enforced. The only exception to the rule is based on three rigid requirements: the floor must be level, the truck must be equipped with swivel wheels at one end, and the paintings must be secured to the truck. *Hand trucks*

Provide adequate manpower

Paintings sometimes are so large that the only possible way to ship them or move them is to remove the canvas from the stretcher and roll it. This is never a very happy situation but it is sometimes necessary. The rolling of a canvas without damage to the painting is a very specialized procedure. The exact sequence of steps involved in the rolling of a large canvas should be reviewed, discussed and agreed upon by those who are to participate in the rolling. Each person should know exactly what he is to do and what part the others will play before the operation begins. Coordination of action is important. A sheet of clear polyethylene should be placed next to the paint surface. For support use a rigid drum of light wood or strong fiberboard. It should be as large in diameter as possible and several inches longer at each end than the painting. With the painting side out, roll it very slowly, making sure that the sheet of polyethylene rolls with the painting. In the process, the inner surface is squeezed and the outer surface is stretched. The greater the *Rolling paintings for shipment*

Use clear polyethylene next to paint surface

Roll around a drum with the painting side out

33

diameter of the drum, the less squeezing and stretching. If paint is squeezed it causes wrinkles and chipping; if stretched, the paint cracks. When unrolled and laid flat, cracks usually minimize and become hairlines or disappear entirely. Unrolling should be done as soon as possible.

Do not tie   When the rolling of a painting has been completed, it should be wrapped in waterproof paper and sealed. *Do not tie a rolled painting with string, cord or rope.* This pulls the canvas and polyethylene sheet unevenly tighter and results in damage to both the painted surface and the canvas.

Backing protects from dirt, blows, and marks   A backing protects a painting. It keeps dirt out to a degree, and it wards off blows to the back side of the canvas which could damage the painted surface. A backing prevents the application of labels directly to the back of a canvas and marking or writing on the reverse side of the canvas. Unless the backing is strong and firm it is practically useless. Attach a backing with screws long enough to hold into the stretcher or frame but short enough so that they do not penetrate the canvas or the front of the frame.

Do not apply tapes, labels, or adhesives   Never apply any kind of tape, label or adhesive to the face of a canvas or to the back side of it. This rule also applies to the front and side surfaces of frames. Gold and silver leaf on a frame, for example, can be totally removed where adhesives have been in contact with them. Any kind of adhesive discolors gilt, gold and silver leaf, as well as most other finishes of picture-frame moldings.

Keep work areas and equipment clean   Before beginning any operation with paintings, be sure working areas are clean. If they are littered, clean them. Never use a hand truck until it has been swept clean or vacuumed. All equipment, tables, benches and floors should be free of dirt, nails, brads, screw eyes, wire, tools, and other debris.

Save pigment particles from losses   If losses of pigment occur during handling or packing of a painting, collect all particles, no matter how minute. They should be placed in an envelope and the envelope documented, giving the date of the damage, title of the painting and the artist and museum number, and when and where the paint losses were collected, describing the circumstances. The envelope and notations should be signed.

Search packing material before discarding   Never discard any packing material until it has been searched. If there is not time when the unpacking is done, save the packing material until it can be searched. Valuable elements of frames and

34

paint have been lost because the packing case and packing materials were discarded before they were searched. Even small paintings have been discarded in packing materials.

If there is any loose flaking paint, the painting should be carried in a horizontal position to prevent flakes from becoming detached and the loss of loose particles of paint. Storage of paintings with flaking should be in a horizontal position until a conservator begins his work.

Store paintings with flaking in horizontal position

Changes in atmospheric humidity, especially sudden changes, cause paintings on wood panels to warp. Atmospheric changes cause wood to alternately absorb and give up moisture. This causes expansion and contraction across the grain of the wood, resulting in warping. When paintings on wood panels are found to be cupped, this condition usually has been brought about by an atmosphere that was too dry. Cradling is used to correct such a condition, since it confines stresses to one plane.

Atmospheric changes cause warping

Cradling confines stresses to one plane

Generally, paintings should be kept in an atmosphere of circulating air with a relative humidity of about 55% at 63 degrees fahrenheit as an ideal to aim at.

Recommended RH

BIBLIOGRAPHY

Agrawal, O. P. *An Introduction to Preservation of Paintings.* Baroda, India, University of Baroda, 1969.

Boskovits, Miklos. *Early Italian Panel Paintings.* Budapest, Corvina Press, 1967.

Bowness, Alan. *Contemporary British Painting.* New York, Frederick A. Praeger, 1968.

Bradley, M. C., Jr. *Treatment of Pictures.* New York, Cosmos Press, Inc., 1950.

Buck, Richard D. "The Use of Moisture Barriers in Panel Paintings," *Studies in Conservation,* Vol. 6 (1961).

Constable, W. G. *The Painter's Workshop.* New York, Oxford University Press, 1954.

Coremans, P., Gettens, R. J. and Thissen, J. "La Technique des Primitifs Flamands, Etude Scientifique des Materiaux de la Structure et de la Technique Picturale," *Studies in Conservation,* Vol. 1, no. 1 (1952), pp. 1-29.

Feller, Robert, Jones, Elizabeth H., and Stolow, Nathan. *On Picture Varnishes and Their Solvents.* Oberlin, Ohio, Intermuseum Conservation Association, 1959.

35

Gettens, Rutherford J. "Preliminary Report on the Measurement of the Moisture Permeability of Protective Coatings," *Technical Studies in the Field of Fine Arts*, Vol. 1 (1932), pp. 63-68.

———— and Stout, George L. *Painting Materials, A Short Encyclopaedia.* New York, Van Nostrand Co., 1942.

Heaton, Noel. *Outlines of Paint Technology.* 3rd ed. London, Charles Griffin & Co., Ltd., 1948.

Hendy, Philip. "Taste and Science in the Presentation of Damaged Pictures," *Problems of the 19th & 20th Centuries, Studies in Western Art*, Acts of the Twentieth International Congress of The History of Art, Vol. IV (1963), pp. 139-145.

Hiler, Hilaire. *Notes on the Technique of Painting.* New York, Watson-Guptill Publications, Inc., 1968.

Keck, Caroline K. *A Handbook on the Care of Paintings for Historical Agencies and Small Museums.* Madison, Wis., The American Association for State and Local History, 1965.

————. *How to Take Care of Your Pictures.* New York, The Museum of Modern Art and the Brooklyn Museum, 1954.

Keck, Sheldon. "The Care of Paintings," *Brooklyn Museum Bulletin*, Vol. X, no. 3; reprint from *New York History*, January, 1953.

Laurie, A. P. *The Painter's Methods and Materials.* Philadelphia, J. B. Lippincott Co., 1926.

Minich, A. and Goll, M. "Mould Growth on Painted Surfaces," *Paint Technology*, Vol. 17 (1952).

Novak, Barbara. *American Painting of the Nineteenth Century.* New York, Frederick A. Praeger, 1969.

Pars, H. H. *Pictures in Peril.* Trans. by Katherine Talbot. New York, Oxford University Press, 1957.

Prown, Jules. *American Painting from Colonial Times to the Armory Show.* Vols. I, II. New York, World Publishing Co., 1969.

Reade, Sir Herbert. *A Concise History of Modern Painting.* New York, Frederick A. Praeger, 1969.

Richmond, Leonard. *Fundamentals of Oil Painting.* New York, Watson-Guptill Publications, Inc., 1970.

Rorimer, James J. *Ultra-Violet Rays and Their Use in the Examination of Works of Art.* New York, The Metropolitan Museum of Art, 1931.

Ruheman, Helmut. *The Cleaning of Paintings.* London, Faber & Faber, Ltd., 1969.

————. *The Cleaning of Paintings: Problems and Potentialities.* New York, Frederick A. Praeger, 1968.

Smyth, C. H., et. al. *Aesthetic and Historical Aspects of the Presentation of Damaged Pictures.* Princeton, New Jersey, Princeton University Press.

Stevens, W. C. "Rates of Change in the Dimensions and Moisture Content of Wood Panels," *Studies in Conservation*, Vol. VI (1961), pp. 21-25.

Stout, George L. and others. *The Care of Wood Panels.* Paris, UNESCO, 1955.

Taubes, Frederic. *Better Frames for Your Pictures.* New York, The Viking Press, 1970.

UNESCO, "The Care of Paintings," *Muesum,* Vol. III, nos. 2-3 (1950); Vol. IV, no. 1 (1951).

2

Watercolors

Watercolor is essentially a simple process in which the only necessary components are a layer of paint and a support. The pigment is mixed with a water soluble medium which dilutes it and evaporates after the paint is applied to the support. During the Middle Ages in Europe, when manuscript illumination was the painter's chief means of expression, the medium used was generally egg white and the common support was parchment; since then, the usual medium in the West has been gum arabic (which derives from the acacia) and the standard support, paper. Throughout the ages, watercolor has been employed by artists to achieve a swift, glowing effect, whether as an end in itself or as a step toward a more laborious work in oil painting or sculpture.

In addition to their esthetic charm, watercolors have proved to have a remarkable permanence; an incredible number of magnificent examples have been beautifully preserved. We find aqueous paint in prehistoric cave paintings, and it was used by the ancient Egyptians to decorate the walls of tombs, mummy cases, and papyrus scrolls. It is the process in which the greatest triumphs of Chinese and Japanese painters have been executed.

After the development of oil painting in the fifteenth century and the invention of the printing press in Europe (with the subsequent change in the entire character of the book), watercolor was relegated to a subsidiary role, primarily for sketching or tinting drawings. However, the eighteenth century saw a revival of interest in England which culminated in the remarkable achievements of J. M. W. Turner and J. S. Cotman in the early nineteenth century. In America, a burst of activity in the first half of the twentieth century followed the magnificent examples by Winslow Homer (1836-1910), John Singer Sargent (1856-1925), Mary Cassatt (1845-1926), and William Glackens (1870-1938). Today, watercolor, once regarded condescendingly as the stepsister of oil painting, has regained its leading place in the painter's equipment.

There are two main types of watercolor, transparent and opaque, although they are sometimes combined. When used with skill and invention, transparent watercolors possess a fresh, luminous quality not found elsewhere. The surface texture is practically that of the paper ground, since watercolor is thinly and often sparingly applied. The light ground shining through the translucent paint contributes to the character of the work.

Opaque watercolor, or gouache, differs from transparent watercolor in that the pigments are mixed with white body color, generally lead white until the middle of the nineteenth century and zinc white thereafter. Since its comparatively thick impasto prevents reflection from the ground through the paint, what it gains in opacity it loses in sparkle and luminosity. However, it does have the advantage of allowing alterations to be made more easily and has a delicate quality of its own, which approaches the sensuous charm of the pastel.

For added strength, the original support of a watercolor is often mounted on cardboard or linen, and this support, as well as the actual support of paper, should have some size incorporated into it to prevent soaking up the paint like a blotter. The danger of perspiration on the support from fingers cannot be minimized, since any trace of grease affects the bind between the paint and the support. Also, the absorbency of the support exercises considerable effect on the appearance of the watercolor. Parchment, for example, which is only slightly absorbent, is particularly suitable for precise and delicate detail, but it is liable to break and detach the color layer if bent. This condition can be observed wherever illuminated manuscripts have been negligently handled and not kept flat.

For good adhesion between support and paint layer, works on heavy, absorbent paper have proved their resiliency with time. The medium penetrates it and yields a softer, airier result than on thin, smooth, close-textured paper. Of vital significance for preservation, the more supple support is a safeguard against separation of the color layer.

One advantage of both transparent and opaque watercolor over oil is that they are quick drying, so that the painter does not have to wait a long interval between applications. On the other hand, his stroke must be swift and sure, and each part of the painting must be final with the first touch. Mastery of the medium is thus more demanding than oil paints, if for no other reason than that rapid application is essential. Oil paints may be applied again and again, colors on top of colors, whereas any reworking makes transparent watercolors appear muddy and dull.

Two disadvantages are the paper support, which is subject to damage and disintegration, and the medium itself, which is limited in the range of pigments which are stable in watercolor. For example, indigo, once much in favor, oxidizes and turns brown when exposed to the atmosphere. If such works are to endure, this aspect of the craft must be respected and its basic weaknesses recognized. The reason that the colors in illuminated miniatures have retained their freshness and brightness is that, whether by design or chance, they have been locked away in portfolios at monasteries, and thus protected from light and air. As for pigments which can be safely used in watercolor, recent research has confirmed their physical properties.

Although today watercolors come ready mixed in tubes and it is no longer necessary to break an egg or hand-grind pigment, the basic procedures are not radically different from the early works, and the aim of the watercolorist is still spontaneity and luminosity. Whether a realist or abstractionist, the technique it-self enforces breadth of treatment on all practitioners.

Figure 16. HEAD OF A BEARDED MAN. Emil Nolde, German, 1867-1956.
Watercolor. This powerful head demonstrates why the watercolor
medium has been employed by artists through the ages to achieve
a swift, glowing effect, whether as an end in itself or as a step toward
a more laborious work in oil or sculpture. In the hands of the German
Expressionist master, its full range is exploited—from transparent
washes to opaque contour lines. The light ground shining through
the translucent pigment contributes to the character of the work.
Courtesy, Fogg Art Museum, Harvard University.

1.

2.

Figure 18. Glazed watercolor, preparation for shipment. The glass is protected with strips of masking tape laid on in alternate directions. A mat of charcoal urethane, cut to size, is set into place to fill the void between an outer fabric-covered frame and its elevated gold leaf frame liner. A solid piece of urethane further protects both frame, glass, and watercolor. *Courtesy, Los Angeles County Museum of Art.*

Figure 17. Painted Limestone Stela from Meseika. Egyptian, First Intermediate Period, ca. 2300 B.C.: 1. a detail of lower part of stela, normal light on panchromatic plate; 2. detail of lower part of stela, ultra-violet light. Examined under the lamp, certain details which were formerly invisible have become apparent. In this instance traces of paint used in the inscriptions and figures have reacted to the rays differently from the bare limestone. For example, Egyptian green paint, which has a copper base and fades easily, is especially strong in its reaction to ultra-violet light. *Courtesy, Museum of Fine Arts, Boston.*

Figure 19. Flatford Mill. John Constable, English, 1776-1837. During the late eighteenth century, the use of transparent watercolor became more complicated. To attain this effect of glowing light, Constable builds up his work in a series of layers. Further washes define details and add touches of varying sharpness and depth of tone. *Figure 20.* Under the Cocoanut Palm. Winslow Homer, American, 1836-1910. Watercolor. The father of the American school of watercolorists, Homer epitomizes the full range and vividness of the medium, employing single transparent washes at full strength and leaving tiny areas of the support uncovered to produce additional sparkle. *Courtesy, Fogg Art Museum, Harvard University.*

Figure 20.

Figure 21. PAINTED CEDAR WOOD COFFIN OF DJEHUTY-NEKHT (detail).
From Bersheh in Upper Egypt, Dynasty XII, ca. 1860 B.C. Harvard-
Boston Expedition. Easel painting was unknown in ancient Egypt,
but the paintings on the side of the Bersheh coffin are similar in conception and execution. They were executed on a small scale with a
free brush technique, with which the artist portrayed the most subtle
shading and exquisite detail. A painter of unusual ability lavished
special care on the inner faces, and the minutely executed elements
of the false door retain the brilliant freshness and enamel-like quality
of miniature painting, against the soft brown tones of the cedar wood
background. *Courtesy, Museum of Fine Arts, Boston.*

RULES FOR CARE AND HANDLING

Most watercolor paintings are on paper, which by its very nature is subject to damage and deterioration. Works of art on paper are probably the most vulnerable of all museum objects to serious damage from light, atmospheric conditions, insects and handling. *Damage to paper*

Direct sunlight, even reflected rays from the sun, and high intensity fluorescent light, all cause fading of colors. Watercolors which have suffered from exposure to strong illumination can seldom be totally restored to their original luminosity and brilliance. Pigments fade and paper becomes brittle from exposure to the sun or strong incandescent lamplight, and this process is more rapid if the paper is not of good quality. Direct sunlight also affects high-grade paper, as well as the pigments on it. The rate of damage is simply slower with better grades of paper. *Fading* *Exposure to light*

Pulp paper, which is made from wood fibers, should never be allowed to come into contact with a watercolor on paper or with any other work on paper. Paper made from wood fibers, ground or separated with chemicals, is the poorest and the cheapest quality. If it is allowed to remain in contact with a good quality of rag paper, the better paper will become discolored by acids in the low-grade paper. Paper takes on the grain of the wood in the form of discoloration when allowed contact with it. For this reason wood should never be used as a backing when framing a picture. *Pulp paper* *Wood discolors*

Mats for watercolors must be made of high-quality rag-content matboard. Watercolors should never be pasted to mats or matboard. They should be hinged, as prints are hinged. Hinging affixes the watercolor to a piece of matboard (the backing or mount) so that the painting can be viewed through the window opening of a mat and will stay in place. The mount also protects the picture from handling and creasing. Mat and backing should be of the same size. The size of the painting determines the number of hinges. Hinges should always be made of Japanese or Chinese rice paper, a tough-fibered paper which will not exceed the thickness or strength of the paper on which the watercolor is painted. *Rag paper for mats* *Backings and mounts protect*

When rematting watercolors, always remove the painting from *Rematting* its mount by lifting the mount *from* the painting, never the painting from the mount. Backing mounts protect the reverse of the watercolor. Mats offer a degree of protection, but the image is exposed by the window opening.

Right and wrong adhesives

Do not use rubber cement or any synthetic adhesive to affix a watercolor to its mat. They all leave indelible stains. Correct matting and mounting is a precise operation extremely important for the preservation of the work. The kind of adhesive used is even more important. The only adhesive which should ever be used with a work on paper is a rice or wheat-flour paste. Never use any other kind. Prepare it just before using it.

Always frame with a mat

Never frame a watercolor without a mat. Do not permit a watercolor to be framed with the painting directly against glass or plexiglass. Direct contact with glazing eventually leaves an impression of the painting on the glass or plexiglass, which means that a part of the original image has been lost.

Do not use pressure-sensitive tapes or water-soluble tapes with watercolors or with any work on paper. All commercial tapes are damaging. Many cause irreparable damage.

Never use scotch or other tapes

Never use scotch tape with a work of art on paper. Scotch tape is probably the most damaging of all commercial tapes. It stains paper and can never be successfully removed without taking a part of the paper with it. The longer it remains on paper, the greater the stain and damage.

Paper clips and staples

Paper clips and staples should never be used on watercolors or other works on paper. Any metal device is damaging. If paintings are received with staples or paper clips attached, remove them immediately. Rust, or oxidation, discolors paper and is difficult to deal with if it has been allowed to remain for a long time. Extreme care is necessary when removing staples, especially if the paper is old and fragile. Do not use a staple remover.

Lift by two upper corners

When picking up an unframed, unmatted watercolor, lift it by its two upper corners, never in any other way.

The safest way to carry unframed, unmatted watercolors, as well as those matted, is in specially designed portfolios or boxes, holding the container flat. If boxes or portfolios are not available, each one should be carried separately on a piece of clean rag matboard. The matboard should be larger by several inches than the watercolor.

Wash hands

Always wash the hands before handling unframed works,

48

whether matted or unmatted. Damp or sticky hands leave damaging deposits. Even if smudges from hands are not visible, they will eventually appear.

Do not allow hands to come into direct contact with watercolors. Oils, secretions, and residue from unwashed hands can mar a painting, sometimes beyond successful restoration. Never handle watercolors unnecessarily. Protect mats by having clean hands.

For maximum protection, watercolors should be framed as soon as possible. Mats should be thick enough to keep the paintings from touching the glass or plexiglass. Mats usually enhance a watercolor painting, but if a mat is not used, strips of rag matboard should be laid into the rabbet of the frame to prevent contact between picture and glazing. *Use thick mats*

Framing protects the picture from dirt and damage by handling, but temperature and humidity must always be controlled. Changes in temperature can cause condensation on the glass, which affects both pigment and paper and increases vulnerability to microbiological activity. *Temperature and humidity*

If not framed, small watercolors should be stored in Solander boxes, map cabinets, or any cabinet with shallow drawers. They should be matted before storing. Each one should have sheets of acid-free tissue paper laid over the entire mat, not just the window of the mat, to protect the picture; mats should also be protected. Sheets of rag paper, rag matboard, or glassine paper may be used between the pictures. If not stored in Solander boxes or drawers, use separation sheets. *Storage of framed or matted works*

Before storing framed watercolors, remove all screw eyes, wires, and hooks. Wire and metal hardware scratch the glass, plexiglass, and adjacent frames. *Screw eyes, wires, and hooks*

Framed works stacked in storage should be separated with pieces of board. These separation sheets should be larger by several inches than the frame. Bristol board or beaver board is good for separating framed pictures. Corrugated board is satisfactory if the paintings are framed properly and sealed well. *Separation boards*

There are certain advantages to using plexiglass instead of glass. Plexiglass will not break, and it is lighter than glass. When a glass is broken, sharp edges or slivers invariably scratch the painting. It is not true that plexiglass filters out all ultraviolet rays and therefore affords greater protection from light than glass. A water- *Plexiglass* color painting under plexiglass or glass should not be exposed to strong light or sunlight. There are, however, different qualities of plexiglass, and some are more protective than others. Naturally, the grade of plexiglass which affords the more protection is the more expensive. Do not use inexpensive grades.

Plexiglass attracts dust   All plexiglass becomes dusty because of static attraction. This feature can become a troublesome nuisance. To eliminate or decrease its tendency to attract dust, plexiglass may be coated with an antistatic film.

Advantages and disadvantages   A distinct disadvantage is that all plexiglass is easily scratched, but on the whole it is preferred because it is unbreakable. Its use in framing has been generally accepted because its advantages outweigh its disadvantages. Glass has become outmoded, particularly when framed works are shipped. Museums no longer ship works of art or circulate traveling exhibitions unless plexiglass is used. They generally request permission from lenders to replace glass with plexiglass for shipment.

Professional framing   When watercolors are sent to a commercial framer, be sure he is an experienced professional who knows what to do and what not to do and is accustomed to handling and framing valuable paintings. His knowledge and experience are important. After he has finished and the picture is returned with the back sealed, it is already too late to check on the work without unframing the picture.

Silverfish   The worst insect enemy of paper works is the silverfish. Their principle diet is paper. Unless there is a constant lookout for these fleeting little pests, their enormous appetite for paper can destroy a watercolor.

Cockroaches   Cockroaches also eat watercolors. A watercolor can be actually eaten off its paper ground by roaches. In the process, a part of the paper goes with the pigments. A few roaches can accomplish an unbelievable amount of damage over night. They work at night

Termites, woodworms, and book lice   and in darkness. Other paper destroying insects are termites, woodworms, and book lice.

Paper must always be kept dry and well aired. Dampness must be avoided. Damp fibers cause mildew and mold. Fungi thrive on dampness, warmth and darkness.

Removing mold   Mold may be removed by a conservator with a camel-hair or sable brush. Even with skill and experience, it is often impossible to avoid rubbing the spores of fluffy molds into the paper. Removal

50

of mold should take place away from unaffected works to avoid spreading the spores and infecting other paper works. Cleaning affected works should be done in open air or in an airy room.

A small storage area or even an entire room may be sterilized with a gaseous fumigation, provided the area is thoroughly sealed. Otherwise, dealing with fungus is ineffective. When commercial exterminators are engaged, they should be cautioned not to use insecticides, which harm paper. Fumigation to destroy insect pests should be done regularly. *Gaseous fumigation* *Insecticides*

Foxing is the term for the brownish, dark spots which appear on paper, usually along the edges. These are caused by mold. Beginning along the edges, they progress inward, unless wrong atmospheric conditions are corrected. Lower-grade papers are more subject to foxing. If a watercolor develops foxing, bleaching by chemical treatment may eradicate the spot, but this highly specialized treatment should be attempted only by experts. *Foxing* *Bleaching by experts*

Watercolors on paper sometimes warp or buckle, even when framed. This distressing condition is always caused by humidity and other atmospheric changes. The only way to eliminate warping is to maintain the same atmospheric conditions that prevailed when the watercolor was hinged, matted, or framed. Air-conditioning and controlled humidity provide the only solution. If a watercolor on paper buckles, leave it alone. With a change of atmosphere, it will return to its original flat shape. Direct attention to the atmosphere. Under no circumstances should the picture be pasted down, dry mounted, put under pressure with weights or stretched over a board or framework. Paper will always be subject to expansion and contraction with each atmospheric change. Any of these drastic measures will weaken the fibrous structure of paper, cause breakage and splitting, and consequent damage. *Buckling and warping* *To cure warping*

The relative humidity must be constantly watched. A constant RH of not more than 50% is usually ideal. If humidity is kept below 65%, safety is assured, but when it approaches 70%, danger is imminent. Between 65% and 70% RH, mold formation may be expected. With an RH above or near 70%, mold is inevitable. If the relative humidity is high, the moisture content of the paper rises, the paper swells, and mold results. Evidence of mildew or mold is a sure sign that the humidity has exceeded the safety zone. *Desired RH*

BIBLIOGRAPHY

Binyon, Laurence. *English Water-Colours*. New York, Schocken Books, Inc., 1969.

British Water Colours. London, Victoria & Albert Museum, 1963.

Buckley, H. and Macintyre, J. A. "The Fading of Water-Colour Pictures," *The Burlington Magazine*, Vol. LVII (July, 1930), pp. 31-38.

Chomicky, Yar G. *Watercolor Painting—Media, Methods, and Materials*. Englewood Cliffs, New Jersey, Prentice-Hall, Inc., 1968.

Cundall, H. M. *A History of British Water-Colour Painting*. London, John Murray, 1909.

Dibble, George. *Watercolor: Materials and Techniques*. New York. Holt, Rinehart & Winston, 1966.

Gardner, Albert Ten Eyck. *History of Watercolor Painting in America*. New York, Reinhold Publishing Corp., 1966.

Haftmann, Werner. *Expressionist Watercolors*. New York, Harry N. Abrams, Inc., 1967.

Kent, Norman. *Watercolor Techniques*. New York, Watson-Guptill Publications, Inc., 1968.

Koschatzky, Walter. *Watercolor: History and Technique*. New York, McGraw-Hill Book Co., 1969.

Kühn, H. "The Effect of Oxygen, Relative Humidity and Temperature on the Fading Rate of Watercolors," *IIC Conference on Museum Climatology*, London, 1967, pp. 79-88.

Torche, Judith. *Acrylic and Other Water-Base Paints for the Artist*. New York, Sterling Publishing Co., 1967.

Whitney, Edgar A. *A Complete Guide to Watercolor Painting*. New York, Watson-Guptill Publications, Inc., 1965.

3

Pastels

Pastels are chalk crayons. The pigments are practically pure and in powder form. They come in the shape of colored sticks, as do wax crayons, but the barest minimum of gum adhesive is mixed with the powder to form a crayon, either round or square.

Pastels may be used as a pencil or they may be rubbed to blend colors with either the fingers or with a "stump," a paper cylinder in pencil form, usually pointed at one end. Stumps are also used with charcoal. If a stump is used, a good deal of the powder is lost. Therefore, most pastellists prefer to use their fingers. Too much use of a stump produces a muddy effect and often destroys the sparkle pastels produce.

With most color media a solvent, such as turpentine, water, linseed oil, or stand oil, is mixed with the pigments. This is not true of pastels. The colors are laid directly on the ground, which is usually paper, or sometimes canvas of a very fine weave. Unless the artist chooses to rub the color in, the pastel remains on the surface and does not soak in. For this reason pastel paintings are extremely fragile. A gust of wind or any slight movement of the air can cause a loss of the pastel powder. They can be easily damaged or destroyed unless they are framed immediately behind glass or plexiglass. This should always be done by an expert who understands the delicacy of the medium.

The artist does very little or no blending of colors, unless a slight shading of colors with fingers or a stump. Some pastellists prefer not to touch the surface at all. The crayons have been prepared by the manufacturer in a wide variety of tones of each color so that a great range is already available.

Pastels are usually applied thinly. Heavy application builds up the powder so that it falls off. Areas of the paper that are left untouched play an important part in the tonal gradations of the total composition. Though a fixative may be used successfully with charcoal to make it adhere to the paper, it is not recommended for stabilizing pastels. It completely destroys the character of the medium and changes the colors. The Impressionist painter Degas, who employed pastel superbly, is reported never to have used commercial fixatives because they gave a shine to the surface.

Pastel is a comparatively modern process. Although it was known in the seventeenth century, it was not until the eighteenth century that it came into widespread use. It has remained continuously in favor ever since.

In France, one of the greatest exponents of the pastel medium was Quentin de la Tour (1704-1788), who used rubbing extensively, while his contemporary, Perroneau, gave more prominence to the unfused touch. In the following century, Degas found the chalky texture a perfect vehicle for effects of line and color pattern.

Italy had its famous pastellists, such as Rosalba Carriera (1697-1757), and England had its share too. Francis Cotes (1725-1770), who had studied with Carriera, was the first to develop fully the use of pastels in England, but it was his pupil John Russell (1745-1806) who brought the medium to perfection and wrote a little known but very authoritative account of eighteenth century practice, *Elements of Painting with Crayons*. In the United States, such famous painters as Mary Cassatt and William Glackens have practiced pastel painting.

The image achieved with pastels is very different from an oil painting. A pastel painting cannot approach the full-bodied effect possible with oil. It is extremely delicate and must be carefully handled if the results are to be successful and spar- kling. Pastels, with a rather obscure history, might be said to be the humblest of all art media, but it is a medium with a dis- tinctive character of its own, one which requires great skill to realize its full beauty.

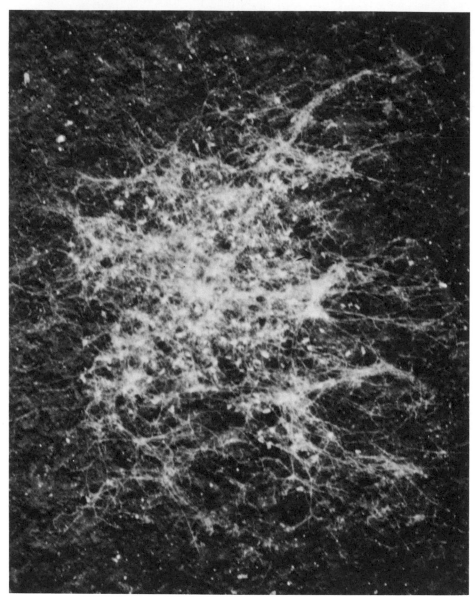

Figure 22. MOLD GROWTH. A detail at 4x magnification of a pastel
surface, 4 diameters in width, showing mold growth. *Courtesy, Clements L. Robertson, Conservator, City Art Museum of St. Louis.*

Figure 23. AFTER THE BATH. Edgar Degas, French, 1834-1917. Pastel. The subtle tones were achieved by soaking the colored chalks. The sensitive modeling and rhythmic contours of the nude form are hallmarks of the great Impressionist as a pastellist. *Courtesy, Fogg Art Museum, Harvard University.*

Figure 24. PORTRAIT OF A WOMAN. Maurice Quentin de la Tour, French, 1704-1788. Pastel. It was the practice of de la Tour, one of the greatest exponents of pastel, to brush over the paper with gum water and sprinkle this with smalt, a vitreous blue pigment. It was this preparation of the surface which gave both a suitable tooth and a tinted ground on which to work. *Courtesy, Fogg Art Museum, Harvard University.*

RULES FOR CARE AND HANDLING

The life of a pastel painting depends on its treatment by owner, museum curator, shipping agent, handler or packer.

Frame immediately

Pastels must be framed immediately with glass or plexiglass if they are to be preserved with their original freshness. The powdery nature of the medium makes them extremely fragile. Even a slight jolt usually loosens the crayon surface, spoiling the painting and altering its entire composition.

Use thick mats and plexiglass

Pastels should always be framed behind mats, preferably a thick rag matboard, so that the crayon does not contact glass or plexiglass. Leave at least a quarter of an inch between pastel and glass, with more space on the sides and back to allow air to circulate. Unless a mat is used, a part of the top surface will adhere to the glass. This not only causes distortion but risks future damage if the pastel is ever reframed or if the protective glazing is broken. In this case, slivers of glass invariably cause irreparable harm.

Avoid reframing

Reframe pastel paintings only when absolutely necessary. Make sure the protective backing is strong and the sealing paper fully protects the pastel from dust and grime. If backings become old and brittle, replace them with clean, fresh rag paper, handling the painting with great care. Only an experienced person should attempt this.

Never touch surface

Never touch the surface of a pastel. The slightest contact, with fingers or any object, results in a loss of pastel crayon and of esthetic quality.

Do not allow rough paper to come in contact with pastels. *Anything* which touches the surface of a pastel damages it permanently, and repair is rarely very successful. Attempts to "retouch" such areas or smudges usually result in additional losses.

Protect unframed pastels and keep them flat

If pastels are received unframed, protect the surfaces with wax paper, place each one in a separate box, keep it flat, and as soon as possible turn it over to a reputable framer who understands their fragility. The slightest jarring during the framing process can cause loss of pastel powder.

Storage

When they are not on exhibition, framed pastels should be

stored flat. Even the slamming of a door can cause the crayon to move and sift downward. Storage in a dark room will injure the painting. Basements are usually fatal. Moderate light, air circulation, and some heat are essential factors in determining the longevity of a pastel.

Dampness is the greatest cause of destruction to pastels. They are easily infected with mildew and mold, a fungoid growth. They should be inspected frequently for any signs of the condition. Any indication of mold warns that the atmospheric relative humidity is above the safety limit. If a pastel is hung on a damp wall, mold is sure to occur on it. If shipped in a damp box it will decay. Most mold growth can be prevented by keeping the relative humidity below 68%, preferably below 65%, and by providing a circulation of air. Thymol vapor cannot remove mildew and mold once it has formed but does kill the mold spores. It acts as a preventive only but offers no permanent immunity. Fungi thrive in dampness, warmth and darkness. Molds usually attack certain pastel colors more than others. Yellows, bone brown, ultramarine blue and some of the more brilliant reds seem to be more susceptible to mold infection. Mold growth may also occur on the binding medium of pastel crayons and on the sizing of the paper. *Infection with mildew and mold* *Inspect frequently for fungi growth* *Humidity*

Amateurs should not undertake the treatment of pastels. If no conservator is on the museum staff, engage a reputable person who is experienced with the medium. Some conservators remove mildew and mold with a tiny camel's hair brush, slightly moistened with pure alcohol. If the mold is old and has formed a horny crust, the conservator must use a scraper, but in most cases when the disease has progressed to this stage, the pastel is already ruined. Alert inspection will forestall this condition. Walter Beck says in his article, "Something About Pastel Technique and Its Permanence,"[1] 95% of mold infection can be corrected if caught in time. *Treatment by conservators only* *Inspection*

Insect pests attack pastels just as they attack prints, drawings in other media, or any work on paper, but with pastels it is principally the paper that insects feed on. Silverfish and roaches attack paper and eventually eat into the pastel image unless checked. Inspect frequently to prevent insects from multiplying. *Insect pests*

1. *Technical Studies in the Field of Fine Arts,* Vol. II, No. 3, Jan., 1934, pp. 119-123.

Avoid displaying in sunlight — Avoid displaying pastels in sunlight or reflected light. While the medium itself is not as susceptible to fading and discoloration as are prints and watercolors, the paper ground of pastels deteriorates if thus exposed. If the paper deteriorates, so will the pastel.

Hang pastels free from the wall — If pastels are hung free from the wall, more ventilation is possible. Attach corks to the four corners of the back of the frame. If this precaution is not taken, a condition of stale air will be created on the picture. Bad air generates mold; this flies to the glass and is returned to pigments. If this continues, a pastel can disappear under a covering of fungi.

Never use staples or clips — Never staple or paper clip a pastel, even if there is a border or margin on the paper ground. Metals stain paper and destroy the quality of the picture.

Remove screw eyes and hooks — Remove all screw eyes, wire and hooks from framed pastels before storing them. It is recommended that pastels be kept flat and not stacked. Screw eyes and hooks prevent storing in a perfectly flat position. They also damage frames.

Fumigation — Regular, professional fumigation of all museum areas is recommended but be sure pastels are protected from fumigants; it is better to remove them from a room which is to be fumigated. Some fumigants alter the colors. Never fumigate a room which has unframed pastels in it.

Avoid sea air — In areas near the ocean the atmosphere contains more salt. Pastels and oils near the water should be protected from this dangerous atmosphere. If the building is not air-conditioned, keep pastels in sealed cases with a circulation of air; make sure the protective sealings on the backs of the frames are secure. Paintings shipped in the hold of a ship sometimes become alive with mold.

Do not use tapes — Never use any kind of tape on or with pastel paintings. Scotch tape and any water-soluble tape usually cause damage beyond repair.

Hand carry — Carry only one pastel at a time, even though small. It is safer to transport them by hand than on dollies or hand-trucks. There is less shock to the painting if hand-borne.

Ultramarine disease — *Ultramarine disease* is a whitish film which develops over the surface of ultramarine color because it has a tendency to hygroscopic action, doubtless because of its heavy clay base. If a picture becomes affected, move it to a drier atmosphere and treat as for mold.

60

BIBLIOGRAPHY

Beck, Walter. "Something About Pastel Technique and Its Performance," *Technical Studies in the Field of Fine Arts*, Vol. II, no. 3 (January, 1934), pp. 119-123.

Beckwith, T. D., Swanson, W. H., and Iiams, T. *Deterioration of Paper: The Cause and Effect of Foxing.* Berkeley, Calif., *University of California Biological Science*, Vol. I, no. 3 (1940), pp. 299-356.

Church, Sir Arthur H. *The Chemistry of Paints and Painting.* London, Seeley, Service & Co., 1915.

Gettens, Rutherford J. "The Bleaching of Stained and Discolored Pictures on Paper with Sodium Chlorite and Chlorine Dioxide," *Museum*, Vol. 5, no. 2 (1952), p. 116.

Lapauze, Henri. *Les Pastels de M. Quentin de la Tour a St. Quentin.* Preface by Gustave Larroumet. Paris.

Murray, Henry. *The Art of Painting and Drawing in Coloured Crayons.* London, Windsor & Newton, n.d.

Richmond, Leonard and Littlejohns, J. *Technique of Pastel Painting.* London, Sir Isaac Pitman & Sons, Ltd., 1946; 1963.

Robert, Karl. *Le Pastel.* Paris, Laurens, 1890.

Russell, John. *Elements of Painting with Crayons.* London, Marlborough Rare Books, Ltd., 1772.

Sears, Elinor Lathrop. *Pastel Painting.* New York, Watson-Guptill Publications, Inc., 1953.

Sprinck, J. L. *A Guide to Pastel Painting.* London, Rowney, n.d.

Williamson, George C. *John Russell, R.A.* London, 1894.

4

Prints and Drawings

PRINTS

The graphic process may be divided into three major categories: the relief method (woodcut and wood engraving); the intaglio method, literally meaning to "cut in" (engraving on metal, drypoint, etching, aquatint, mezzotint) and the surface method (lithography). These categories differ mainly in the manner in which the primary surface is used. In the relief method, the lines or spaces are engraved as negatives to leave the design in relief, whereas in intaglio or lithography the line or space engraved possesses a positive value and represents the design itself. It is from this original surface that the resulting print or impression is taken or pulled.

The technique of relief printing is probably the simplest and certainly one of the earliest processes employed by man. While the exact origins of prints are disputed, prints were known in the Orient long before their advent in the Western world. It is only with the discovery of the printing press, after 1450, and the use of paper instead of parchment, that prints became more widespread throughout Europe.

The first European woodcuts were for textile designs and playing cards; it was not until after the 1470's that woodcuts came into their own as an independent medium depicting both

62

religious and secular themes. In a woodcut the artist works on a plank of soft wood (e.g. cherry, pear, maple, American white wood, etc.) cut along the grain, onto which he draws his design. The parts of the design which are not to be printed black are cut away, thus leaving part of the wood surface raised in relief. The instruments used for the cutting are sharp knives, hollow-type "V" tools, or various shaped gauges. Next, the raised surface of the block is inked, covered with paper and put into a press or pressed by hand. The result is that the inked surface is transferred onto the paper—hence the woodcut. Linoleum, which offers a very malleable surface, can be treated in the same way as wood.

The wood engraving was invented in the eighteenth century as a variation to the woodcut. The principal departure in the appearance results from the fact that the wood block is generally engraved crosswise rather than plankwise with the grain. To attain the desired effect, the harder and closer grained woods (box, holly, etc.) are preferred. The instruments employed are called burins or gravers, which have a lozenge-shaped point. Like the wood and lino-cut, this is a relief method; the print is taken from the raised surface after engraving. Also there is greater delicacy of treatment as a result of the harder wood and the finer tools used. The delicacy and precision of the line often requires greater pressure from the press.

In the intaglio methods, as opposed to the relief, the surfaces are cut into with a sharp instrument. The lines thus created are the ones that are blackened and transferred onto paper. In the process of engraving on metal the artist, with his burin or engraving tool, cuts into the polished surface of a plate. The plates are generally copper with a highly polished surface but may also be zinc, iron, silver, steel, brass and even pewter. By pushing the tool before his hand, the artist creates a clear, fine, tapering line. The burr, which is turned up as he cuts, is removed with a scraper before the plate is inked, thus leaving a clean furrow. Thicker lines are achieved by either deepening the furrow, leaning the graver to one side or cutting more lines alongside the original furrow. Dots and short lines, called flicks, are used to create shading. Cross-hatching is another way of adding dimension to the print. In engraving, unlike woodcuts, mistakes can be erased by means of a scraper or burnisher.

The process of etching, which originated in the shops of armors, was not used for picture making until the sixteenth century. Rembrandt, in particular, is noted for his superb etchings. Here, the line is obtained by corroding or eating the plate with acid or some mordant. The plate is first polished with an oil rubber, very carefully cleaned with whitening or chalk and then covered with a thin layer of etching ground, a protective film which is made by mixing various amounts of gums and resins. This ground resists the acid. The etching ground may be laid in several ways. The most common of these is to bring a ball of solid ground placed in a porous silk bag into contact with the heated plate. The substance melts, oozes from the bag and is spread over the plate evenly by a dabber or roller. The plate is next smoked so that the melted ground becomes black. This helps the etcher see the lines he is opening. Before the plate is dipped in acid, the back of the metal plate must be sealed. The etcher now is ready to open up the lines. The instrument he uses is an etching-needle. These needles vary in thickness. Wherever the needles have laid bare the plate, the acid bites. The longer the plate stays in the acid, the deeper and therefore darker the lines become. In contrast to the engraved lines which usually taper, the etched lines are blunt and rectangular. The plate is now ready to be inked and printed.

The process of drypoint, often referred to as drypoint etching, is actually more related to intaglio engraving than to etching; however, it often may be used in conjunction with etching. In this process the lines are scratched onto the metal plate with either a pointed piece of steel or a diamond point. Unlike engraving or woodcutting, the instrument is drawn across the plate and not pushed before the hand. As this is done, a burr is raised alongside the incised line or furrow. The burr is not scraped away or smoothed over and consequently later holds ink. It is this burr which gives the drypoint plates their rich velvety textures. After fifteen or more printings the burr generally begins to wear away. The print, however, will still retain the delicacy characterized by the dry-pointed lines.

In the aquatint process, line and tone are combined. The tone or tint in the aquatint, which is related in principle to etching, is achieved by the acid biting through a porous ground consisting of either sand or some powdered resinous substance that is evenly coated over the plate. Because the plate is only partially protected from the acid by this ground, the acid can bite through the ground. The effect is one of a grainy texture. Goya was one of the great masters of this medium.

In mezzotint the effects are similar to those characteristic of aquatint but are of a richer, more velvety tone. This process was used often in the eighteenth century for reproductive purposes. The results in mezzotint are achieved by a process which is exactly reverse of the other engraving processes. The artist proceeds in a negative manner to work out the lighter portions and highlights on a plate which has a dark base. The dark base is achieved by a tool called a rocker. This instrument with sharp, tiny cutting teeth is held in the artist's hand at right angles to the plate and rocked all over the plate's surface creating even indentions with a burr to each indentation. Next, using a scraper the artist removes those portions of the burr where there is to be light. The more the surface is scraped and burnished, the lighter the plate will print, since less ink will be held in those portions.

The inking and printing of intaglio plates (engraving, drypoint etching, aquatint and mezzotint) can be discussed concurrently. In these processes ink is forced into the lines which have been cut or eaten into the metal. Next, the plate is wiped clean with a very fine, soft cloth (often silk) or with the palm of one's hand, leaving ink remaining only in the furrows. Then a damp sheet of paper is placed over the plate and both plate and paper are put in a press under heavy pressure. This results in the paper being pressed inside the incised lines of the plate which contain the ink. When the press is released, the ink in the furrows has been transmitted onto the paper, leaving an impression, a print of the etching or the engraving on the paper.

Lithography was invented in 1798 by Aloys Senefelder, a German. It is based on the antagonistic reaction between grease and water. In lithography, the artist draws with a greasy chalk or crayon on the grained surface of a piece of porous limestone (or zinc or aluminum plate). The stone is moistened with water which is repelled in the places where there is grease. Next, a greasy ink is rolled over the limestone. The grease on the roller is attracted to the grease previously put on the slab and likewise is repelled wherever the stone is wet. Paper is placed over and then pressed onto the stone. The surface drawing made by the greasy ink adheres to the paper. This process, which allows much freedom and flexibility, was widely used by nineteenth- and twentieth-century artists.

During the twentieth century alone, there have been startling innovations in printing. Today one may see collage printing (the use of textures such as cloth, paper, wire, sand, etc.), stencil prints or serigraphy (prints made through screens of silk), and finally the incorporating of photography into the print, alongside the more traditional forms of printing.

DRAWINGS

"Drawings are invaluable, not only because they give, in its purity, the mental intention of the artist, but because they bring immediately before us the mood of his mind at the moment of creation." These words by Goethe point up the need to understand more about the various technical resources available to the artist in his ancient preoccupation with drawing, which offer an immediate and yet varied outlet to his imagination.

Drawings may generally be divided into two categories—fine drawing media and broad drawing media. Along with these two categories which separate the different kinds of technical resources, one must consider the varying aims of the artist. For him there are three different types of drawings. The first is the occasional sketch when he draws something at random which strikes his interest or imagination, "The fragmentary passages that come without thought or composition," as Odilon Redon phrased it. Next, there is the preparatory study which is done consciously as part of the preparation for a given major work. Thirdly, there is the drawing for its own sake. Only a few artists have the skill and linear clarity to not only master but excel in this form of expression. Ingres (1780-1867), in particular, is an outstanding exponent of this challenging medium.

Within the fine drawing media one finds metalpoint drawing. The metalpoint styluses may include silverpoint, goldpoint, copperpoint, leadpoint, and brasspoint, with silverpoint the most commonly used. While metalpoints were known to the Romans, it is not until around 1400 in Italy that one finds silverpoint mentioned as a drawing medium. In this medium it is necessary to use paper with an abrasive ground (generally bonedust) in order for the silver to leave its mark. Often artists tint the ground for heightened plasticity in the drawing. The characteristics of the medium are its delicacy and its fine clarity of line which allow careful and exact details.

Chiaroscuro drawings are those drawings in which the artist, reversing the normal procedure of applying dark strokes upon light paper, uses deeply colored halftone as a background and places emphasis on the white strokes which model the figures or delineate the contours. The term chiaroscuro comes from Vasari and others who referred to that method of depicting figures by using light values over a darker halftone or by having figures partially emerge in atmospheric light from a deeply shadowed background. The visual effects rendered by this reversal are quite unusual and striking although the tools employed are such common ones as pen and ink, brush and watercolors, greasy crayons, etc.

The use of pen and ink as accompaniments to various texts is both ancient and popular, but it was not until the Middle Ages that pen and ink was used for independent graphic work. This widespread use is certainly due in large measure to the great adaptability of pens to the varied styles of each epoch and every artist. There are three basic types of pens: quill pens (used frequently in early pen drawings); reed pens (older than the quill but not common until adopted by Rembrandt and others in the seventeenth century); and metal pens (invented in the nineteenth century and generally used now). While the metal pen expressly conveys the artist's intent, the reed and quill pens are more likely to add their own accidental touch to the drawing. In addition, these pens each can have a wide range of points. The inks used in the past were either made from oak apples and vitriol, which turned brown with time, or a pine-soot solution called *bistre* which also turned brown, or lampblack or candleblack dissolved in gum water to make a black wash. The coloring matter from cuttlefish, sepia, came into use in the eighteenth century. Today, one generally uses waterproof carbon black, India ink or sepia. The main characteristic held in common by these various inks is their ability to flow evenly, insuring the artist uninterrupted line.

Pure line is the characteristic of ink drawings. While these lines may be short and wide or long and thin, or even minute flecks, they cannot be successfully used to produce soft tones and gradual transitions. A pen drawing speaks boldly and directly from the artist's hand to the viewer's eye.

Within the broad media of drawings, chalks and crayons are included. Natural chalks are those mineral substances taken from the earth and made into sticks. Fabricated chalks are prepared from pastes composed of water-soluble binding media mixed with dry pigment, rolled or pressed into sticks, then dried. Crayons are made from powdered pigments and mixed into pastes with binders containing oleaginous or fatty substances. The most commonly used chalks are black argillite and red chalk. It was not until the fifteenth century that this substance became popular, mainly in Italy and Germany. Chalk (similar to charcoal in that they both are soft and both smudge) differs from the latter by being less sensitive and adhering better to the support. During the Renaissance, Baroque, and Rococo periods chalk was widely used as it is very suitable for chiaroscuro and for giving plasticity to form. The soft quality of red chalk was much used by Leonardo da Vinci, the master of sfumato. It is in the treatment of broad areas of tone, accentuated highlights, and plasticity of form, rather than in contours and lines, that one notes the painterly quality of this medium. While the support of chalk may be white or tinted paper, pasteboard or linen, the support must be of a somewhat uneven surface so that the color will adhere.

Crayons can range from dry to greasy. With the decline in the use of natural red chalk, various substitutes were discovered. Conté crayon is particularly appreciated for its chalky stroke yet partial resistance to smudging. The effects of crayon can range also from the soft and painterly to a more defined and linear.

Among the most popular drawing media, charcoal, which comes from lime or willow-wood, holds a decided place. One of the oldest materials used in drawing, charcoal's modest characteristics and its simplicity of preparation have made it a common medium for the artist. Since charcoal smudges very easily it is generally used for the occasional or preparatory sketch. Not until the 1500's was a serviceable fixative invented. The fact that it allows the artist to make innumerable corrections and alterations has fostered an approach of experimental freedom in the charcoal drawing. It can be used in both a linear manner or for shading. In addition various tones of grey can also be achieved along with very black lines.

RULES FOR CARE AND HANDLING

Any work of art on paper is easily damaged and may be considered the most vulnerable of the many kinds of art objects found in museums. By its very nature paper is especially subject to damage and deterioration.

Hazards for paper works are varied

The greatest hazards to works of art on paper are sudden changes of temperature, humidity, strong light, water, dampness, extreme heat, attacks by insects, dirt and dust, the kinds of adhesives used, and handling.

Do not touch unnecessarily

An important rule is: never allow hands to come in contact with prints and drawings unless it is absolutely necessary. Never shuffle through them as if they were a deck of cards.

Pick up by upper corners

When handling is necessary, always wash the hands first. Pick up a print or drawing only by its upper corners, never in any other way.

Move individually on rag matboard

The safest way to carry prints and drawings, either matted or unmatted, is in specially designed portfolios or boxes. Solander boxes are recommended. Failing this, carry each one separately on a piece of clean rag matboard. The matboard should be larger by several inches than the print or drawing.

Store unframed examples in shallow receptacles

The ideal situation is to have all prints and drawings framed and hanging in temperature and humidity controlled storage areas or on walls. Museums all seem to share a common problem, lack of space, so this situation is seldom if ever possible. A generally accepted means for the storage of unframed prints and drawings is the Solander box, made especially for the purpose, or in map cabinets or any cabinet with deep, shallow drawers.

Separation sheets and acid-free tissue

Acid-free tissue paper should be laid over the face of each print or drawing. Sheets of a synthetic film which is not permeable by moisture may then be placed between each print or drawing. A high quality rag matboard serves the same purpose and acts as a dust catcher as well. (Glassine paper should be avoided because it is too acid.) The only exception is prints and drawings which are matted with such deep set mounts that there is no possible chance of anything touching the surface. Even if the mats are deep

70

Figure 25. FAIRFAX AND MUSTARD. Nicolas Krushenick, American, born 1929. 1. a color lithograph being inked; 2. pulling of the print. Lithography is based on the antipathy of oil and water. The image is made with a greasy crayon or ink. The stone is then moistened, the water becoming an even film except where the lithograph crayon or ink has been applied. When an inked roller is applied to the wet surface, the ink adheres only to the greasy areas. *Courtesy, Los Angeles County Museum of Art.*

1.

2.

Figure 26. Cut from "De Biblia mit vlitigher" Lubek. Anonymous, German, 15th century. Woodcut, 1494. Famous as the most beautifully illustrated early book, this Bible contains many illustrations by an unknown artist, possibly of Dutch origin, who was the greatest master of the woodcut technique prior to Dürer. *Courtesy, The Metropolitan Museum of Art.*

Figure 27. RUE TRANSONAIN, LE 13 AVRIL 1834. Honoré Daumier, French, 1808-1879. Lithograph. Contrast the rich velvety tones of the painterly shading obtained in the lithograph with the harsh simplicity of the early woodcut. *Courtesy, Los Angeles County Museum of Art.*

Figure 28. Empress Catherine II of Russia. After H. Benner, engraver Joseph Macoú, 1771-1837. 1. shows disfiguring marks caused by mold infestation; 2. shows the engraving after fumigation and restoration. The cleaning process has improved the quality of the work of art itself as well as removing "foxing." *Courtesy, Research Laboratory, Museum of Fine Arts, Boston.*

1.

2.

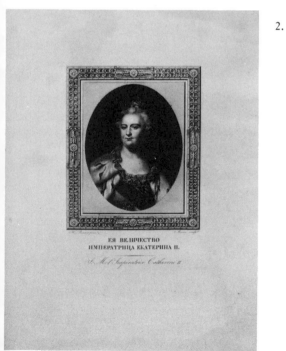

Figure 29. Pᴏᴛ-ᴅᴇ-Nᴀᴢ. Honoré Daumier, French, 1808-1879. Lithograph. This fine work bears dramatic evidence of age and neglect. Note marring effect of foxing and stains caused by tape. *Courtesy, Conservation Center, Los Angeles County Museum of Art.*

1.

Figure 30. Two studies of hands demonstrate difference in density and texture resulting from use of various tools. 1. graphite on tracing paper, which has been affixed to laid paper, shows the clear precision of this technique, which nineteenth-century draughtsman Ingres manipulated so well; 2. charcoal heightened with white chalk, used here for its soft, crumbling effect, by the eighteenth-century artist, Quentin de la Tour. *Courtesy, Fogg Art Museum, Harvard University.*

2.

Figure 31.   *Figure 32.*

LA FAMILLE   FAMILIA

Gravée d'Après le tableau original peint par   Sculpta juxta Exemplar quondam magnitudinem
Watteau de la même grandeur de l'estampe   à Wattaevo depictum

Figure 34.

Figure 31. GOD APPEARING TO NOAH. Engraving after Raphael. Marcantonio, ca. 1488-1530. The most famous of the sixteenth-century Italian engravers. Marcantonio was the artistic shadow of Raphael; his prints after the master played an important role in the dissemination of the Raphaelesque design throughout Europe. *Courtesy, The Metropolitan Museum of Art. Figure 32.* THE RISEN CHRIST BETWEEN SS. ANDREW AND LONGINUS. Andrea Mantegna, Italian, 1431-1506. Engraving. The greatest fifteenth-century painter to make prints with his own hand, Mantegna was also the first important artist to have a considerable number of engravings made after his designs. In his prints he raised the medium to a major status (unacknowledged at this period). *Courtesy, Fogg Art Museum, Harvard University. Figure 33.* ADAM AND EVE. Albrecht Dürer, German, 1471-1528. Engraving, 1504. *Courtesy, Los Angeles County Museum of Art. Figure 34.* LA FA-MILLE. Antoine Watteau, French, 1684-1721. Illustration engraving. The first important "publication" of

Figure 33.   *Figure 35.*

paintings and drawings of any major artist was the "Oeuvre Complet" of Watteau. Here reproduction engraving reached one of its greatest excellencies both in the technique of translation and in familiarizing the world with the designs of a famous master. *Courtesy, The Metropolitan Museum of Art. Figure 35.* Seated Clowness. Toulouse-Lautrec, French, 1864-1901. Color lithograph. Lautrec's contribution to color lithography was to close the gap between the artist's hand on the lithographic stone or the etching plate and the completed print. At the same time, he widened the technical range of lithography by treating the stone with a new informality. In this example, he speckled its surface with ink by flipping the ink-soaked brush bristles of a stiff brush above it and dabbing the surface in any way he chose. Actually, he combined and invented variations on conventional lithographic techniques in order to give them variety. *Courtesy, Fogg Art Museum, Harvard University.*

Figure 36. WOMAN STANDING WITH HAND ON HIP. Jean-Honoré Fragonard, French, 1732-1806. Fabricated red chalk on white paper. Said to represent the artist's sister-in-law and assistant, Marguerite Gerard, this drawing is one of the rare examples executed with crayons before the nineteenth century. *Courtesy, Fogg Art Museum, Harvard University. Figure 37.* NUDE FEMALE. Auguste Rodin, French, 1840-1917. Drawing, pencil outline with brown and black watercolor washes. The control of fluid line is integral to the miraculous craftsmanship of the sculptor Rodin. Such audaciously naturalistic poses served as preliminary drawings for his final work in stone or bronze. *Courtesy, Priscilla Lucier, Boston.*

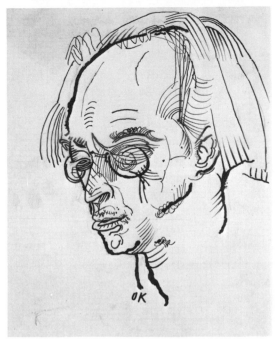

Figure 38. PORTRAIT OF THE POET, HERWARTH WALDEN, 1910. Oskar Kokoschka, Austrian, born 1886. Drawing. The power of this work lies in expressive, emphatic blacks and whites and in the rude directness of cutting. The effect of primitive simplicity is reminiscent of early fifteenth-century woodcuts which influenced Kokoschka and other German Expressionists.

Figure 39. PORTRAIT OF CLAUDE GOUFFIER DE BOISY. François Clouet, French, ca. 1510-1572. Natural black and red chalks on white paper. The elegance and refinement of Clouet's line was particularly suitable to his aristocratic subjects. Despite its provenance, which included transportation to Italy and England, this work is in a fine state of preservation. *Courtesy, Fogg Art Museum, Harvard University*.

*Contact only
with a
high-quality
rag paper*

and thick, separation sheets of acid-free tissue should be used to keep the works clean and free of dust. Separation sheets, mats, and mounts should always be of a high-grade rag product.

*Mold and
insects*

Desired RH

Paper is highly subject to attacks by insects and mold growths. Paper works should always be kept dry and well aired. For the preservation of any work on paper, constant relative humidity of not more than 50% should be maintained at all times. Mold formation usually occurs when relative humidity approaches 70%. It is imperative that the humidity be kept below this point, preferably below 65%. Damp paper fibers are food for mildew and mold. If

*Fungi thrive in
dampness,
warmth, and
darkness*

the relative humidity is high, the moisture content of paper rises, the paper swells, and damaging mold growths appear. Any sign of mold is a warning that the atmospheric conditions are beyond the safety limit. Fungi thrive in dampness, warmth and darkness.

*Separate
affected works*

Fungus molds should not be removed from prints and drawings in a room where there are unaffected paper works. Infected specimens should be dealt with in open air or in a large, airy room. Conservators sometimes use a camel's hair or sable brush to remove mold. The spores in the fluffy growth may be scattered about even with careful use of a fine brush so it is important that this procedure be undertaken away from healthy prints and drawings. Even with skill and experience, it is sometimes impossible to avoid rubbing mold spores into the tissue of the paper.

*Fumigate
regularly*

Gaseous fumigation to sterilize a room containing mold infested prints and drawings and insects is effective only if the room is thoroughly sealed. The regular fumigation of all areas is recommended whether or not mold and insect damage is evident.

*Silverfish eat
paper*

The main diet of silverfish is paper. Frequent inspections should be made to prevent these pests from multiplying and destroying prints and drawings. Unfortunately, many old, valuable prints have been trimmed to the platemarks by uninformed individuals, perhaps in some cases to make them fit a handy frame or mat. When trimmed prints are attacked by silverfish, the actual image is eaten away and the print spoiled, for these pests seem to always begin work at the edges.

*Roaches eat
pigment and
paper*

Roaches eat watercolor paints, also paper. A watercolor drawing may be literally eaten off the paper by roaches. Extreme heat, water, and dampness must be avoided at all times for these are the conditions in which insects thrive. The presence of gelatin in starch

80

increases the danger of damage, but the greatest insect activity is *Avoid extremes*
associated with dampness and warmth.

Sunlight and strong fluorescent lamps harm any work of art on
paper. Faded prints are beyond restoration, and often faded watercolors are too. The effect of sunlight on paper is easily recognized,
if one recalls the effect of sunlight on newspaper, the cheapest pulp
paper. In only an hour or two of exposure to the sun it will be- *Sunlight and*
come discolored; longer exposure makes it brittle at a fast rate. *strong*
Newspapers are printed on newsprint, the poorest quality of paper, *lamplight*
but natural sunlight and high-intensity lamps, especially fluorescent *damage*
lamps, also affect a good quality of paper in time. The process is
simply slower. A poor quality of paper—made from wood fiber *Danger of pulp*
either ground or separated by chemicals—should never be allowed *paper*
to come into contact with a work of art on paper. Low-grade
paper discolors prints and drawings and also mats, just as paper *Matboards of*
takes on the coloration of the grain of wood when left against it. *high-quality*
Mats must always be of a high-quality fiber paper made of cotton
or linen rag.

Paper is subject to *foxing*, that is, brownish spots caused by *Foxing*
mold. These discolorations usually begin along the edges of the
paper and progress inward. Rag paper is less susceptible to foxing
than other papers but any paper will develop the condition if
temperature and humidity are not controlled. Persistent stains, such
as foxing, present special problems. Sometimes it is necessary to *Cleaning and*
resort to chemical treatment to clean and bleach paper, but this *bleaching of*
should always be done by an expert. Cleaning treatment and bleach- *stains*
ing are not often necessary with Japanese prints and drawings
because of the soft texture and the delicate but sturdy nature of
the paper.

Never use paper clips or staples in connection with prints and *Do not use*
drawings. Do not allow clips, staples or anything metal to remain *staples or*
on a work of art on paper. If prints or drawings are received with *paper clips*
clips or staples, remove them immediately. The removal of staples
is very dangerous and tedious if the work is not to be damaged in
the process. Great care should be exercised in removing them. Do
not use a metal staple remover.

Remove all screw eyes, wires and hooks from framed prints and *Screw eyes,*
drawings before storing them. Screw eyes, hooks and wires damage *wires, and*
frames, glass and plexiglass which is easily scratched. *hooks*

81

How to mount and hinge

The correct mounting of prints and drawings is extremely important. They should always be fastened to a backing, or mount, with pieces of Japanese paper or Chinese rice paper, never with any other kind of paper. This process is referred to as *hinging*. When rehinging a print, never tear off or soak off old hinges. Attempts to remove them may also take away a part of the paper with the hinges unless done expertly. However, old hinges sometimes cause buckling.

Never use scotch tape, rubber cement, or pressure-sensitive tapes

The kind of adhesive used with paper hinges is of the utmost importance. The only safe adhesive is one made either with a rice flour or pure starch paste. Prepare it at the time it is to be used. All other adhesives stain and damage. *Never use scotch tape.* It can never be removed without taking layers of paper with it, and it stains beyond repair. *Do not use rubber cement.* It leaves an equally, if not worse, damaging stain. Pressure sensitive tapes and water soluble tapes must not be used. They too are very damaging and sometimes cannot be removed without actually tearing the paper.

How to remove from backing or mount

When removing a print or drawing from its mount, or backing, remove the mount *from* the print or drawing, *not* the work of art from the mount.

Prints and drawings should always be on a matboard backing and matted. An unmounted, unmatted print or drawing framed directly against glass leaves an impression of the work on the glass clearly indicating that a part of the image has been lost, thus diminishing the quality as well as value.

Do not frame directly against glass

Matting, hinging, and framing should always be done by an experienced professional. If a commercial framer is engaged, be sure he knows exactly how to handle the works—what to do and what not to do.

Seal the backs of frames

When framing, always seal the frame at the back to prevent dust entering. With temperature and humidity control, prints and drawings are well protected from fungi activity and microbiological attacks.

Buckling

If a print or drawing buckles in its frame it is owing to atmospheric changes and humidity variances and will often stabilize itself. If there is buckling, the mat is often too tight in the frame. Instead of worrying about the buckling or warping, check tightness of frame and correct the temperature and relative humidity. When atmospheric conditions return to the safety zone, or to the condi-

82

tion of atmosphere when the work was framed, the buckling will correct itself. Never attempt to correct buckling by dry mounting, pasting or pressure. To avoid warping and buckling, prints and drawings should be kept in the same atmosphere at all times.

The advantages of framing a print or drawing with plexiglass instead of glass outweigh the disadvantages. Plexiglass does not break as glass does; when glass breaks on a framed print or drawing, slivers of glass will cause damage. On the other hand, plexiglass is easily scratched, and it attracts dust by reason of static electricity. There are, however, more expensive grades of plexiglass which do not have this disadvantage. See Chapter 2, "Rules for the Care and Handling of Watercolors." *Advantages and disadvantages of plexiglass*

BIBLIOGRAPHY

Allen, Virginia. *Tamarind: Homage to Lithography*. Greenwich, Conn., New York Graphic Society, 1969.

Auvil, Kenneth. *Serigraphy: Silk Screen Techniques for the Artist*. Englewood Cliffs, New Jersey, Prentice-Hall, Inc., 1965.

Azechi, Umetara. *Japanese Woodblock Prints: Their Techniques and Appreciation*. Japan Publications, 1966.

Binyon, Laurence and Sexton, J. J. O'Brien. *Japanese Color Prints*. Boston, Boston Book and Art, 1969.

Braby, Dorothea. *The Way of Wood Engraving*. New York, Oxford University Press, 1953.

Brunner, Felix. *Handbook of Graphic Reproduction Processes*. New York, Hastings House Publishers, Inc., 1968.

Chaet, Bernard. *The Art of Drawing*. New York, Rinehart & Winston, Inc., 1969.

Chieffo, Clifford T. *Silk-Screen as a Fine Art*. New York, Reinhold Book Division, 1968.

Faithorne, William. *The Art of Graveing and Etching*. Reprint with a new introduction by Jacob Kainen. New York, Da Capo Press, 1968.

Gross, Anthony. *Etching, Engraving and Intaglio Printing*. New York, Oxford University Press, 1969.

Hill, Edward. *The Language of Drawing*. Englewood Cliffs, New Jersey, Prentice-Hall, Inc., 1967.

Hillier, Jack. *Japanese Color Prints*. New York, Phaidon Press, 1966.

Hind, A. M. *A History of Engraving and Etching*. London, Constable & Co., Ltd., 1923.

———. *Guide to the Processes and Schools of Engraving.* London, The British Museum, 1933; 1952.

———. *Introduction to a History of Woodcut.* 2 vols. London, Constable & Co., Ltd., 1935.

Hutter, Heribert. *Drawing: History and Technique.* New York, McGraw-Hill Book Co., 1968.

Ivins, William M., Jr., *Prints and Visual Communication.* Reprint of 1953 edition. New York, Da Capo Press, 1968.

Marsh, Roger. *Monoprints for the Artist.* New York, Transatlantic Arts Books, 1969.

Meyers, Francis S. J. *Charcoal Drawing.* New York, Pitman Publishing Corp., 1965.

Narazaki, Muneshige. *The Japanese Print: Its Evolution and Essence.* 1st edition, Tokyo; English adaptation by C. H. Mitchell, Palo Alto, Calif., Kodansha International, 1966.

Plenderleith, H. J. *The Conservation of Prints, Drawings and Manuscripts.* London, Oxford University Press, 1937.

Sotriffer, Kristian. *Printmaking: History and Technique.* New York, McGraw-Hill Book Co., 1968.

Turk, F. A. *The Prints of Japan.* New York, Marlboro Books, 1967.

Twyman, Michael. *Lithography, 1800-1850: The Techniques of Drawing on Stone in England and France and Their Application in Works of Topography.* New York, Oxford University Press, 1969.

Weber, Wilhelm. *The History of Lithography.* New York, McGraw-Hill Book Co., 1967.

Zigrosser, Carl. *Six Centuries of Fine Prints.* New York, Crown Publishers, Inc., 1937.

———, and Gaehde, Christa M. *A Guide to the Collecting and Care of Original Prints.* 4th printing. New York, Crown Publishers, Inc., 1967.

———, The Directors of The Print Council of America, and others. *Prints, Thirteen Essays on the Art of the Print.* New York, The Print Council of America, 1962.

84

5

Sculpture

Sculpture is that branch of the arts which deals with organizing mass or volume. In form, it may exist in three dimension (as distinct from painting which is two-dimensional) so that the viewer may walk around it; or it may be a relief attached to a background from which it projects; or it may be an intaglio, sunk into the ground. The material of sculpture naturally imposes certain elements of stylistic treatment, and the success of the finished product depends on the suitability of the artist's concept to the material he has chosen to represent it. For example, a hard, unpliable material like basalt imposes a largeness and dignity by the very nature of its rigid substance; it does not lend itself to capturing quick impressions.

The use of stone, wood and ivory involves carving, or cutting away, from the original block of material until one attains the desired shape. Working in clay involves the opposite approach; that is, building up a shape. This plastic material which can be freely and quickly modeled is preferable for a spontaneous expression (which can be made durable by firing). Metals also entail a building-up process, since they usually presuppose the use of clay or wax and the pouring of molten metal in the casting.

ART OBJECTS

Through the ages, sculptors have used many materials to represent observed or imagined subjects—marble, stone, wood, clay, horn, ivory, gems and metals. In fact, man has used anything he has found that he could shape, reshape, combine, or mold as a means of self-expression or communication. Today more than ever before he is using any material at hand for sculpture.

In one form or another, terra cotta or baked clay was one of the earliest substances used in sculpture. Primitive races made extensive use of clay to model small figures. The earliest civilizations of Egypt, Greece, India, and China worked in clay, but it was always the material at hand, the material in greatest abundance, that was most used. In Egypt, stone was a favorite material. Some of the Egyptians' greatest work was in limestone and sandstone quarried nearby. In Greece and Rome marble was native to the country and of a superior quality. Sculptors soon mastered it to fashion monuments of great beauty.

The first great monumental style to develop in the world was that of Egypt. From predynastic times on, Egyptian religious beliefs advanced the art of sculpture as a magical means of insuring an after-life for the dead. Painting and sculpture both enhanced those vast architectural projects, the pyramids, designed to protect burials throughout the Old, Middle, and New Kingdoms.

Across the Mediterranean, the Aegean cultures of Crete and Mycenae, from the nineteenth to the twelfth century B.C., influenced future trends in Europe and thus in all Western civilizations. From its archaic beginnings in the eighth century B.C., Greece rapidly developed the technique of sculpture with the hand chisel to a climax in the Gold Age (450-400 B.C.). The desire for perfection of the human form became a cult, fostered by the life-style of the age. Contests and games were held in which athletes competed for prizes of laurel wreaths, and commemorative statues were erected in bronze and marble to glorify the victors. Above all, the Greeks dedicated majestic statues to their gods in temples throughout the Greek world.

86

When the Romans conquered Greece in 146 B.C., many bronze and marble statues were looted and taken to adorn the palaces and civic buildings of Rome. Native sculptors imitated the Greek forms, but the practical Romans replaced Greek idealism with their own brand of realism. The resulting images lacked the Greeks' dynamic integration of form and surface, since the Romans employed the mechanical drill instead of the hand chisel.

The conquest of northwest India by the Greeks under Alexander the Great spread the Hellenistic influence in its wake. The imprint of classical art is apparent in the Greco-Roman sculpture of Gandhara and in objects excavated in Afghanistan. However, reproduction of natural form was alien to Indian philosophy, so sculpture soon reverted to traditional abstraction and interpretation of spiritual essence. When a native dynasty was restored in the Gupta period (320 A.D.), magnificent conceptions of the Buddhist deities were created and continued to be produced.

In China, sculpture has always played an important role in the artistic achievement of the country, but it was the infusion of Indian religion into traditional Chinese forms which led to its zenith in the T'ang dynasty (618-907 A.D.). Bronze inlaid with gold and silver, gilded wood, and stone were utilized for serene and majestic religious figures, meticulously worked. By the Sung dynasty (960-1280), delight in decorative detail replaced the spiritual energy of the earlier style, and forms became more suavely elegant and naturalistic.

After the Roman Empire, during the Dark Ages in Europe, sculpture became the handmaiden of Christianity. In the eleventh century, the church grew richer and more powerful. As an integral part of the Medieval cathedral, subject matter was largely dictated by ecclesiastical doctrine. Sculptors, who were formed into guilds, worked anonymously for the glory of God.

During the Renaissance, Italy was the fountainhead of fine sculpture. Whereas sculptured figures during the late Gothic period were primarily decorative elements in churches, sculptors

87

in the fifteenth and sixteenth centuries revived the dignity of man in free-standing form. Their work demonstrates the rise of individualism and naturalism in a secular society in contrast to the dominantly religious outlook of the Middle Ages. The influence of such masters as Donatello in the fifteenth century and Michelangelo in the sixteenth inspired a horde of followers.

Baroque sculpture reached heroic dimensions to conform to the grandiose proportions of architecture. A vast number of flamboyant marble figures disregarded the classical precept that a supreme example of marble sculpture should be so contained within the block of marble that it could be rolled down a hill without damage to any part of it. In reaction, the artists of the neo-classic period such as Canova and Thorwaldsen revived the ideals of Greece and Rome. The movement was sparked by excavations of classical remains at Pompeii and Herculaneum which reflected a general upsurge of interest in archaeology.

In the twentieth century nonrepresentational sculpture has gained world wide acceptance. An awakened appreciation of primitive sculpture of Africa and other exotic arts has been a prime influence on modern sculpture. Sculpture of this century can be characterized with one word, *diversity*. With radically new esthetics, sculptors have explored new directions in style, technique, meaning and form. Every technological innovation of science and industry has been exploited. Although the traditional wood, stone and bronze of the past have continued in use, the repertoire has expanded to include materials unknown before the present day. Much of twentieth century sculpture demands engineering skill as well as artistic skill.

Today one finds interesting applications and combinations of materials such as plastics, chromium, neon lights, plexiglass, mirrors, wood, ball bearings, stone, steel. Movable parts that are electrically controlled (often intended to be set into motion by the viewers), sound devices, discarded nylon hose and other articles of wearing apparel are incorporated into many contemporary works. One even finds artificial limbs, automotive parts, photographs, sponges, bedsprings, stovepipes, light globes

88

and lighting devices, hardware, bits of fur and fabrics, and other ephemera.

Because of the diversity of industrial materials and of mechanical equipment, far more sculpture has been produced since 1900 than in any other comparable period in the history of mankind. Sculptors today do not have to labor for long periods as did sculptors of the past, cutting each piece by hand from a block of stone or wood. Large and massive, or small and delicate in nature, the most distinctive sculpture of today owes its particular stamp to the technological advances of our time.

It is inevitable that with such a wide variety of materials many creations are merely novel, superficial or incidental. Amid radically different theories and diverse forms, still one can discern a pattern which reflects man's quest for meaning in his inner life and a place in the world. Mysterious as some approaches may appear, sculpture of this century has been compelling and stimulating.

The movement, care, and preservation of sculpture made up of combinations of unrelated materials present very special problems and demand special consideration. Each piece is a unique case within itself, to be evaluated individually and solved separately. Much modern sculpture has detachable parts to facilitate movement and shipment. Often the assembly or disassembly of such pieces is so complex that specific directions from the artist, or consultation with him, are necessary. Frequently, the artist must be on hand to direct the packers or handlers. This requirement is sometimes imposed by the artist himself.

For obvious reasons, the following recommendations are for the most part confined to sculpture which was not produced in recent years.

Figure 40. CYCLADIC STATUETTE. One of the earliest examples of sculpture in existence from the Bronze Age, Greece, this primitive marble figure of a woman made in the Cycladic Islands between about 2500 and 2000 B.C. is a miracle of survival through the ages. Close examination shows tattoo marks on face and bears evidence of root marks from burial. *Courtesy, Museum of Fine Arts, Boston.*

Figure 41. MELEAGER. Style of Scopas, Greek, 4th century B.C. A dramatic find of the late nineteenth century and one of the first Greek originals to be purchased by a museum in the United States was this marble statue, excavated in 1895 by Edward Forbes, co-founder of the Fogg Art Museum. Its fragments were found in a basin on the estate of Marquesa Sachetti on the Via Aurelia outside Rome. Samples of the marble from the head and torso were analyzed by William J. Young of the Boston Museum and compared favorably. Traces of marble struts on the left hip, thigh, and buttock were helpful clues in the reconstruction of the parts with modern dowels and cement. In 1961-62, the figure was cleaned and rejoined by the conservation department of Fogg, and the head reset at a different angle. *Courtesy, Fogg Art Museum, Harvard University.*

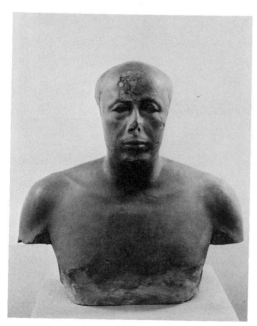

Figure 42. BUST OF THE VIZIER ANKH-HAF. Reign of Chephren, builder of the Second Pyramid, Giza, Dynasty IV, 2625-2600 B.C. Painted limestone. The major achievement of the artists of the Fourth Dynasty was the development of portrait sculpture, and the bust of Ankh-haf delicately modeled in limestone is perhaps the finest portrait to survive from the Old Kingdom. The high percentage of salt in the limestone caused the surface to become deliquescent when the bust was exposed to the high humidity of its new environment. Although it had survived for thousands of years in the preservative climate of Egypt, it began to disintegrate as the salt recrystallized in the drying-out process. Details of features modeled in plaster were painted in red oxide-of-iron watercolor. Ankh-haf is now protected in a separate glass case which automatically regulates the humidity. *Courtesy, Museum of Fine Arts, Boston.*

2.

1.

Figure 43. RELIEFS FROM PALACE OF ASSURNASIRPAL II. Nimrud, Assyria, 9th century B.C. Gypseous alabaster. 1. complete installation of five panels in special display gallery; 2. panel of winged genius. Excavated more than a century ago by British archeologist Sir Austen Henry Layard, these low reliefs were acquired and shipped from England in 1966. At some time in the past, old breaks were closed with iron dowels inserted and cemented into the abutting edges, causing oxidation to take place and weakening the repaired areas. As a result, separation and additional breakage occurred under pressure. In the process of transport, the movement of the parts allowed adjacent surfaces to grind against each other, chip and crack. The fragments which arrived in Los Angeles required physical rejoining of ruptures before presentation to the public. *Courtesy, Los Angeles County Museum of Art.*

1.

2.

3.

Figure 44. SPHINX. Attic, ca. 530 B.C. Marble. Once the crowning
member of a grave monument, this finial is the finest piece of Archaic
sculpture in the Boston Museum collection. 1. and 2. reveal traces of
color which emphasize the important part played by the painter in
the development of Greek sculpture. On the finial, particularly, the
color on the decorative patterns is well preserved; and on the sphinx,
there are traces of blue and green, as well as red and black, on the
feathers of the wings and on the breast. Such excellent color preservation is rare. 3. shows the bronze dowels put into base (upside-down
view) to attach fragments. The lead by which the sphinx was fastened
to the base is largely preserved, and a pour-hole at the back of the
finial indicates where lead was poured to secure this member to the
shaft below. *Courtesy, Research Laboratory, Museum of Fine Arts,
Boston.*

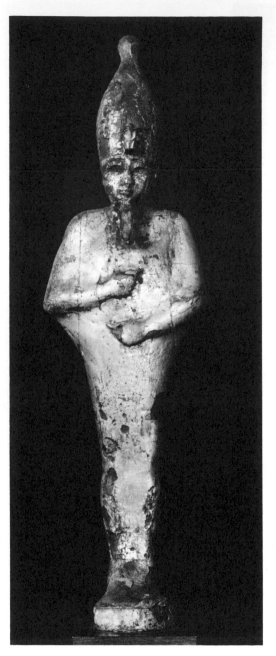 

Figure 45. OSIRIS. Egyptian (New Kingdom), 1580-633 B.C. Gilded wood. This gilded wood sculpture had gilt losses when it was acquired by the Los Angeles County Museum of Art. Total restoration (complete re-gilding) would destroy a part of the sculpture's esthetic value. Extreme care must be exercised in the handling of it to prevent further losses and steps taken to prevent additional gilt losses from sudden changes of temperature and incompatible humidity. *Courtesy, Los Angeles County Museum of Art.*

Figure 46. VIRGIN AND CHILD. Ile-de-France, early 13th century. Polychromed oak. (The highly developed drapery style of the statue with its deep-cut folds is characteristic of Early Gothic cathedral sculpture of northern France, but only in the works of the greatest masters does one note such understanding for the organic function of the body as well as grace, gentleness, and serenity.) Careful cleaning by the Research Laboratory revealed polychrome paint, including dragon's blood (a dark, resinous pigment known from the time of Pliny). The date of the statue was confirmed by the carbon 14 test. *Courtesy, Museum of Fine Arts, Boston.*

Figure 47.

1.

2.

Figure 48.

Figure 49.

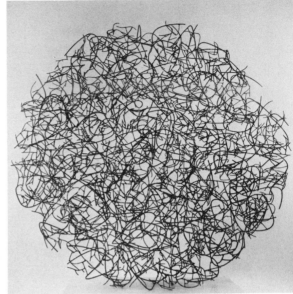

Figure 50.

Figure 47. KUAN-YIN. Chinese, Sung Dynasty, 12th century. Wood. After restoration and removal of paper and five layers of opaque over-painting, including two layers of gold, this carved wooden statue appeared in its original rich range of colors. Note particularly details such as the *urna* in the middle of the forehead, which is not apparent in 1 but becomes visible in 2. *Courtesy, Museum of Fine Arts, Boston. Figure 48.* GO-ZANZA MYO-O. Japanese, Fujiwara Period, 897-1185. Wood. This wood sculpture formerly had eight arms; the legs are also missing. Ravages of time, temperature, humidity—and possibly human handling—brought about the present condition. The sculpture was carved in the single-block technique, characteristic of ninth-century sculpture. The grain of the wood has been effectively used in the chest area and natural lines of the wood have aided in the modeling of the body and faces. Changes in atmospheric climate cause little change along the grain of wood, but expansion across the grain results in warping. In part, this may account for the better preservation of those portions which remain. *Courtesy, Los Angeles County Museum of Art. Figure 49.* ROOSTER. Sascha Brastoff, American, born 1918. *Courtesy, Los Angeles County Museum of Art. Figure 50.* VIBRATION. Claire Falkenstein, American, born 1908. Welded metal sculpture requires special handling and special storage. Shipment by van, with the sculpture blanketed, is the safest method for this particular sculpture. *Courtesy, Los Angeles County Museum of Art.*

Figure 51. NUDE FEMALE. Edgar Degas, French, 1834-1917. Projecting areas require special attention and special padding to prevent damages.

Figure 52. This case was designed especially for the shipment of the bronze sculpture. Note the constructed wood support for the base of the sculpture and the padded wood bracing. Before shipment the space within the crate was filled with a shock-mitigant material. Instructions for unpacking were lettered on one end of the crate. *Courtesy, Los Angeles County Museum of Art.*

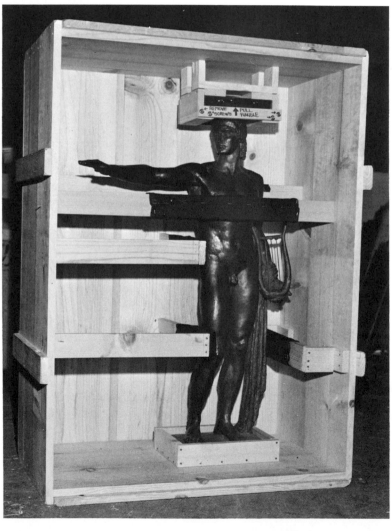

RULES FOR CARE AND HANDLING

Never move one piece of sculpture with another or with any other objects. A slight movement of a dolly in the wrong direction could cause sculpture to move independently resulting in damage.

Move each piece by itself

With highly polished surfaces, there is the danger of insecure grasp if gloves are worn, but they are recommended when handling most types of sculpture. Marble, alabaster, limestone, terra cotta and other media tend to absorb dirt and grime. When hands come in contact with polished metal sculpture the salt content in perspiration causes discoloration even if the residue is not visible.

Wear gloves except with highly polished surfaces

Regardless of size, weight or media, all sculpture should rest on heavy but soft pads while being moved. Pieces should be kept in place by means of blankets, padded blocks, battens, padded wedges or a combination of these. Extra precautions prevent harmful movements during transit. With some pieces it is advisable to lash the sculpture to the truck or dolly but only after padding has been applied, never next to the sculpture. Heavy, cumbersome pieces require special equipment such as hoists.

Use pads, battens, blankets, and wedges

Blankets, pads and other materials used in moving sculpture must be perfectly clean. Dirt becomes imbedded in these protective coverings if they are used for long periods of time. New protective coverings are a good investment. Sculpture which rapidly absorbs grime and dust should be covered with tissue paper or clean soft cloth, even if the padding appears to be clean. Using dirty cushioning in direct contact with sculpture is as harmful as dirty gloves or dirty hands.

Protective coverings must be clean

Over padding and excessive use of cushioning materials is sometimes as unwise as no padding, depending on the shape, medium, weight and other considerations. It can create unequal pressure within the structure of the object itself, thereby causing breakage by self-weight.

When moving sculpture, its weight should be evenly distributed. With some sculpture, because of size, weight or the physical structure of the museum, it is necessary to devise unusual, special handling procedures and methods of transportation in order to obviate

Weight should be evenly distributed

99

damage and relieve abnormal strain on parts which were designed for positions other than those in which the sculpture must be moved.

Projecting parts require special attention

Projecting areas require special attention and particular padding to prevent damage or breakage. With some pieces, vulnerable parts are obvious. Points of figurative sculpture, which always demand special attention, extra support, and extra padding, are the neck, arms, legs and hands.

Lift, do not drag, sculpture

Lift, never push or drag, a piece of sculpture. Terra cotta sculpture, in particular, should be gently handled. If dragged or pushed, extreme damage or breakage often occur.

Plan action

Know exactly how a piece of sculpture is to be handled before beginning its movement. If it is small, have a carrying box near

Take moving device to the sculpture

before picking up the piece. *Do not take the sculpture to the box. Take the box to the sculpture.* If a sculpture is large enough to require a dolly or hand truck, bring the moving device to the area instead of taking the sculpture to the transportation. No matter what the device, have it near the sculpture before touching it. This simple precaution will lessen the chances of dropping and of breakage.

There was a time when the general rule for transporting sculpture was that it be moved in a horizontal position, never upright. Today there is such a variety of sculptural media and so many different kinds of sculpture that no rigid rule can be enforced. Even when museum personnel adhered to the horizontal position rule, it was

Specific characteristics determine positions for moving

seldom the position the sculptor intended. Now size, shape, weight and media dictate the position in which sculpture should be moved with maximum safety. Sometimes an upright position is the only feasible one; sometimes, owing to contour, weight and size, a horizontal position is immediately recognized as the safest. Brittle pieces are usually moved upright. Mortised wood, often with protruding elements, should remain upright. Sometimes the medium, not the shape or size, is the determining factor.

Sculptures with bases are special problems

If a sculpture is permanently secured to a pedestal or base and is to be moved without separation of the two, consideration must be given to the weight of the pedestal or base in relation to the weight of the sculpture. What may appear as a secure arrangement in a

Movement

gallery should not necessarily be considered safe for movement. Consider the example of a rather heavy piece attached to a pedestal. Assume that it is against a gallery wall. Perhaps it has been on exhibi-

100

tion for a long time and has had a barrier so that the public could not reach it. (Without the barrier possibly a casual contact might topple it.) It is never wise to take such chances in public areas. Mankind is always capable of ignoring barriers. *The base, if of lesser weight than the sculpture, should have ballast, even if a barrier is provided.* Now, consider that this piece is to be moved. No accident or incident has occurred while it was on exhibition. *Do not move it in either a horizontal or upright position before adding ballast to the hollow base.* The ballast should fill the base to capacity whether movement is made in an upright or horizontal position.

Add ballast to the base if lighter than sculpture

If a piece becomes chipped or broken during movement, all fragments should be carefully collected and preserved, no matter how small. Every fragment is valuable for restoration or repair. Expert conservators can accomplish remarkable feats if pieces are preserved. They may or may not use the fragments, but when it is possible to use them, repairs can be almost totally indiscernible. Even when the fragments are not used, they may be valuable to the restorer as an index to color, shape, composition, chemical content, and in other ways.

Collect and preserve fragments broken off sculpture

The most experienced museum professional is often confronted with problems never met before. No matter how many years of experience, consultation with other professionals is advisable when deciding on the safest procedures for the movement of a piece of sculpture. Problems with movement are not always confined to weighty sculpture or to those of unusual shapes. Discussions and a consolidation of past experiences are wise prior to moving a piece of sculpture.

Do not assume you know everything

Any condition not already known and recorded and any condition occasioned during movement should be reported and recorded before further movement. Conditions of any nature, severe or slight, should be made known immediately to those in authority. Serious conditions should be carefully documented both in writing and photographically.

Report and document conditions immediately

Most collections include wood sculpture. The conservation and care of wood is a matter of importance. The most common form of deterioration of wood in temperate climates is dimensional changes resulting from variations of relative humidity. Changes in atmospheric environment cause wood to alternately absorb and give up moisture. Changes in atmospheric humidity cause little change along

Changes in humidity cause wood to warp

101

the grain of wood, but expansion and contraction *across* the grain results in warping.

Insects are the greatest menace to wood in a museum; termites are the most injurious of the wood-feeding insects. If timber pests are not controlled at an early state, a wood sculpture may literally fall to pieces. The presence of a light-colored powder usually is the first indication of attack by insects. Unless wood objects are carefully examined and inspected on a regular basis, they may deteriorate beyond repair. Fumigation is the only way to prevent and eradicate wood-boring insects.

Holes in wood do not always indicate that insects are still alive. They sometimes die before wood is totally destroyed, but it should never be assumed that insect activity has ceased. If there is any doubt, assume the worst and take steps to check the destruction. A wood sculpture should be brushed carefully with a soft brush. After brushing, treat the sculpture with an insecticide or fumigate it. Small wood sculpture can be treated in a fumigation tank with which

Fill holes with beeswax

most large museums are equipped. All holes should be filled with a soft wax so that new attacks by insects will be apparent in case some of the pests were not killed with fumigation or a new horde attacks the wood. The insecticide DDT can be stirred into melted beeswax, then bleached or colored to match. Waxing by immersion has been developed on a large scale at the Walters Art Gallery, Baltimore,

Spraying is not effective

Maryland, by David Rosen.[1] Spraying has not been very effective for killing pests which bore into wood.

Do not store different media together

Storage and atmospheric conditions are special studies. All sculpture cannot be stored together safely, nor can there be definite rules because of the variety of component materials used for sculpturing. It is not possible to recommend atmospheric conditions for sculpture per se. Specialists disagree on a maximum and minimum temperature range and desired RH. The consensus among authorities seems to fall within the following recommendations for desired environment:

Desired RH for metal

Metal sculpture should be kept at a low RH, below 40%. Most steel, brass, aluminum alloy, and organic materials can be stored with safety at about 45% RH. Above this, rust and corrosion can occur.

Stone sculpture should be maintained at below 50%; *wood sculpture* at about 55%; *plaster sculpture* at less than 50%. *Ceramic*

1. "The Preservation of Wood Sculpture: The Wax Immersion Method," *Journal of the Walters Art Gallery*, 1950-1951, pp. 45-71.

sculpture differs. The desirable RH atmospheric condition for ceramic sculpture depends on the degree of firing but no ceramic sculpture should be exposed to high relative humidity.

BIBLIOGRAPHY

Ashton, Dore. *Modern American Sculpture.* New York, Harry N. Abrams, Inc., 1968.

Bazin, Germain. *The History of World Sculpture—An Illustrated Survey from Pre-history to the Present Day.* Greenwich, Conn., New York Graphic Society, 1968.

Buck, Richard D. "A Note on the Effect of Age on the Hygroscopic Behavior of Wood," *Studies in Conservation,* Vol. I, no. 4 (October, 1952), pp. 39-44.

Charbonneaux, J. *Greek Bronzes.* New York, The Viking Press, 1962.

Cheney, Sheldon. *Sculpture of the World.* New York, The Viking Press, 1968.

Craven, Wayne. *Sculpture in America.* New York, Thomas Y. Crowell Co., 1968.

Fagg, William and Plass, Margaret. *African Sculpture.* London, Dutton & Co., 1964.

Hager, Werner. (Intro.) *Baroque Sculpture.* New York, McGraw-Hill Book Co., 1968.

Hammacher, A. M. *Evolution of Modern Sculpture: Tradition and Innovation.* New York, Harry N. Abrams, Inc., 1968.

Hanfmann, George. *Classical Sculpture.* Greenwich, Conn., New York Graphic Society, 1967.

Lee, Sherman E. *Ancient Cambodian Sculpture.* Greenwich, Conn., New York Graphic Society, 1969.

Licht, Fred. *Sculpture, 19th and 20th Centuries.* Greenwich, Conn., New York Graphic Society, 1967.

Lynch, John. *Metal Sculpture.* New York, Studio-Crowell, 1957.

Maillard Robert (Ed.). *Dictionary of Modern Sculpture.* New York, Tudor Publishing Co., 1962.

Nichols, Henry W. *Restoration of Ancient Bronzes and Cure of Malignant Patina.* Chicago, Field Museum of Natural History, Museum Techniques Series No. 3.

Packard, Elizabeth C. G. "The Preservation of Polychromed Wood Sculpture by the Wax Immersion and Other Methods," *Museum News,* Vol. 46, no. 2 (October, 1967), Technical Supplement No. 19, pp. 47-52.

Panofsky, Erwin. *Tomb Sculpture: Its Aspects from Ancient Egypt to Bernini.* New York, Harry N. Abrams, Inc., 1969.

Plenderleith, H. J. "Technical Notes on Chinese Bronzes with Special Reference to Patina and Incrustations," *Transactions of the Oriental Ceramic Society*, Vol. XVI (1938-1939), pp. 33-35.

Rogers, L. R. *Sculpture.* New York, Oxford University Press, 1969.

Rood, John. *Sculpture in Wood.* Minneapolis, University of Minnesota Press, 1968.

Rorimer, James J. "Forgeries of Medieval Stone Sculpture," *Gazette des Beaux-Arts*, Vol. XXVI (1944), pp. 195-210.

———. "The Restoration of Medieval Sculpture," *Metropolitan Museum Studies*, Vol. V, Part II (1936), pp. 170-181.

Rosen, David. "The Preservation of Wood Sculpture: The Wax Immersion Method," *Journal of the Walters Art Gallery* (Baltimore), (1950-1951), pp. 45-71.

Salvini, Roberto. *Medieval Sculpture.* Greenwich, Conn., New York Graphic Society, 1970.

Savage, George A. *A Concise History of Bronzes.* New York, Frederick A. Praeger, 1969.

Stamm, Alfred J. and Hansen, L. A. "Minimizing Wood Shrinkage and Swelling," *Industrial and Engineering Chemistry*, Vol. XXVII (1935), pp. 1480-1484.

———. and Seborg, R. M. "Minimizing Wood Shrinkage and Swelling: Treating with Synthetic Resin-Forming Materials," *Industrial and Engineering Chemistry*, Vol. XXVIII (1936), pp. 1164-1169.

Williamson, Moncrieff. "A Combination Shipping, Display and Storage Unit for Small Sculptures," *Museum News*, Vol. 41, no. 6 (February, 1963), pp. 34-36.

Wilpert, Joseph. "Early Christian Sculpture: Its Restoration and Its Modern Manufacture," *The Art Bulletin*, Vol. IX (1926), pp. 110-141.

6

Ceramics

The term *ceramics*, or *pottery*, in its widest definition, refers to all objects fashioned of clay and baked or hardened by firing. In its moist condition, clay is pliable and can be formed into any shape. When dried by exposure, it retains its shape; when baked at a high temperature, a permanent and irreversible change takes place. It becomes one of the most durable substances known.

However primitive they may be, receptacles or containers have always been necessary to man. Pottery has an advantage over basketry, skins, gourds, and other natural objects because it can be used over fires as cooking vessels and yet not be burned or rendered useless. Perhaps the discovery of clay's numerous uses stemmed from the practice of lining baskets with clay so they could hold liquids and small solids, and an accidental fire left the clay standing solid after the basket had been destroyed.

Primitive man used the clay he found easiest to obtain—that on top of the ground or in shallow river beds. Even before the dawn of recorded civilization, the art of forming vessels by hand was practiced by all peoples throughout the world. Crude specimens of Neolithic man's pottery designed for food utensils, drinking cups, and cinerary urns have been excavated, as well as similar vessels in the graves and barrows of the Old and New Worlds. All of these were baked in an open fire and, if decorated, have a geometric decoration stamped into the clay before firing.

From humble domestic vessel to grand palace, clay has served the multiple needs of mankind. In the Tigris-Euphrates valley it provided the material for building the magnificent glazed-tile residences of kings, and it was also the vehicle for recording the first writing, cuneiform, which the Mesopotamians incised into clay tablets before firing. From predynastic China to imperial Persia, funerary ceramic ware reveals the progress of man and attests to the universality of the art.

Through the centuries, the potter's wheel and tools for shaping pots and objects gradually evolved. The Egyptians and the Chinese both claim to have invented the potter's wheel. The former regarded it as a tool of the gods and believed that Ptah, the creator, fashioned the "egg of the earth" on such a wheel. Wherever it originated, the potter's wheel greatly facilitated the manufacture of pottery and has been in constant use ever since.

The Egyptians are also credited with discovering how to glaze, that is, apply superficial layers of a molten material onto a clay object. Glazes are of two types, lead silicate and feldspathic. Some of the earliest glazes were colored glass containing copper or iron and appear on beads and plaques; but as early as 2000 B.C. the Egyptians were making seven different colors in glazes. The typical turquoise, yellow, and green glazes of Egypt and Assyria still retain their brilliance today.

Both lead silicate and feldspathic were used in China in the Han Dynasty (205 B.C.-220 A.D.). The feldspathic glaze was China's unique discovery which, combined with their skillful construction of kilns, led to the Chinese invention of porcelain. Their feldspar glaze contained some iron which imparted the characteristic green color of feldspathic celadon ware, now classified as Yüeh.

In the Ming Dynasty (1368-1644), a wide range of colored

glazes and enamels were developed. With great technical ingenuity the Chinese craftsmen developed combinations of colors for both monochrome and polychrome decorations of Ming wares.

However, China's outstanding contribution to the ceramic art is the invention of porcelain. Its history dates from the manufacture of hard shell-like porcelain from kaolin during the Han Dynasty (205 B.C.-220 A.D.). It is characterized by a glassy fracture, clear ring when struck, uniform thickness, and resistance to fire, water, and all acid except hydrofluoric. From the earliest days, the Chinese have ranked fine porcelain as one of their most precious materials, along with jade. Westerners admire the translucence and high vitrification that makes it impossible to scratch it with a knife.

By the fifteenth century, Chinese porcelain was imported into European countries. The unusual hardness (it is almost infusible) and rare translucence excited the Florentines particularly. Working under the patronage of Francesco de'Medici, they attempted to imitate the Chinese work and produced a translucent ware called Medici porcelain.

During the Renaissance, the Italians reached the highest peak of achievement in the potter's art, developing a type called *majolica*, an earthenware coated with an opaque tin glaze or enamel on which decoration could be applied. A similar type, called *faience*, was made at Lyon, France, in the sixteenth century by Italian potters; thriving faience centers mushroomed throughout France in the following centuries.

Attempts by Europeans to imitate Chinese porcelain resulted in an artificial porcelain which was fired at a low temperature and made translucent with a previously fired glassy mix, called "frit." These were known as soft paste (*pâte tendre*). They comprised the characteristic French porcelain made at St. Cloud, Vincennes, etc. for nearly a hundred years and were widely adapted in Spain, England and Italy.

The secret of manufacturing true hard-paste porcelain was discovered by Johann Friedrich Böttger in Meissen, Saxony, in

107

1707. Following the lead of the Meissen factory, others sprang up to satisfy the enormous demand in the eighteenth century. Vienna, Berlin, St. Petersburg, Sèvres, Limoges, and Bristol were leading competitors. Porcelain manufacture throughout the continent and in England developed to a great degree in the eighteenth century.

In the United States, there was little success during Colonial days in producing ceramics for domestic use, although there are records that bricks and roof tiles were made by white settlers in the seventeenth century. Dishes for everyday use and porcelains for entertaining company were imported, mainly from England. As the United States became more settled by Europeans, the demand for dishes of all kinds increased. More and more potters tried to supply the demand, but at first only the plainest wares were made; crockery of glazed earthenware or stoneware served as articles for domestic use. Neither is translucent like porcelain. The term "china" is still used for all kinds of table dishes and ornamental pieces, because the first porcelain that Westerners saw came from China.

Stoneware, a hard nonporous pottery, was particularly suitable for kitchen and dairy use in the New World. At first the demand for it was supplied by potters from Vermont to Maryland. Later, it was produced in great quantity and variety in the Ohio valley where its form and decoration continued to be outstanding until about 1880. Until the 1850's ceramics in the United States were decorated freehand. In the 1860's stencils came into use for decoration.

During the latter half of the nineteenth century, the pottery of Christopher Webber Fenton, who began his operations in Bennington, Vermont, in the 1840's, took the lead in producing several kinds of porcelain. One was Parian, a fine, hard, flat white, unglazed porcelain, which is a version of *bisque*. Parian statuettes, ewers and vases were a mark of distinction in homes between the 1850's and 1900.

While the United States did not contribute any important new technique to ceramics, much American ware has charm

108

and individuality. With little scientific knowledge, potters had to discover methods by trial and error. Some enterprising manufacturers imported Europeans—skilled workmen from France, England and Germany—to improve their products. The American Ceramic Society, founded in 1898, coordinates ceramic interests and fosters research to further progress. Because emphasis was put on science and technique at the expense of design, form and color, the ever-changing taste of the American public became prejudiced in favor of imported ceramics. This time there was a good reason: the absence of that intangible quality which is the mark of an original artist and is absent in the work of a copyist.

Collectors appreciate the importance of fine pottery and porcelain as social documents which deserve the utmost care to preserve them from the vicissitudes of time. Although the agencies which corrode metal have little effect on fired clay, still there are varieties which are exceedingly fragile, such as the delicate porcelains of the Orient and Europe. In these areas, the craft of the restorer is increasingly valuable since completely undamaged pieces are becoming rarer.

Most experts agree on the desirability of restoration of some kind, if not on the extent. The stress today is on confining restoration to those parts which have been damaged and protecting pieces against the tendency of over-zealous restorers to paint over large, undamaged areas to disguise a trivial repair. Equally commendable is the general condemnation by ceramic authorities of the use of sprays to confuse the searching eye of ultraviolet radiation. Properly applied, good restoration is an invaluable aid to conservation and only becomes the object of criticism when its purpose is to deceive.

RULES FOR CARE AND HANDLING

Do not lift by projecting elements

Do not lift or carry a ceramic object by its handles, rims or any other projecting part. Handles, although usually designed for ease in carrying the object, should not be used in museums. Often handles, rims and other projections have been broken off and restored or replaced, and so the mended or reconstructed area must

Weak areas

be regarded as weakened and must not be subjected to undue stress or strain and the chances of a rebreaking.

How to carry by hand

Pieces of ceramics small enough to be carried by one person should be carried with one hand on the bottom and the other hand at the side and toward the top but not at the topmost part or rim. Never try to carry more than one object at a time by hand.

Be sure hands are clean before touching. Many glazed pieces are not entirely covered with glaze, leaving the baked portion partially exposed. Fingerprints on such areas can mar their beauty and are all but impossible to remove.

Gloves not recommended

It is not generally recommended that gloves be worn. Smooth surfaces make handling with gloves difficult and risky. If gloves are worn, extra care must be exercised to avoid slipping from grasp. Even when gloves are worn, wash hands first.

Comparative fragility

The fragility or stability of ceramics is due to a number of things. Clay varies in chemical composition and impurity content. Even different pieces from the same clay can vary widely depending on the temperature, duration of firing, and the method used. Inadequate firing often results in soft, porous examples which are more liable to damages.

Resistance is high

Baked clay, genuine ceramic ware, is highly resistant to chemical action. It rivals gold in permanence if it has been fired properly, is fully glazed, and does not contain impurities or foreign substances. If clay is baked at a sufficiently high temperature, the possibility of deterioration is about the same as stone. Pottery baked at low temperatures is more fragile and more sensitive to external agents.

Unfired clay

Unfired clay, depending on its constituents and the manner in which it is dried, is generally more fragile than fired clay. It can be strengthened by applying a thin coat of cellulose lacquer and allowed to dry for several days.

110

Figure 53. MADONNA OF VICTORY. Johann Martin Mutschele, German, 1733-1804. Schrezheim faience, white glazed. The extreme sophistication in complex forms, attained by German potters in the eighteenth century, is well exemplified in this dramatic figure with windswept drapery. Made for the niche over the door of the Prinzen Inn of the Deutsche Orden at Wolframs-Eschenbach, it is the most important creation of German faience at the museum, where it is individually displayed. Contours and certain details were purposely left unglazed. *Courtesy, Museum of Fine Arts, Boston.*

Figure 54. ITALIAN PLATE. Francesco Xanto Avelli, Italian, ca. 1532. Examination of this majolica plate (figure 1) made at Urbina in 1532 for the Pucci family of Florence by Francesco Xanto Avelli of Rovigo, a celebrated master in his field, reveals lines of partial or complete fracture and the addition of a varnish-like surface along the lines of fracture. The broken plate has been skill-fully repaired and retouched. The answer to the question "To what extent?" comes clearly under ultra-violet (figure 2), and the camera has recorded the difference of reaction between the original glaze and the work of the restorer. *Courtesy, Research Laboratory, Museum of Fine Arts, Boston.*

Figure 55. THE MADONNA AND CHILD. Benedetto da Maiano, Florentine, 1442–1497. Terracotta relief. Enhancing details with paint on terracotta is characteristic of this Renaissance sculptor's technique. Traces of white still cling to surface; adhesion is secured with fixative. *Courtesy, Isabella Stewart Gardner Museum, Boston.*

1.

2.

Figure 56. AMPHORA. Pottery, late XVIII Dynasty, ca. 1350 B.C. This majestic vase retains traces of prized "Egyptian blue." *Courtesy, Museum of Fine Arts, Boston.*

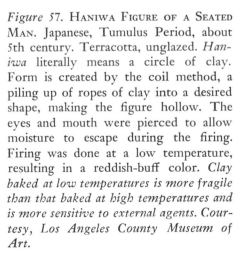

Figure 57. HANIWA FIGURE OF A SEATED MAN. Japanese, Tumulus Period, about 5th century. Terracotta, unglazed. *Haniwa* literally means a circle of clay. Form is created by the coil method, a piling up of ropes of clay into a desired shape, making the figure hollow. The eyes and mouth were pierced to allow moisture to escape during the firing. Firing was done at a low temperature, resulting in a reddish-buff color. *Clay baked at low temperatures is more fragile than that baked at high temperatures and is more sensitive to external agents. Courtesy, Los Angeles County Museum of Art.*

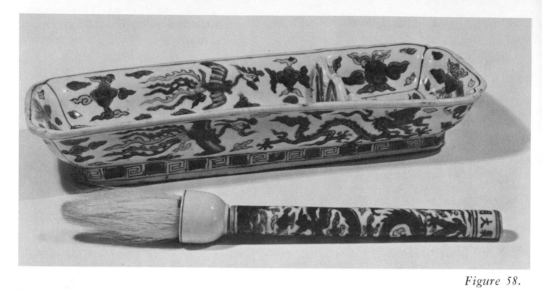

Figure 58.

Figure 59.

Figure 58. PORCELAIN BRUSH AND STAND. Chinese, Ming Dynasty, Wan Li Period. Chinese porcelain was the much-coveted "white gold" of the eighteenth century in Europe and the New World. Collectors literally paid for its weight in gold, and Augustus the Strong of Saxony once gave the King of Prussia a regiment of dragoons for a particularly fine set of Ming vases from the same period as examples illustrated above. Even after the Meissen alchemist Boettger discovered its "secret" in 1709, true chinaware retained its fascination. *Courtesy, Fogg Art Museum, Harvard University.*

Figure 59. PORCELAIN GROUP. English (Chelsea), 1750-1753. Lady in Eastern costume standing with a Chinese child by a pot of boiling water. Separate figure of a Chinese boy with a bowl. *Courtesy, Museum of Fine Arts, Boston.*

Figure 60. OINOCHOE. Greek, 6th century B.C. Ceramic black-figured. *Courtesy, Los Angeles County Museum of Art.*

Figure 61. TEA BOWL. Chinese, Sung Dynasty, 960-1279. Chien ware (stoneware). *Courtesy, Los Angeles County Museum of Art.*

Figure 62. DISH. Hispano-Moresque, first half of the 15th century. Earthenware. *Courtesy, Los Angeles County Museum of Art.*

Figure 63. FLORAL PUNCH BOWL. Chinese, 18th century. Export Ware, Porcelain. *Courtesy, Museum of Fine Arts, Boston.*

Figure 60.

Figure 61.

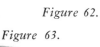

Figure 62.

Figure 63.

Figure 65.

Figure 64.

Figure 66.

Figure 64. Fan-Spout Ewer. Persian, 10th century B.C. Clay. *Courtesy, Los Angeles County Museum of Art.*

Figure 65. Bowl. Persian (Rhages), 11th-13th century. Pottery. *Courtesy, Los Angeles County Museum of Art.*

Figure 66. Well-Jar. Chinese, Han Dynasty, 206 B.C.-A.D. 220. Pottery. *Courtesy, Los Angeles County Museum of Art.*

Glazed pottery is more permanent than unglazed. Vitreous glaze film is waterproof, but if a piece is not totally glazed, or if glazing is imperfect, the body of the ware, in addition to being subject to damage by fingerprints, may also be attacked by soluble salts. Salts tend to crystallize and eventually cause glaze to flake. The principal enemy of ceramics is water with salt in solution. All porous clay pieces become quite frail under wet conditions. *Glazed pottery is more permanent than unglazed* *Principal enemy is salt*

Unbaked clay objects should never be cleaned with any solution. Gently blow away any dust accumulation or brush it off with a soft brush; this is the only safe method of removing dust particles from unbaked clay. *Remove dust from unbaked clay by brushing*

Baked clay objects, even if unglazed, may be cleaned by washing them with a detergent water solution, if care is taken and they are not allowed to soak in water. *Washing with detergent*

A glazed piece which is cracked or "crazed" should not be washed. "Crazing" denotes fractures in the glaze which result from the rate of expansion and contraction of the glaze and the body of the object. It is comparable to "crackle" in paint or "checking" in wood finishes. Hot water should be avoided in cleaning all ceramics in any condition. *Avoid hot water*

If several pieces are moved at one time, the tray, cart or carrying box used for transfer should be carefully padded. *Separate pieces with padding in box*

Each piece should be separated from the others within a carrying box to prevent abrasion, chipping and breakage. Cotton batting can be used for most pieces unless they have a rough surface. Pieces with incising should *not* be wrapped with cotton, which tends to cling to rough areas and is tedious and difficult to remove. Wrap such objects first in clean tissue paper or a clear polyethylene sheet and then pad them. *Wrapping*

Do not overcrowd a carrying device. Do not *pack* objects in the container. Even with sturdy pieces, overcrowding can cause mended fractures to separate. *Do not overcrowd*

Always unpack ceramics on a padded table so that any detached parts or fragments may be recovered and will not be lost or damaged. *Unpack on padded table*

Never allow a piece of ceramic to protrude beyond the top or edges of a carrying box, tray, hand truck, storage shelf or bin. The chance of damage is greatly increased when any portion of a ceramic piece protrudes. *Do not allow to protrude*

Guard against Guard all ceramics against exposure to high relative humidity,
exposure to regardless of their size, firing, glazing, or physical condition. It is
high RH difficult to establish a recommended favorable RH range for ceramics, but authorities do agree that the desired relative humidity
depends largely on the degree of firing and type of ceramic surface.

Desirable RH The degree of firing often cannot be established by observation,
depends on and usually this information is unavailable. Based on the general
firing acceptance of a constant RH of about 40% for glass and less than
50% for enamels, a safe conclusion is that ceramic wares should be
maintained in an RH atmosphere range between 40% and 55%.

BIBLIOGRAPHY

Bacci, M. *European Porcelain*. New York, Marlboro Books, 1969.

Barber, Edwin Atlee. *The Ceramic Collectors' Glossary* (Reprint of the Walpole Society publication of 1914) New York, Da Capo Press, 1967.

Berges, Ruth. *Collector's Choice of Porcelain and Faience*. New York, A. S. Barnes & Co., 1968.

Billington, Dora. *The Technique of Pottery*. London, B. T. Batsford, Ltd., 1963.

Charleston, Rober J. (Ed.) *World Ceramics*. New York, McGraw-Hill Book Co., 1968.

Colbeck, John. *Pottery: The Technique of Throwing*. New York, Watson-Guptill Publications, Inc., 1968.

Cox, Warren E. *The Book of Pottery and Porcelain*. New York, Crown Publishers, Inc., 1944.

Cushion, John Patrick, in collaboration with W. B. Honey. *Handbook of Pottery and Porcelain Marks*. New York, Pitman Publishing Corp., 1957.

Dodd, A. E. *Dictionary of Ceramics*. New York, Philosophical Library, 1964.

Fink, Colin G. "Incrustations on Porous Pottery: A New Method of Cleaning Without Loss of Pigment," *Technical Studies in the Field of Fine Arts*, Vol. II, no. 2 (October, 1933), pp. 58-61.

Godden, Geoffrey A. *An Illustrated Encyclopedia of British Pottery and Porcelain*. New York, Crown Publishers, Inc., 1966.

Green, David. *Pottery, Materials and Techniques*. New York, Frederick A. Praeger, 1967.

Hillier, Bevis. *Pottery and Porcelain, 1700-1914*. London, Weidenfeld & Nicolson, 1969.

118

Honey, William Bowyer. *European Ceramic Art from the End of the Middle Ages to About 1815*. London, Faber & Faber, 1949.

Koyama, Fujio, and Figgess, John. *2,000 Years of Oriental Ceramics*. New York, Harry N. Abrams, Inc., 1962; 1968.

Nelson, Glenn C. *Ceramics: A Potter's Handbook*. 2nd ed. New York, Holt, Rinehart & Winston, Inc., 1965.

Savage, George. *Eighteenth Century German Porcelain*. 1968.

Schwartz, Marvin D., and Wolfe, Richard. *A History of American Art Porcelain*. New York, Renaissance Editions, 1968.

Shaw, Kenneth. *Ceramic Colors and Pottery Decoration*. New York, Frederick A. Praeger, 1969.

Taggart, Ross T. "Relief Ornamented Ceramics, An Historical Survey," *Bulletin of the Nelson Gallery and Atkins Museum*, Kansas City, Mo., Vol. IV, no. 3 (1963).

Wills, Geoffrey. *English Pottery and Porcelain*. London, Guinness Superlatives, Ltd., 1968.

Winterburn, Mollie. *The Technique of Handbuilt Pottery*. New York, Watson-Guptill Publications, Inc., 1968.

Wuthenau, Alexander von. *The Art of Terracotta Pottery in Pre-Columbian Central and South America*, 1970.

7

Oriental Scroll and
Screen Paintings

The Chinese have always regarded the art of calligraphy as equal to that of painting. Early Chinese writings speak of painting as one of the six branches of calligraphy, the branch offering expression of matter through form. Chang Yen-yüan wrote in his *Li Tai Ming Hua Chi*, or *The Origin of Painting*, completed in 845 A.D., that, since there were no means of transmitting ideas, writing was invented, "and, as there was no way of showing the shapes, painting was introduced, all in accordance with the purpose of Heaven and Earth and the ancient Sages." Chinese painting, more than any other Chinese form of art, sums up the attitude of the Chinese toward nature and the physical world, thus providing a synthesis of Chinese thought. In painting the natural scenes about him, he regarded man as no more important than birds and animals, so human figures were infinitesimal parts of landscape paintings, never the center of attention.

Since no comparable development took place in the Western world, it is sometimes difficult to appreciate and evaluate Chinese calligraphy; at all times there is control of the brush which is always used with complete mastery and ease. Furthermore, the close affinity between the two arts, painting and calligraphy, must be grasped, if one is to understand and appreciate Chinese and Japanese paintings to the fullest.

As Chinese painting matured, it gradually invented a system of spacing which was unique in the art of the world. Pictorial forms were reduced to bare essentials. No subject was thought too slight to depict if seen with true vision. Landscapes seemed to the Chinese a loftier subject than the human form, because it expressed the wholeness of the world, of which man is but a part. Suggestion is paramount. Empty spaces are eloquent. The creation of a mood is the aim, with the painter assuming that the viewer will possess the sensibility to participate. Behind this idea lies the conception that art in essence is a communication between mind and mind, a fusion of thoughts and emotions, which could never be expressed through language. The dominant aim is that the work of art should plant a fertilizing seed to blossom in the beholder's mind.

Unfortunately, very ancient Chinese paintings are rare, but the practice of repeating famous compositions, copying them exactly or with slight variations, imparts a general idea of their style. In Japan, collections of original paintings, both Chinese and Japanese, have been preserved for centuries.

Most Chinese paintings are on silk or on a soft, absorbent paper. Painters sized their silk by mixing alum dissolved in water with glue, later beating the silk. Many of the masterpieces of China are in monochrome or subdued tones. Chinese ink is a remarkable substance with a capacity for an infinite range of tones from the deepest lustrous black to a faint, silvery grey. It is a form of carbon combined with glue and comes in sticks or cakes. In addition to ink, both mineral and vegetable pigments were used by Chinese painters. Even when Chinese paintings are in color, ink is usually the foundation of the composition.

The beginnings of the art of painting in Japan are as much a mystery and myth as the beginnings of the Japanese race itself, but it is generally conceded that Japanese painting owes a great debt to China. The Japanese mind also approached the subject of painting through calligraphy. Judging from the works now

121

in existence, it is evident that many techniques and styles were derived from the Chinese.

Japanese painters also painted on silk and paper. Strength of brush strokes is the first essential for both Chinese and Japanese. Differences of "touch" were as personal to each painter as his own voice. A wet brush laid to a sheet of paper or a piece of silk must be handled boldly, rapidly and without hesitation. Since silk and paper are highly absorbent, strokes once applied cannot be corrected.

Whether on silk or paper, most of the paintings are in the form of hanging scrolls, hand scrolls, or screens. The purpose of a *hand scroll* is to allow the viewer to unroll it little by little and enjoy the pictorial text scene by scene. They are never hung but are kept rolled and stored in their own boxes, opened only for inspection. To view, one unrolls the scroll horizontally from right to left. The hand scroll, or *emaki*, consists of a single long sheet of paper or a number of such sheets joined lengthwise. A cover is pasted at one end and a roller at the other. The sheets are wound around the roller, which is made of wood, bone, or ivory. The leisurely rolling motion is timed by the viewer. Spread out in museum show-cases, scrolls are seen in toto, contrary to their essential character.

Like the hand scroll, the *hanging scroll* is also kept rolled in a wooden box and only exposed for a particular showing. Its box is highly prized and is given the same care as the painting, particularly if it is the one originally made for it. The mounting of a hanging scroll is a matter of science, rule, and proportion, and may be done in many different ways. The hanging scroll painting is usually mounted with a border of brocade. A round stick at the bottom weighs it so that it hangs well and evenly. Such paintings may hang alone but often are in pairs or sets of three. Seldom does a set consist of more than four.

The disadvantages of keeping an important painting rolled and boxed are easily recognized, but in ancient Japan there were reasons for this practice. In case of fire, a large number of pictures could be quickly removed by the arm load. Boxes also served to add a degree of protection if fire should come near them or reach them.

Many of the important works of master painters were executed on or for screens. There are many different kinds of screens. The folding type may consist of from two to as many as forty-four leaves. The most common format is a pair of six-fold screens, each about twelve feet long and about six feet high when extended.

Folding screens were known in China as early as the second century B.C. In the century preceding the Christian era, screens were carved and inlaid with jade and other precious materials. Unfortunately, there exist no examples of screen painting from the Sung, Yüan or Ming periods. It is possible that some of the paintings from those periods which were made for screens are now mounted as single scrolls.

A new type of screen was introduced from Korea sometime during the fourteenth century which revolutionized the general scheme of composition. Heretofore, screens had consisted of a group of separate panels tied together by means of cords, and each panel had a separate design and brocade border. In contrast, the leaves of the Korean screens were joined by paper hinges built into the framework before the silk or paper was attached. This provided a continuous surface for painting, whereas previously a continuance of design was interrupted by the frame and the individual brocaded borders of each panel.

Paintings for folding screens set the painter a difficult task in composition for not only is it necessary that each panel should be a perfect composition in itself, but it must play its part in the composition of adjoining leaves and in the composition of the whole. Any part of the screen might be extended, leaving the remainder folded, so that any combination of leaves must present a complete and satisfactory arrangement.

It was the Japanese who brought painted screens to the highest level of achievement. During Japan's Edo period, 1615-1868, pigments instead of ink began to be used. Colors became bold and brilliant; areas of gold and silver were introduced.

Some paintings for screens were done in China during this same period, but the Chinese were best known for screens of lacquer, carved teakwood, often set with jade or plaques of porcelain, and for those with panels of silk, tapestry or embroidery.

The framework of both Chinese and Japanese screens is usually wood with metal fittings of many shapes and sizes. Besides folding screens, there are screens of one large surface mounted in a frame and standing on feet. Other large works were on sliding panels or doors. They were never covered with glass, contrary to the Occidental fashion of protecting paintings of high value with a glazed frame. Oriental paintings are also mounted in albums, but the production of screen and scroll paintings has predominated in both China and Japan.

Figure 67. DENSE FOREST ON KUN-SHAN.
Kung Hsien, Chinese, active ca. 1656-1682,
Ch'ing Dynasty. Hanging scroll painting, ink
on paper. Kung Hsien, a master of monochrome ink painting, was particularly skilled
in the use of rich, heavy masses of black ink
contrasted with lighter washes of fluid greys.
The massing of brush strokes and the almost
completely covered surface of the paper are
characteristic of his style. *Courtesy, Los Angeles County Museum of Art.*

 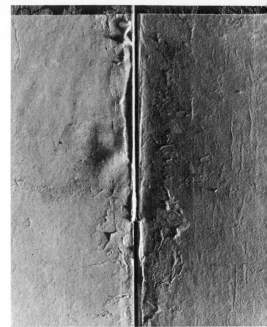

Figure 68.   *Figure 69.*

Figure 68. Detail of a damaged sixteenth-century six-fold screen, painting on mulberry paper which had already been remounted several times. With each remounting, it is inevitable that a small strip of the paint surface along the hinges will be lost. Here, a strain on the paper hinges has caused them to rip away from the framework, tearing the paper and causing paint loss. *Courtesy, Los Angeles County Museum of Art.*

Figure 69. Detail showing lifting of paint from backing due to damaged, strained paper hinges on a sixteenth-century six-fold screen. *Courtesy, Los Angeles County Museum of Art.*

Figure 70. UNTITLED (detail of a painting). Tibetan, 17th-18th century. Color on silk. *Courtesy, Los Angeles County Museum of Art.*

Figure 71. BUDDHIST PAINTING. Japanese, Kamakura Period, 14th century. Color and gold on silk. *Courtesy, Los Angeles County Museum of Art.*

Figure 70.

Figure 71.

RULES FOR CARE AND HANDLING

I. General Rules for Scrolls and Screens

Do not touch the surface of paintings or brocade borders

Never touch the surface of scroll and screen paintings. Silk and paper soil easily. Scroll and screen paintings often have borders of fine brocade. These are equally subject to damage and staining from contact with hands. Do not touch them. Brocades which border scroll and screen paintings are also rare and valuable. They should be given equal care and respect.

Paper and silk absorb deposits

Wash hands

Unclean hands can cause permanent damage to scroll and screen paintings. Most of them are on silk or fibrous paper. Just as fine grained silk or paper "drank up" ink and colors applied to them when the paintings were executed, dampness from hands can enter the fibers of these grounds. Moist hands leave an oily deposit which is all but impossible to eradicate without damaging painting or border. If hands are dirty and moist from perspiration and natural oils, damage from deposits is increasingly serious and the problem of removal is compounded. Always wash hands immediately before handling a scroll or screen.

Do not use tape on scrolls

Never use any kind of adhesive tape on or with scrolls and screens. All tapes are damaging. They leave ugly stains and residue; attempts to remove them are seldom totally successful. Boxes made especially for storing scrolls should not be marred with tapes or any kind of identification marking.

Never use rubber cement or any synthetic adhesive

Under no circumstances should rubber cement or any synthetic adhesive be used with or on a scroll or screen. Do not allow rubber cement to be near them.

Protect from sun and strong illumination

Protect scroll and screen paintings from sunlight, reflected rays from the sun and from strong artificial illumination, especially fluorescent lamplight. The sun and artificial light cause the fading of colors, embrittlement of paper, rotting of fabric fibers and warping or blistering of wood and lacquer.

Regular fumigation recommended

Paper and textiles are attacked by insect pests. Wood is subject to damage by wood feeding insects. Make regular inspections for conditions. Engage a professional exterminator to fumigate on a regular basis to eliminate any chance of damage by insect attack.

128

All restorations, repairs and cleaning should be referred to a *Use* conservator. Conservators are specialists in the conservation and *experienced* care of paper, ancient fabrics, woods, inks, color pigments and *conservators* other components of scrolls and screens.

The relative humidity for scroll paintings should be slightly *Relative* higher than recommended for most other works on paper. Gen- *humidity must* erally, about 55% is recommended. Screens particularly should be *be steady* kept in a higher RH than recommended for other paper works because of the complicated construction of them.

It is important to maintain the same relative humidity. It should never be allowed to fluctuate. Temperature and humidity control are determining factors in the preservation and life of scrolls and screens.

Experiments on Chinese screens and paper have revealed that dark colors absorb the greatest amount of heat; lighter greens, greys and white reflect heat waves. The gold on Japanese screen paintings was found to also reflect heat waves, bringing about a very uneven *Circulate air* range of temperature. Because of this danger to screens, the solution *around screens* arrived at was to situate them so that air space exists behind them and to pass a current of air directly over them, thus controlling heat and humidity.

II. Scrolls

Always carry, move and store scrolls in their own boxes. Unless *Carry and store* they are on exhibition, do not allow them to remain out of their *in boxes* individual boxes. Every scroll has a box made for its protection. Use it for that purpose.

When transporting boxed scrolls within the museum always move them in a flat position, never standing on end or at an angle. When *Move in flat* a scroll is in a horizontal, flat position it will rest within its con- *position* tainer as it was intended that it should. If it is not kept flat the painting will be forced against the inside walls of the box. Even if the box is lined, as they frequently are, repeated contact with the inside of the box will eventually cause a scroll to become damaged by a repetition of movement and contact.

If more than one boxed scroll is moved at the same time on the *Separate with* bed of a hand truck or dolly, separate each one with a cushioning *cushioning* *material*

material to eliminate transmittal of travel shock. Arrange them so there is no movement. Scroll boxes are also valuable; protect them from contact with each other and contact with other objects and surfaces to prevent scratches, abrasions and general wear and tear.

Hand carry horizontally   When hand carrying a scroll in its box, hold it in its natural, flat, horizontal position. Never move a rolled scroll unless it is in its box. Eliminate unnecessary contact with hands.

Never allow boxed scrolls to protrude beyond the edges of a carrying device. When they are moved on a hand truck there is always a chance that it will contact a wall, door facing or a passing person.

Keep sharp objects away   Keep sharp objects, tools with sharp edges, and all objects with points away from scrolls whether they are rolled, unrolled or in their boxes. Pencils and pens should not be used or left near scrolls.

Do not allow writing or marking pens near scrolls   Many currently popular marking pens and other felt tipped markers contain a fluid which is more indelible and damaging than ink used in the now almost obsolete fountain pen. Any ink is damaging. Sometimes attempts to remove ink stains result in damage to fabrics. In the case of scroll paintings, the paper is as absorbent as fabric; damage from inks and dyes is a serious damage.

Remove box lids with care   Do not use a sharp pointed object to pry off the lid of a scroll box. Any instrument used for this purpose will damage the box; if it should slip and enter the box it might damage the scroll as well.

Never expose to tar paper   Under no circumstances should tar lined paper be used with or near scroll paintings. It should not be left in the same room with them. Changes in atmosphere cause the consistency of tar to melt or alter. The vapor from it can be damaging. Some insect repellents in vaporous form also cause the lining of tar paper to ooze, run or give off fumes.

Protect in storage   When storing boxed scrolls protect them and their containers from dust accumulation by wrapping them in acid-free tissue paper or by laying a sheet of glassine paper over them. Dust is abrasive. In time, it will change the surface of a scroll box. Unless dust covers are provided, box surfaces become roughened even if dust is removed from time to time. No matter how well constructed a scroll box is or how tight fitting the cover seems to be, dust will filter to the inside and come to rest on the scroll. There is dust in air-conditioned buildings.

Do not smoke   Never smoke while working with scrolls. Do not smoke in the

130

same room with them even if they are in their boxes. The risk is too great to permit smoking. Aside from the danger of fire, cigarette smoke leaves an oily, yellowish film on anything.

It is extremely important that a hanging scroll be properly unrolled. First, the scroll painting should be hung in place, then unrolled very gradually and very, very slowly. Undue tension on the backing of the painting must be avoided at all times. *Inexperienced handlers should receive repeated demonstrations from experts before being permitted to unroll a hanging scroll.* Following instructions, demonstrations and practice with a simulated scroll, first attempts should be supervised. In Japan, a hanging scroll is reverently handled and preserved with care. If its life is to be prolonged in good condition, it must receive the same respect and treatment.

Unrolling hanging scrolls requires practice

Equal care must be exercised with the unrolling of a hand scroll but the method differs from that for a hanging scroll. Unrolling a hand scroll is more difficult to master. With a hand scroll, rhythmic rolling at both ends takes place simultaneously. As the right side is rolled inward (rolling to the left as one faces the scroll), the left portion is rolled outward, also to the left. As with hanging scrolls, exactly the right pressure must be applied and maintained throughout the rolling procedure for maximum protection of the painting. Any fold or crease rolled into the scroll is usually a permanent damage, especially if it is allowed to remain creased very long. Instructions and demonstrations by an expert should be mandatory before handling a valuable hand scroll. A unique scroll of high value should never be subjected to possible damage from inexpert handling and rolling. Practice with a simulated hand scroll. Constructing a mock scroll is a fairly simple matter and worth the time, effort and cost of materials.

Unrolling hand scrolls is a special technique

Learn on mock scroll

If a scroll painting is preserved much depends on how it is handled, particularly the specialized technique of rolling and unrolling. Unless rolling and unrolling are expertly done the painting will suffer. Haphazard, incorrect rolling could destroy some paintings in the course of a dozen or less repetitions. Edges must be kept perfectly even. Do not tamp the ends in an attempt to even them. Too great tightness in the roll must be avoided. Use a practice roll under supervision until the technique has been mastered.

Keep edges even

All scroll paintings are equipped with ties for holding the scroll at exactly the correct tension, prevent movement within the roll and

Learn tying of knots from an expert

131

prevent its unrolling. The correct tying of knots on these cords in order to maintain exact tension is also a specialized technique. It can only be learned from an experienced handler. Securing the ties on scrolls must be precise and accurate. It can be learned by experience and practice. With a practice scroll made for learning scroll techniques, the dangers of incorrect tying will be obvious.

III. *Screens*

Preceding precautions and recommendations apply to screens

The preceding precautions for the care and handling of scrolls—cleanliness, conditions of work areas and storage areas, the danger of instruments and implements, tar paper in proximity, smoking and other recommendations—all apply to Oriental screens as well.

Store and move screens flat

Screens should also be stored flat. Never stand them in storage areas. Do not lean them. For exhibition purposes they cannot lie flat but they should be retired from exhibition frequently and stored in a flat position for a period of "rest."

Protect from dust

Screens should be protected from dust accumulation. Dust is damaging to the paintings and to the framework. Cover screens with glassine paper or a sheet of plastic film unless the framework has lacquer. Do not use plastics with lacquer; use clean rag paper or acid-free tissue.

Move screens in a flat position, *always folded*. Never transfer or move a screen while it is in a standing position, even if it is folded. When folding a screen, remember that old paper hinges fold one way only.

Do not stack

Never stack folded screens, one on top of another. This precaution should be observed when storing them and when moving them on hand trucks. The framework of a screen may appear to be sturdy but it was never intended to bear any weight.

Move one screen at a time

Always move one screen at a time on a hand truck. The bed of the truck should be larger than the screen so that the screen does not protrude beyond the edges. Unless equally supported, uneven pressure is applied to the screen's framework. Allowing a screen to protrude beyond the hand truck is also dangerous because of the chance of colliding with a door, wall, piece of furniture or some other damaging surface or object. Avoid speed when pushing a hand truck. Two men should always accompany a loaded hand truck.

Move load slowly with two men

Do not use rope, twine or string to lash a screen to a hand truck. Harsh cord or rope scratches the framework. Tying a screen down tightly puts undue stress and strain on both painting and framework. If movement or shifting is inevitable and tying is indicated for safety, use a soft cloth tape. *Tie to hand truck with soft cloth tape*

A folded screen should never be carried by two men, one at each end. Weight should always be evenly distributed. Lifting and carrying a screen by its ends puts an abnormal strain on all parts of the framework and on the painting. *Do not lift folded screen by its ends*

Often, the paintings on a screen are in a better state of preservation than the framework. For various reasons screens are often structurally weak. Examine the framework. Know its condition, including any repairs or restorations. Compensate for structural weaknesses by giving them added care to prevent stress and strain at weak areas. *Compensate for structural weaknesses*

The leaves of early folding screens were tied together with cords threaded through holes in the edges of the panels. In the fourteenth century the elements began to be joined by means of paper hinges which were built into the bodies of the panels, permitting a tighter joining of the leaves. When handling a screen, always eliminate undue tension on its hinges. This is one of the reasons a folding screen should never be leaned or placed at an angle. Leaning is an unnatural position for a screen and strains hinge joints. *Avoid strain on hinges*

Changes in atmosphere and relative humidity cause wood to warp. If the framework of a folding screen warps measurably, damage will also occur to the paintings on the leaves of the screen. Maintain a close, regular check on atmospheric conditions. *Atmospheric changes warp frame*

BIBLIOGRAPHY

Bussagli, M. *Chinese Painting*. New York, Marlboro Books, 1969.

Carter, Dagney. *Four Thousand Years of Chinese Art*. New York, Ronald Press Co., 1948; rev. ed., 1951.

Edmunds, W. H. *Pointers and Clues to the Subjects of Chinese and Japanese Art*. New York, E. Weyhe, Inc., 1934.

Goepper, Roger. *The Essence of Chinese Painting*. Boston, Boston Book and Art, 1969.

Jenyns, Soame. *A Background to Chinese Painting*. New York, Schocken Books, 1966.

Lee, Sherman E. *Japanese Decorative Style*. New York, Harry N. Abrams, Inc., 1961.

————. *A History of Far Eastern Art*. Englewood Cliffs, New Jersey, Prentice-Hall, Inc., 1964.

Lin Yutang. *The Chinese Theory of Art*. London, Heinemann, 1967.

March, Benjamin. *Some Technical Terms of Chinese Painting*. Baltimore, Waverly Press, Inc., 1935.

Paine, Robert Treat, and Soper, Alexander. *The Art and Architecture of Japan*. Baltimore, Penguin Books, 1955.

Rosenfield, John M. *Japanese Arts of the Heian Period*. New York, The Asia Society, Inc., 1967.

Rowley, George. *Principles of Chinese Painting*. Princeton, New Jersey, University Press, 1947; 1969.

Sickman, Laurence and Soper, Alexander. *The Art and Architecture of China*. Baltimore, Penguin Books, 1956.

Silcock, Arnold. *Introduction to Chinese Art and History*. New York, Oxford University Press, 1948.

Sirén, Osvald. *Chinese Painting*. 7 vols. New York, The Ronald Press Co., 1956.

Swann, Peter C. *Chinese Painting*. New Haven, Yale University Press, 1967; New York, Universe Books, Inc., 1969.

Toda, K. *Japanese Scroll Painting*. Chicago, University of Chicago Press, 1935.

Wang Chi-Yuan. *Oriental Brushwork*. New York, Pitman Publishing Corp., 1965.

Warner, Langdon. *The Enduring Art of Japan*. Cambridge, Mass., Harvard University Press, 1952.

Willette, William. *Foundations of Chinese Art: From Neolithic to Modern Architecture*. New York, McGraw-Hill Book Co., 1968.

Yamasaki, K. "Technical Studies on the Pigments Used in the Ancient Paintings of Japan," *Proceedings of the Japan Academy* (Tokyo), Vol. XXX (1954), pp. 781-785.

8

Metal Objects

Metal objects (including sculpture) are made of silver, gold, copper, brass, bronze, iron, steel, pewter, chromium, aluminum, and other alloys and elements, and combinations of alloys and metals.

All metals have durable qualities in varying degrees. Metals can be fused, cast in a mold as a solid or hollow piece and manipulated in many ways by mechanical processes. They can be drawn into fine wires, even into minute threads. Heated, they can be hammered, welded, twisted, bent and fashioned into numerous forms and shapes. Metals may be plated, one metal wholly or in part covering another. As openwork or grilles, they provide visibility and at the same time strength. Metal objects may be decorated and ornamented by *repoussé* (a pattern in relief on one side and an *intaglio* on the other), chasing (surface ornamentation by tracing or engraving the metal), damascening (inlaying with other metals), enamelling, or *cloisonné* (design in enamel produced by laying out the pattern with strips of flat wire and filling the interstices with enamel paste fused in place). Pliny records one of the oldest methods of silver decoration, *niello*, in which the engraved design is filled with a black lead compound consisting of lead, copper, silver, and sulphur.

Man discovered metals about 10,000 B.C., late in the Mesolithic-Neolithic period. Silver was used in the famous lyre (ca. 3000 B.C.) found at Ur of the Chaldees at a time when silver was a rarity in Egypt. Before 2475 B.C. the Egyptian goldsmith had developed his skill to a remarkably fine degree. He had learned to cast, chase, solder, hammer, and plate gold, often combining it with other metals and stones. Egyptians continued to make lavish use of gold during the Middle Kingdom and Empire (2160-1090 B.C.). Although great amounts of gold were used for furniture, it is not surprising that the robbers who entered Tutankhamen's tomb concentrated first on the silver. Indeed, silver was not available in any quantity in Egypt until Greco-Roman times.

Metals are usually durable and easily cared for. They are not subject to damage by light or biological action. Processes which cause deterioration are usually slow. With most metals the principal foe is oxidation. Not all oxidation is undesirable, however. Controlled oxidation is sometimes used to protect metals. Original forms may often be preserved only by oxides. Ancient bronzes, for example, are sometimes so eroded beneath the oxide that it is wise to leave the oxidation crust undisturbed. Many of the corrosion crusts contain carbonates, basic chlorides and basic sulphates in addition to oxides. The tarnishing and darkening of silver, for example, is caused by the formation of a thin film of silver sulphide.

Iron and steel will rust. The process is slow but very destructive. Copper and its alloys—brass and bronze—are highly vulnerable. Lacquer, if expertly applied, is the only coating which will prevent brass, bronze, and copper from corroding. Again, it is sometimes desirable to preserve objects in their oxidized states, if the patina is uniform or if it serves as evidence of the object's antiquity, as proof of the time and conditions of its origin.

Bronze disease attacks copper, bronze and brass. It takes the form of a sudden outbreak of small areas of corrosion distinguished by powdery, light green spots. Bronze disease is caused by the presence of cuprous chloride which reacts to dampness and the presence of oxygen (causing corrosion and metal deterioration). Objects can sometimes be treated effectively by soaking them for long periods in sodium sesquicarbonate which makes the chloride inactive.

Pewter also suffers from a disease in the form of a black corrosion and a roughening of the surface.

Silver is a soft metal which requires extra precautions in cleaning it. No matter how soft the abrasive cleaning agent or cloth may be, polishing will remove some of the silver surface each time it is done. Nearly all commercial polishes are too harsh to be recommended for use. A piece of gum camphor placed in a tight container will retard oxidation but, happily, some oxidation enhances the decorative effect of relief patterns on silver. Tarnish-proof bags and containers are available for storage of silver pieces.

Gold is also a very soft metal, but is more durable than silver and does not corrode at all. The care of gold objects usually involves only the removal of grime and dust from the surface. Rinsing in warm, soapy water suffices to remove any dirt accumulation.

Tin and lead are soft metals. Tin becomes oxidized after prolonged burial in the ground and above ground. Under normal atmospheric conditions it is stable and resistant in circumstances where lead is subject to corrosion. Many organic acids which affect lead have no action at all on tin.

All metals have one feature in common, they must be kept as dust-free as possible, because accumulations of dust build up into a film which can be difficult to wash or polish off. Besides, this coating will eat into the metal surface and cause pitting which cannot be removed. Variations in temperature are of little importance, but variations in humidity and impurities in the air exert varying degrees of destruction on metals.

Some experts advocate that all metal objects should be kept in glass cases, correcting the atmosphere within the case by placing inside small open containers filled with silica gel. An effective drying agent, it indicates when it is spent and no longer able to absorb the moisture in the case by turning from deep blue to pink. When silica gel becomes pink, it can be reconditioned to its original blue by heating in an oven.

Figure 72. Bronze Aegis. Egyptian, Dynasty XXII, 950-730 B.C. 1. shows aegis (symbol of power carried by the pharaoh) before electrolysis; 2. shows aegis after removal of incrustation by electrolysis to reveal gold and paste inlay. *Courtesy, Research Laboratory, Museum of Fine Arts, Boston.*

Figure 73. Suits of Armor. 1. Early 16th-century Maximilian armor for combat. German, 1510. Metal; 2. A half suit of armor for a page. Italian, 1575. According to the curator of the John Woodman Higgins Armory, Albert J. Gagne, the most acceptable method of cleaning dirt or rust is to use very fine mineral or steel wool, applied directly to the armor. This is accomplished by careful rubbing. After the surface has been thoroughly cleaned, soft paste wax is applied, allowed to dry, and then polished. A second coat of wax is applied and polished to insure the full coverage and protection of the metal against moisture. This process is slow, but the results are most satisfying. *Courtesy, the John Woodman Higgins Armory, Inc.*

Figure 74.

Figure 74. BUST OF SASANIAN KING, SHAPUR II (?). Iranian, ca. 4th century. Silver-gilt. A truly royal work of art both in its material, silver-gilt, and subject, this majestic head reflects the high level of craftsmanship in the mighty Sasanian dynasty, which ruled Persia from A.D. 226 until 651. Its gleaming surface demands frequent maintenance and constant protection. It is necessary to insure a sulphur-free environment. *Courtesy, Metropolitan Museum of Art.*

Figure 75. ROSPIGLIOSI CUP. Attributed to Jacopo Bilivert, Netherlandish, active in Florence, ca. 1550-1585. Gold, enamel, and pearls. Characteristic of the opulence of Renaissance goldsmith's work, this dazzling example is one of the greatest treasures in the collection. Before stylistic and technological analysis, it was attributed to the celebrated Cellini because of its highly imaginative design and superb craftsmanship. *Courtesy, Metropolitan Museum of Art.*

Figure 76. HERMES HOLDING A RAM. Greek, early 5th century. Bronze statuette. *Courtesy, Museum of Fine Arts, Boston.*

Figure 77. HELMET. Etruscan, 3rd century B.C. Bronze. A pleasing green patina covers most of the surface of this helmet, but evident traces of "bronze disease" will eventually destroy both patina and metal unless stopped. This specimen with cheek pieces is part of a collection of bronzes excavated by Professor A. Castellani near Perugia, Italy, toward the end of the nineteenth century. *Courtesy, Los Angeles County Museum of Art.*

Figure 78. ONE OF A GROUP, CITIZENS OF CALAIS. Auguste Rodin, French, 1840-1917. Bronze. The rigid frontality of the archaic Greek statuette and dramatic asymmetry of the realistic nineteenth-century statue demonstrate by their contrasting postures the variety of stylistic effects that can be achieved by the bronze casting technique. *Courtesy, Fogg Art Museum, Harvard University.*

Figure 79.

Figure 80.

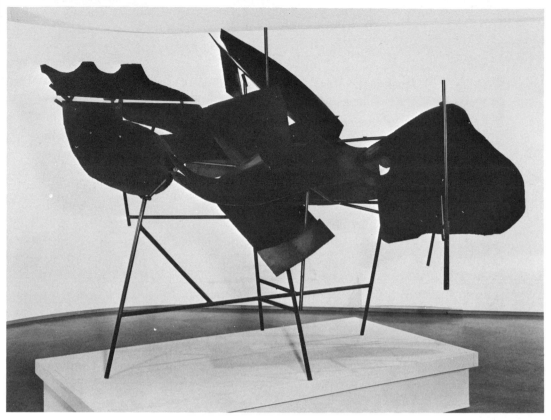

Figure 81. THE DUCHESS OF ALBA. Reuben Nakian, American, 1897. Welded sheet steel and rods. Large metal objects of monumental size and weight require planning and special handling equipment to move them. *Courtesy, Los Angeles County Museum of Art.*

Figure 79. Two small metal objects packed in a rigid plastic box lined with polyurethane cushioning; size of box, 5″ x 7″ x 2″ deep. *Courtesy, Los Angeles County Museum of Art.*

Figure 80. Storage room for brass, copper, and pewter. *Courtesy, Colonial Williamsburg Foundation.*

RULES FOR CARE AND HANDLING

Carry small metal objects in trays or boxes

Pieces should not touch

Small metal objects may be carried with safety in a carrying box or tray. When several pieces are transferred together, be sure no piece touches another. Separate each object with some cushioning material so that objects do not suffer abrasion by rubbing against each other during movement. Wadded tissue paper is satisfactory for separating them. If cotton must be used, as a shock mitigant, first wrap the object in tissue paper. For silver and bronze, Saran wrap is effective, if the wrapping is done in a dry atmosphere and the objects are not subjected to cold.

Not not allow objects to protrude beyond carrying device or shelf

Secure objects during transit

Never allow an object to protrude beyond the edges of a carrying box, tray, dolly or hand truck. This also applies to storage in trays, shelves or cupboards. Carrying boxes should never be overcrowded. Even to save steps and time, do not crowd the objects in the container. Arrange the packing and loading of carrying devices so that there is absolutely no movement inside during transit. Never carry more than one object at a time by hand. The object may be as small as a finger ring or a spool of thread, or as large as a chair. No matter what its size, only one object should be carried at a time.

Wear gloves unless piece is small or intricately designed

It is advisable to wear white cotton gloves when handling metal objects, but there are exceptions to the rule, of course. Some objects are so small or fragile that the gloves would increase risk. Still, fingerprints on objects can be avoided by wearing gloves. There can be no set rules for handling all metal objects. Situations, sizes, intricacies of design and shape, facilities and equipment—all enter into the matter. Each handling movement must be weighed and evaluated in relation to the object and the distance it is to be moved.

Pad storage areas against possible abrasion

Use tarnish-resistant cloth for silver

Clean silver before storing

Do not use electric buffers

All storage areas (shelves, trays, boxes, drawers, cabinets) should be adequately padded to avoid scratches or abrasions. Cabinets, shelves, and containers for storing silver pieces should be lined with tarnish-resistant cloth to lessen the possibility of a reaction with sulphur compounds. A container of activated charcoal helps prevent tarnish if placed inside the storage area.

Always clean silver objects before storing them, then place in plastic bags or Saran wrap. Do not use mechanical machine buffers to polish metal objects, as they are extremely hazardous.

Very small metal objects should be stored in individual boxes or envelopes, identified on the outside. A brief description and the identifying museum number on the outside of the container avoids exposing the metal to the atmosphere and unnecessary handling.

Store small objects in individual containers

Identify each container

As durable as metals are, they do require attention on a regular basis. Metal objects should be inspected periodically for *bronze disease*. Affected pieces should be removed immediately and treated by an expert. The condition known as bronze disease usually does not develop if there is a dry atmosphere. Dampness should be avoided with all metal objects. Extensive experiments have been conducted by many institutions, such as the Department of Chemistry at Columbia University, on the care and cleaning of bronze objects. Depending on the original condition of the object, the results in many cases have been amazing. Corroded surfaces have been restored to something approaching their original state, revealing delicate surface details and inscriptions. Heavy incrustations have been removed by electrolysis, leaving the surface undisturbed. This process must, of course, be undertaken only by experienced specialists.

Inspect for bronze disease

Avoid exposure to dampness

Pewter is a very soft metal, easy to dent or scratch, and requires different care from other metals. Modern pewter bears little resemblance to old pewter. Today it is a tarnish-resistant alloy (about 90% tin) which requires a minimum of cleaning. To keep modern pewter in perfect condition requires nothing more than dusting and an occasional washing to remove any slight darkening or fingerprints. Wash in warm water with a mild soap. Use a soft cloth and a soft-bristled brush to reach crevices.

The care of modern pewter and old pewter differs

Fingerprints are a real hazard to old pewter if it is touched before it is completely dry. Antique pewter should be thoroughly washed before it is polished. Buffing pewter is not recommended. It should not be necessary unless it is old and in poor condition.

Fingerprints are a hazard to old pewter

Do not use tape to secure the lids of metal pieces. All tapes leave a residue on the metal, which is a foreign matter and almost always damaging.

Do not apply tape

Arms and armor should ideally be kept in air-tight cases. If this is not feasible, they should be covered when in storage. Arms and armor are generally protected by an oil, but unless further protective measures are taken, dust settles, absorbs the oil, falls off the object, and leaves it unprotected. Wax and silicone products are

147

considered by some authorities to be more effective than oil as a protective coating.

Do not polish plated metals often

Many copper and brass pieces are plated with another metal, usually silver. Each time such pieces are polished some of the plating is removed. Lacquering solid copper and brass pieces cuts down

Lacquer on metals prevents patina

on polishing time, but it does not permit a patina to develop. Once a lacquer finish is cracked, the surface will craze, and air will seep under it, causing the finish to peel and discolor. Removal of lacquer depends entirely on the kind of lacquer used for protection. One method is to place the object in boiling water in which washing soda has been dissolved, one cup to two gallons of water.

Desired RH

Atmospheric conditions for metal objects call for the same degrees of temperature and relative humidity as for metal sculpture. Low relative humidity is desirable below 40%, but usually a range between 40% and 45% is safe.

BIBLIOGRAPHY

Berghoff, H. L. *Metals Handbook*. New York, American Society for Metals, 1948.

Caley, Earle R. *The Composition of Ancient Greek Bronze Coins*. Philadelphia, The American Philosophical Society, 1939.

"Caring for Your Collections: Metals and Leather," *History News* (American Association for State and Local History, Madison, Wisc.), Vol. 17, no. 9, Technical Leaflet I, July, 1962; Vol. 18, no. 8, Technical Leaflet No. 10, June, 1963.

Ellsworth, Harold D. and Gettens, Rutherford J. "Examples of the Restoration of Corroded Bronzes," *Bulletin of the Fogg Art Museum*, March, 1936, pp. 35-38.

Fink, Colin G. and Polushkin, E. P. "Modern Methods for the Preservation of Ancient Metal Objects," *Metropolitan Museum Studies*, Vol. II, Part 2 (1930), pp. 236-238.

Foster, Kenneth E. *A Handbook of Ancient Chinese Bronzes*. Claremont, Calif., 1949.

French, Hollis. *A Silver Collectors' Glossary and A List of Early American Silversmiths and Their Marks* (reprint of the Walpole Society publication, 1917), New York, Da Capo Press, 1967.

Hackenbroch, Yvonne. *Bronzes and Other Metalwork and Sculpture, The Collection of Irwin Untermyer*. New York, The Metropolitan Museum of Art, 1962.

Helft, Jacques (Preface by.) *French Master Goldsmiths from the Seven-*

teenth to the Nineteenth Century. New York, French & European Publications, 1966.

Jacobs, Carl. *Guide to American Pewter*. New York, McBride Co., Inc., 1957.

Mori, H. and Kumagat, M. "Damage to Antiquities Caused by Fumigants, I: Metals," *Scientific Papers of Japanese Antiques and Art Crafts*, Vol. 8, 1954.

Nichols, Henry W. *Restoration of Ancient Bronzes and Cure of Malignant Patina*. Chicago, Field Museum of Natural History, Museum Techniques Series No. 3.

Organ, Robert M. "A New Treatment for 'Bronze Disease'," *The Museums Journal*, Vol. 61 (1961), pp. 54-56.

Plenderleith, H. J. "Technical Notes on Chinese Bronzes with Special Reference to Patina and Incrustations," *Transactions of the Oriental Ceramic Society*, Vol. XVI (1938-1939), pp. 33-35.

—— and Organ, Robert M. "The Decay and Conservation of Museum Objects of Tin," *Studies in Conservation*, Vol. 1, no. 1 (1953), pp. 63-72.

Price, L. E. and Thomas, G. J. "Selective Oxidation as a Fundamental Principle in Metallic Protection," *Nature*, May 7, 1938.

Savage, George A. *A Concise History of Bronzes*, New York, Frederick A. Praeger, 1969.

Schur, S. E. *The Use of X-ray Fluorescence in Analyzing Bronzes*. Cambridge, Mass., Massachusetts Institute of Technology, 1960.

Todd, William. *Conservation of Metals, Archaeological*. Toronto, Department of Travel and Publicity, 1961.

Vernon, W. H. J. and Whitby, L. "The Open-Air Corrosion of Copper," *Journal of the Institute of Metals*, Vol. XLII (1929), pp. 181-202; Vol. XLIV (1930), pp. 389-408; Vol. XLIX (1932), pp. 153-167.

White, William Charles. *Bronze Culture of Ancient China*. Museum Studies No. 5. Toronto, University of Toronto Press, 1956.

Young, William J. "Electrolytic Restoration of Metals," *The Encyclopedia of Electrochemistry*, Clifford A. Hampel, Ed., 1964, pp. 479-483.

9

Enamelled Objects

Enamelling is one of the richest and most fascinating arts that man has ever devised. An enamel is a lead glass to which some metallic oxide has been added to give it color or opacity. It is applied thinly to a metal base, usually copper, gold or silver, and fused in an oven. Pure, or almost pure, metals are the best ground to receive and retain enamels.

We do not know when the art of enamelling first began. It is thought that the first enamelling was created by fusing glass beads to copper, gold or silver for use as jewelry in Egypt. Until recently it was thought that examples of ancient Egyptian enamelling did not still exist. However, the Boston Museum has two such pieces, a small gold ibis, which is published with a photograph on page 109 of W. S. Smith, *Ancient Egypt as Represented in The Museum of Fine Arts, Boston,* and a particularly fine bracelet which is published by Dows Dunham in *Royal Tombs at Meroe and Barkal.* In each case, it is a blue vitreous material, fused in place, containing silver, iron, copper and potassium.

During Medieval times in Europe, enamels were regarded as semiprecious materials and were widely used to decorate crowns and rings, liturgical boxes and decorative plaques. Important

150

centers flourished during the eleventh and twelfth centuries in the great abbeys of the Meuse, Moselle, and Rhine valleys. At some centers, notably Limoges in France, the enameller's art gradually reached the proportions of an industry. At first the pyxes to hold wafers for the Mass, book covers, incense boats, basins, candlesticks and other vessels were fashioned individually, but later they were mass-produced. In early examples the forms are set with an incised metal field; later the forms themselves are incised in the metal and placed within an enamelled reserve. In both they are cast separately in relief and fastened to the background. The cool deep tones of Limoges, predominantly blue, are reminiscent of thirteenth century French stained glass.

One of the most beautiful developments of the art occurred in Italy early in the fourteenth century. The technique developed here became known as *basse-taille*. At about the same time, another process called *plique-à-jour* came into practice. Both techniques demanded highly skilled artisans, but because of the difficulty in successfully manufacturing the plique-à-jour, few early examples remain for study. One of the finest specimens is in the Victoria and Albert Museum in London. It consists of two bands of emerald green enamel on a silver beaker in the form of miniature stained glass windows.

At the end of the fifteenth century, two revolutionary discoveries were made. Until then, enamel had been held in place (to form the design) by strips of metal, or the *cloison*, very much as a mounting holds a jewel in a ring; all enamel had been sunk into cells, or *cloisons*. Now it was found that enamel could be fused on both sides of a metal object and that after it had been fused, another enamel could be superimposed and fused to the first layer. These discoveries allowed a degree of shading of colors to give three dimensional depth. The process is known as *grisaille*.

The art of enamelling apparently did not reach China until long after the craft was popularized in Europe. It was probably introduced by Arab traders or traveling craftsmen. Limoges

151

ART OBJECTS

enamels were taken to China by early French missionaries to be copied during the reign of Louis XIV when K'ang Hsi was Emperor. Chinese enamels of this time often betray signs of the French influence in motifs and decoration. Similar commissions were sent out about the same time from England, Holland and other European countries. Orders were executed with rare fidelity by Cantonese workmen and brought to Europe by the ships of the Dutch and English East Indian Companies. When not busy with European orders, Cantonese workers supplied clients in India, Persia and other countries of western and southern Asia.

Processes of Enamelling

The base of enamel is called *flux*, known in France as *fondant*. It is a clear, colorless, transparent, vitreous compound composed of silica (the dioxide of silicon, SiO_2, a hard, glassy mineral, found in a variety of forms, as in quartz, sand, opal, etc.), minium (red oxide of lead, Pb_3O_4, also called *red lead*), and potash. While in a state of fusion, the flux is colored by the addition of oxides of metals which stain it throughout its mass.

Enamels are hard or soft according to the amount of silica in proportion to the other components of the composition. They are hard when a very high temperature is required to fuse them. The harder the enamel, the less subject it is to being affected by atmospheric conditions. Atmospheric agencies can produce a decomposition of the surface of soft enamels, gradually penetrating the entire enamel. Enamels containing a great amount of soda or potash are more likely to crack and are less cohesive. If red lead (minium) is in greater proportion, liability to cracking is diminished. The brilliance of enamel depends on the perfect combination and proportions of its component parts. From its lump form, enamel is pulverized. The resulting powder is then subjected to a series of baths in distilled water. After

the metal ground has been thoroughly cleaned, the enamel preparation is carefully and evenly spread over the parts of the
metal to receive it. It must just cover the ground. Metals are
cleaned by immersion in acid and water. Nitric acid is used for
copper, sulphuric acid for silver, and hydrochloric acid for gold.
The metal is then further cleansed of any traces of acid with a
brush and water and finally dried in a warm sawdust. After the
preparation is dry, it is then put into a furnace and heated to a
bright, pale red. When the piece glows red all over, it is removed from the furnace. Unlike pottery or glass, the firing of
enamel takes only a few minutes.

The following enamelling processes are described in the
order in which they were known and practiced. Variations have
been introduced into all of the processes, but each remains
basically the same as when it was discovered.

Champlevé Enamelling

Champlevé enamelling involves the cutting away of troughs
(or cells) in the plate. This leaves a metal line which forms the
outline of the design which will be enamelled. Pulverized
enamel mixtures are laid in these cells and then fused by heat.
After the heating process, the piece is smoothed with pumice
and a corundum file. Further smoothing and polishing is done
with crocus powder and jeweler's rouge.

Cloisonné Enamelling

Thin metal strips are bent and shaped to form the outline
of the pattern or design. These are affixed to the metal ground
with silver solder or by the enamel itself during the fusion
period. The bands, or strips, of metal produce cells for receiving
the pulverized enamel as in the *champlevé* method. The remainder of the process is identical with that of *champlevé*.

153

Basse-taille Enamelling

This process is a combination of engraving, carving and enamelling. The metal is first engraved with a design and then carved into a *bas-relief*. *Bas-relief* usually refers to a sculpture in which the figures or design project only slightly from the background. With enamelling, *bas-relief* is used to indicate below the surface of the metal. When the enamel is fused, it is level with uncarved parts of the metal, and the design shows through a transparent enamel.

Plique-à-jour Enamelling

This type of enamelling is identical with *cloisonné* except that the bands, ribbons, wires or strips of metal formed to enclose the enamel and form the design are not soldered to the base or ground but are soldered only to each other. These are then merely placed onto the metal which will become the ground. After fusion and cooling, the metal boundaries for the design are removed.

Painted Enamelling

The metal ground for painted enamels may be copper, silver or gold, but it is usually cooper. This type differs from any of the preceding in both method and result. The metal is cut to the desired size and shape with shears and then slightly domed with a hammer or burnisher. After the ground has been cleaned with acid and water, the enamel is laid equally over both front and back and then fired. After the first coat of enamel is fixed to the ground, the design is carried out on the fused enamel surface by laying in white enamel or any opaque enamel.

154

Figure 82. Pyx. French, 12th century. Champlevé enamel on bronze. Losses of enamel years ago, just above the lid of the ciborium, between the two figural patterns, permit a clear view of the cutting away of the metal. *Courtesy, Los Angeles County Museum of Art.*

Figure 83. Song of the Three Worthies. Mosan, ca. 1150. Champlevé enamel on gilded copper. The plaque's peculiar, slightly curved shape, and the inscription along its semicircular border, suggest that it once formed part of a large ensemble. *Courtesy, Museum of Fine Arts, Boston.*

Figure 84. LID OF A SILVER-GILT BOX. Italian, late 19th century. An example of *plique-à-jour* enamel. *Courtesy, Los Angeles County Museum of Art.*

Figure 85. OVAL DISH. Bernard Palissy, French, 1510-1590. Lead-enamelled earthenware. The practice of enamelling pottery or brick goes back to ancient Mesopotamia; in Renaissance Europe, the French craft achieved a great artistic triumph. *Courtesy, Museum of Fine Arts, Boston.*

Figure 86. DISH. Pierre Courteys, French, 16th century. *Grisaille* enamel on copper, before 1591. An example of *grisaille* enamelling showing the degree of shading possible with this revolutionary fifteenth-century development. *Courtesy, Los Angeles County Museum of Art.*

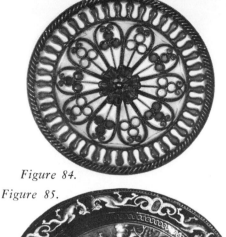

Figure 84.

Figure 85.

Figure 86.

1.

2.

Figure 87. 1. Kohl Pot For Eye Paint; 2. Ibis. Egyptian, Dynasty XVII. Until recently it was thought that such examples of ancient Egyptian enamelling had not survived the ravages of time. The specimens illustrated above are both of a blue vitreous material, fused in place, containing silver, iron, copper, and potassium, and are among the earliest examples in existence. *Courtesy, Museum of Fine Arts, Boston.*

Figure 88. An enamelled plate "floated" in a shock-absorbent material for shipment. Before the case is filled with more material, the object should be wrapped. Note that the shipping case is lined with another type of shock-absorbent material. *Courtesy, Los Angeles County Museum of Art.*

Figure 88.

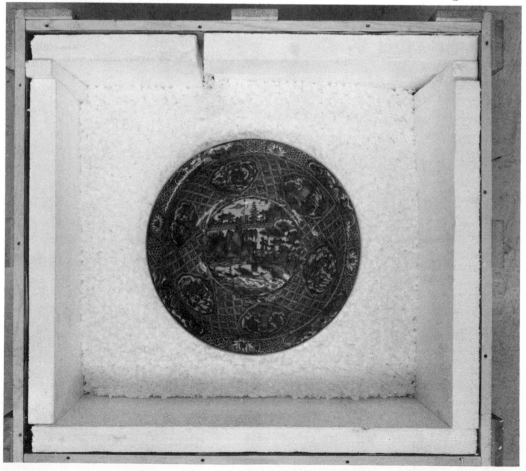

Figure 89. THE ENTOMBMENT. Possibly from the workshop of
Nardon Penicaud (ca. 1470-1542/43) or that of Jean I Penicaud
(active ca. 1510-1540). Limoges enamel plaque. The deep luminous tones of the enamels make this plaque a superb example
of the skill of the Limoges workshop. The brilliant colors of the
figures in enamel are delicately appliqued to the chased metal
base. *Courtesy, Isabella Stewart Gardner Museum, Boston.*

Figure 90. 1. Enamelled vase showing damaged area of enamel losses, caused by dropping; 2. Detail. The damaged area, outlined in black, shows the white area which was originally covered with colored enamel. Within the black outline is the copper surface exposed by total loss of enamel. Such abrasions and indentations to the metal could only have occurred as the result of a severe blow. Extra precautions should be taken in handling of such damaged or chipped objects. Do not handle near areas of enamel loss nor allow cotton to come in contact. *Courtesy, Los Angeles County Museum of Art.*

Grisaille Painted Enamelling

In this process, the white enamel is mixed with water or turpentine, spike oil of lavender, or essential oil of petroleum. The white is painted thickly in the light parts and thinly in the grey areas, over a dark background. This results in a slight sense of relief and enables the enamel worker to obtain a wide range of light and shade.

Colored Painted Enamelling

In the colored painted method white is colored by transparent enamel spread over the *grisaille* treatment. Parts are heightened with touches of gold after the firing. Other parts, if desired, may be made more brilliant by the use of foil, over which transparent enamels are painted and then fired.

Miniature Enamel Painting

Miniature enamel painting is not true enamelling. In fact, the colors are compounds of raw oxides or other forms of metal with a little flux added but not combined. Colors are painted onto a white enamel and caused to adhere to the surface by partially fusing the enamel component.

RULES FOR CARE AND HANDLING

Enamelled objects are subject to chipping and flaking. Caution *Chipping and* should be exercised during handling so that objects receive no blows, *flaking* do not come in contact with sharp or hard surfaces, or in contact with each other.

Always unpack and handle enamelled objects on padded surfaces. *Unpack on* Cotton batting, thick cloth, or velvet are protective. These materials *padded surface* are also recommended as linings for carrying devices and storage bins or shelves.

Do not overcrowd boxes or trays. Never *pack* pieces into a con- *Do not pack* tainer or storage area. When several objects are moved within the *pieces into* museum, separate each one with a shock absorbent material. Be sure *containers* no piece touches another. For small pieces, velvet-covered blocks *Keep objects* are excellent to separate pieces during movement or storage. They *from touching* are easily made. Lumber scraps in a variety of sizes and shapes can be covered with velvet. Padded blocks can be adjusted to make the box compartmented and provide maximum shock absorption and prevent chipping.

For wrapping enamels, first use tissue paper, wax paper, mulberry *Wrapping* paper, or a soft cloth. Cotton batting can be used to pad the objects.

Never lift or carry a piece of enamelware by handles, rims or *Lifting* other projections. Instinctively, one lifts a plate by its rim or edge. Do not lift an enamelled plate this way. Ease one hand under the plate or bowl, support the weight of the piece with that hand and lend balanced support by putting the other hand underneath and toward the bottom edge.

Extra care should be exercised with the handling of objects which *Carrying* have suffered breakage or chipping of the enamelled surface. Once an enamelled surface has been damaged, further enamel loss can be extensive unless extreme caution is practiced in handling. Avoid *Extra* touching a piece near the area or areas of enamel loss. A slight chip- *precautions* ping of the enamel can increase so that the historic importance and *Do not pick up* intrinsic value is diminished. *where chipped*

Do not allow enamelled objects to protrude beyond the storage *Never allow to* area or beyond the transporting device when they are moved within *protrude* the facility.

161

ART OBJECTS

Fingerprints   Fortunately, fingerprints are not damaging to enamelled objects and are easily removed. On the other hand enamel readily retains impressions of prints from hands. Remove them with a soft cloth before objects are put on exhibition or in storage.

Gloves not recommended   In some cases, wearing gloves when handling enamelled objects is wise, but it cannot be generally recommended that gloves be worn. Wearing gloves eliminates fingerprints, but an enamelled surface is slick and smooth. Depending on size and shape, some pieces are subjected to possible danger if gloves are worn by the handler. Gloves are protective but they can also cause trouble. One must evaluate the situation in each case. *Never wear gloves if the piece is chipped.*

Keep cotton away   Do not allow cotton to come in contact with enamelled objects which have been chipped. It adheres to the rough edges of damaged areas and contributes to progressive flaking, either by the very contact of the material or during the process of removing the cotton particles from areas of enamel loss.

Move pieces of similar size together   Insofar as possible, move enamelled objects of approximately the same size together. It is not wise to attempt moving larger objects with small pieces, no matter how carefully padded against shock and contact.

Storage   Store enamelled objects on wooden shelves or in cabinets. Small pieces should be stored in padded boxes or lined and padded drawers.

Humidity   The desired relative humidity for enamelled objects is under 50%.

BIBLIOGRAPHY

Amiranashvili, Shalva. *Medieval Georgian Enamels of Russia*. New York. Harry N. Abrams, Inc., 1966.

Bates, Kenneth F. *The Enamelist*. Cleveland, World Publishing Co., 1967.

Cunynghame, Henry H. S. *On the Theory and Practice of Art Enamelling Upon Metals*. 3rd edition. London, Methuen & Co., 1906.

Fisher, Alexander. "The Art of Enamelling Upon Metal," *The Studio* (London), Vol. 22 (1906), Part I, pp. 242-254; Vol. 23, Part II, pp. 88-96; Vol. 25, Part III, pp. 108-118.

Garner, Sir Harry M. *Chinese and Japanese Cloisonné Enamels*. London, Faber & Faber, 1962.

Hildburgh, W. L. *Medieval Spanish Enamels*. London, Oxford University Press, 1936.

Kovacs, Eva. *Limoges Champlevé Enamels in Hungary*. Budapest, Corvina Press, 1968.

Lansing, Ambrose. "Masterpieces of Enameling," *Bulletin of the Metropolitan Museum of Art*, Vol. XXXV, no. 12 (December, 1940), pp. 99-103.

Millenet, Louis-Elie. *Enamelling on Metal*. New York, D. Van Nostrand & Co., Inc., 1951.

Newble, Brian. *Practical Enamelling and Jewelry Work*. New York. The Viking Press, 1967.

Ross, Marvin C. "Early Restorations of Mediaeval Enamels," *Technical Studies in the Field of Fine Arts*, Vol. II, no. 3 (January, 1934), pp. 138-143.

Wessel, Klaus. *Byzantine Enamels*. Greenwich, Conn., New York Graphic Society, 1968.

Winter, Edward. *Enamel Painting Techniques*. New York, Frederick A. Praeger, 1970.

———. *Enamel Art on Metals*. New York, Guptill, 1958.

10

Ivory Objects

The term *ivory carving* includes all sculpture in bone and vegetable fossil and imitation ivory, as well as ivory of elephant tusks. From earliest times, bone has been the most available in many shapes and could be fashioned into a great variety of useful objects—arrow-heads, fish-hooks and other tools and instruments to aid early man to survive. Ivory, which is composed of a more compact grain, is the more desirable for fine decorative work, although its standard shape and small size restricts its use, for the most part, to delicate ornamental objects on a small scale. The notable exception is its use by the great Greek sculptor, Phidias, in the fifth century B.C. for such huge and majestic statues as Athena of the Parthenon, Athens, and Zeus at Olympia, both destroyed by the barbarian hordes who swept over Europe after the fall of Rome.

Ivory is a versatile medium. It can be carved, stained, etched, painted, gilded, inlaid with metals or with precious and semi-precious stones. It can also be used for inlaying and veneering. It is one of man's oldest mediums for artistic expression, personal adornment, and usefulness. It is often difficult to distinguish ivory from bone when worked and decorated, since the main inorganic constituents are the same. Only microscopic examina-

164

tion by an expert can reveal in cross section the difference in cellular structure. Sometimes, inspection with a pocket lens can accomplish the same end without sectioning. Unlike bone, ivory requires no preparation prior to carving.

The quality of ivory varies according to the district from which it comes. Ivories of considerable age have a yellow color, and this is prized by collectors as a form of natural patination which enhances its appearance. It is often artificially applied by the Japanese *netsuke* carver, for example, to embellish his surface effect or to deceive the buyer on the age of his wares. Sometimes the greyish color of burnt ivory is intentional, as in the case of some of the Nimrud ivories. Staining may be due to a variety of causes, adventitious and otherwise, and can be removed by appropriate chemical treatment.

Whenever and wherever a material is required for the finest carving, ivory has been in great demand. It is ideal for carving figurines and statuettes, as well as small plaques and reliefs on diptychs and bookbindings. Among the earliest specimens extant are those from the Dordogne in France, the work of cave dwellers. They date from the time when the mammoth and the reindeer roved in southern Europe. From the first dynasty of Egypt (3400 B.C.) boxes and other vessels, have survived. A magnificent cache, now in the British Museum, London, was unearthed by the excavation of Nimrud in Mesopotamia in 1952. During the excavation Professor Malloran was able to recover a number of the ivories by drying them slowly and uniformly to prevent serious cracking and preserve their shape.

In the Aegean Age, ivory was used by the sculptors of Crete for their exquisite figurines of ivory and gold. The Museum of Fine Arts, Boston, is fortunate in owning one of the most famous, the Minoan Snake Goddess, dating from the sixteenth century B.C. She has been reconstructed by Dr. William Young, the museum's conservator, from hundreds of slivers (the fragile material splits so easily) and her parts rejoined; the body was made originally in two pieces with the arms attached by pegs. From the glory that was Greece, no example of the great chryselephantine statues survives, although contemporary documents praise their grandeur. Among the varied purposes the Romans utilized ivory for, the most important was the diptych, a tablet for commemorating an important event. It is formed by hinging two slabs of ivory together, the outer faces being decorated and the inner ones hollowed and filled with wax. The practice of signalizing such occasions continued well into the early Christian era.

Throughout the entire Medieval period, ivory carving was continuously practiced and attained a high degree of perfection. It provides evidence of the continuity of tradition at a time when there was little monumental stone sculpture, owing to the Iconoclastic movement under Leo the Isaurian, which forbade the creation of images and destroyed those existing. Fortunately the Iconoclastic edicts did not include the small figures to which the ivory carver was limited by the scale of his material. Thus, masterpieces of decorative religious art, representing the greatest achievement of the period, are the book covers for illuminated manuscripts, devotional tablets and shrines, pyxes, crosiers, crucifixes, and panels of doors. Although primarily at the service of the church, the ivory worker was allowed to represent secular or pagan themes, and a vast number of fine caskets, hunting and drinking horns (called oliphants), combs, mirrors, seals, and chessmen attest to his skill.

Byzantine ivory carving was copied by craftsmen in the West, resulting ultimately in a fusion of Latin and Byzantine styles. Most distinctive are the Carolingian ivories which illustrate the attempt of Charlemagne (742-814) to regenerate his kingdom intellectually and spiritually. In the characteristic ivory of the tenth century one detects the growing trend toward monumental scale, reflecting the influence of the major arts, but at the end of the century a type of ivory appears which is so clearly based on the miniatures of manuscripts that they have been termed "the pictorial group." The painted models provided a variety of subjects which are a welcome change from the rigidly frontal forms of the diptychs. Through the eleventh century, ivory carving was the most important sculptural expression.

During the Romanesque period of the twelfth century, ivory carving continued but primarily as an adjunct in decorating large objects. It became subordinate to stone and reflects the monumental style of cathedral sculpture in the broader proportions of figures, gestures, and drapery folds. In the later Middle Ages or Gothic period, the varied forms of ivory become increasingly self-sufficient, often intended as the central object on the altar of a small chapel or private shrine. The growing secularization of the arts put ivory to new uses, such as decorating jeweled caskets and mirror cases with scenes of love, sport, jugglery, and other pursuits of the age.

In the High Renaissance the art of ivory carving subsided, but during the Baroque period it regained its popularity, particularly in Germany and the Netherlands for elaborate tankards. During the eighteenth century in France, leader in decorative arts on the continent, an important school of ivory carving was established at Dieppe, and at the end of the century ivory was appropriated by the goldsmith for elegant "objets d'art" in Paris.

In India, native habitat of the elephant, ivory carving has been practiced from ancient times to the present day. The Hindu pantheon has supplied subject matter for free-standing figures as well as carved plaques. Great quantities of boxes and other decorative objects have been exported to the European market from southern India.

The ivories of the Orient best known to westerners are those of China and Japan. The abundance of the supply of ivory in China may partly explain its importance as an art medium. Next to jade, it was considered a mark of luxury. Articles of ivory were used for personal adornment as well as for utilitarian purposes. Indeed ivory was in such demand that tusks had to be imported from Siam, Burma, India, and Africa.

In 1680 the emperor K'ang Hsi established imperial ateliers within the palace at Peking and brought craftsmen from all over

167

the empire to produce work of superior quality. Ivory carving is still an important industry in Canton, Peking, Shanghai, Amoy, and Suchow, most of which goes to foreign markets.

Japan's contribution to ivory carving is a style known as *bachiru*. In this technique, the finished surface is first generally dyed or stained, and then designs carved into it. The carved portions can be left plain or colors added. Other methods of the technique include carving an unstained piece and then applying colors.

Most familiar to the Western collector is the carved ivory *netsuke* which began to be produced in the seventeenth century. A *netsuke* is an ornamental piece fastened to the cords of a purse, tobacco pouch or medicine case. The *netsuke* was used to stabilize the container and became a traditional item in the Japanese male costume. These boxes and pouches were carried as substitutes for pockets, which Japanese clothes lack. Usually from one to three inches in height, *netsuke* became a medium for sculptural representation of both mythological and religious subjects ranging in mood from frightening to humorous. These pieces became very popular and were worn by rich merchants as a display of wealth and replaced wooden *netsuke* which were typical of the Ashikaga period, 1394-1573. They were also made of lacquer, metal and stone. The majority of existing ivory *netsuke* are from the nineteenth century, when a realistic style was developed to please customers in the European and American markets.

Soon after Admiral Perry signed the Kanagawa treaty with Japan in 1854, these ivory objects were exported in great quantities to other countries. Foreign collectors were so attracted by them that for a time the demand made Japanese ivory carvings one of the country's leading exports. This was encouraging to the carvers because the native demand for *netsuke* had waned when the cigarette eliminated the need for tobacco pouches. As a result the craft deteriorated in quality and standard.

Ivory carving was not neglected on the North American continent. The American Indian tribes found gleaming ivory

168

Figure 91. SNAKE GODDESS. Minoan, ca. 1600-1500 B.C. Gold and ivory. Very few examples of sculpture in the round have survived from the great Minoan civilization in Crete, and this exquisite figure is by far the finest and largest piece known, although it measures only 6½ inches in height. It was reconstructed from approximately 50 fragments by William J. Young, conservator of the Museum of Fine Arts laboratory. Breaks between first and second flounces date from original manufacture; arms were also put on separately. Decorative pattern incised into gold by tracer tool has regained its original precision. *Courtesy, Museum of Fine Arts, Boston.*

Figure 92. OLIPHANT. South Italy (Salerno?), late 11th century. Ivory. Carved from elephant tusks, oliphants were used in the Middle Ages as hunting and signal horns as well as for drinking vessels. This magnificent example served the latter purpose and was most likely a "Tenure Horn" symbolizing the legal transfer of land. The fantastic beasts, plants, and mythological subjects depicted on these horns are derived from Byzantine and late Classical art and iconography. In the new Medieval gallery of the Boston Museum, it is carefully protected by a glass case from heat and humidity. *Courtesy, Museum of Fine Arts, Boston.*

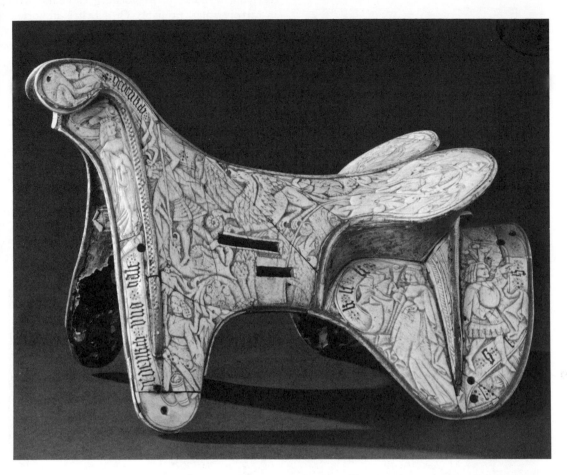

Figure 93. KNIGHTLY SADDLE. Tyrol (?), ca. 1450. Staghorn, carved and partly colored, lined with birch bark. This is a rare example in this country of a Gothic saddle decorated with figures in low relief. Twenty-one such saddles have survived. Depicted against a background of inhabited scrollwork are St. George and the Dragon, and men and women in fashionable secular costume holding inscribed ribbons with initials and legend in German. The refined courtly style of the carving, which is related to contemporary German prints, suggests an origin in Tyrol. The saddle is recorded from 1520 to 1966 as an heirloom of the Hungarian family of Batthyani. *Courtesy, Museum of Fine Arts, Boston.*

Figure 94.

Figure 94. CHRIST IN MAJESTY. German, 10th century. Ivory. This Ottonian plaque shows Christ receiving a model of Magdeburg cathedral from an earthly ruler, probably Otto I. It is important to recognize the vital part played by this minor art (actually minor only in scale) in the subsequent course of Western art.

Figure 95. PENDANT: CORONATION OF THE VIRGIN. Eastern France, early 15th century. Polychromed ivory under rock crystal. The intricate carving and coloring of this exquisite piece demonstrate why ivory has been a universal favorite since prehistoric times. It is the medium that provided the link in the history of sculpture between the Middle Ages and the Renaissance. *Courtesy, Museum of Fine Arts, Boston.*

Figure 96. CAROLINGIAN IVORY PLAQUE. Anonymous, Northern France, 9th century. *Courtesy, Museum of Fine Arts, Boston.*

Figure 95.

Figure 96.

Figure 97. Figure Cut From a Plaque:
Virgin and Child. Byzantine, 11th century. Ivory. The fine texture of ivory
provided the Byzantine artist with a
perfect medium for delicate carvings intended for both secular and religious use.
In this statuette, the figures have been
reduced to an austere and stylized formula consistent with the architectonic
bias of ecclesiastic sculpture. *Courtesy,
Metropolitan Museum of Art.*

Figure 98. 1. An example of *bachiru*, Japan's great contribution to the art of ivory carving; 2. Detail, showing typical *bachiru* method with color added after the figure was carved from a piece of unstained ivory.

Figure 99. 1. BRUSH HOLDER. Ivory, Japanese. Particular care must be taken in the handling of ivories which have detailed carving and piercing. Do not use cotton wadding or absorbent cotton for packing. Particles of cotton become lodged in the crevices and interstices and are difficult to remove. 2. Detail. *Courtesy, Los Angeles County Museum of Art.*

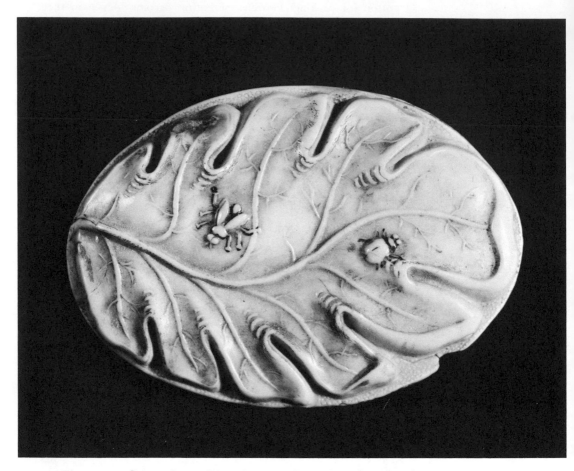

Figure 100. Carved Ivory Leaf. Japanese. Ivory loses its natural color if it is exposed to sunlight very long. Natural light should not strike ivory objects at any time. Old ivory often takes on a yellowish color; this is natural patina and usually enhances the appearance. *Collection of the author.*

teeth of animals very attractive, and the brave decorated himself and his clothing with them. In the Arctic and sub-Arctic regions the walrus, elephant and narwhal were killed by Indians for their ivory. It was in the Eskimo-inhabited areas that the art of carving ivory attained its highest development on this continent. The Eskimos carved for functional as well as ornamental purposes. The earliest such carvings come from the Bering Sea region, but examples are not numerous.

RULES FOR CARE AND HANDLING

Never carry
by hand

Do not carry museum ivory objects in the hands; always move them in a box or tray. Ancient ivories are extremely delicate and easily damaged. The condition, shape, contours and size of each piece should be evaluated before moving.

Do not wrap
carved ivories
with cotton

Particular care must be given to ivories which have detailed carving and piercing. Such intricate features often include restored areas and are subject to breakage. Do not wrap ivory objects with cotton wadding, absorbent cotton, or any such soft material which may allow particles to become lodged in the crevices and interstices of the ivory. Fragments are easily lost in cotton.

Pad with velvet

Velvet is an excellent material to use as padding and as a shock-absorbent material. Shallow trays fully lined with velvet are recommended for moving and storing small ivories. Velvet pile offers just the right amount of protection and does not cling. Storage bins lined with velvet are also recommended.

Line storage
bins and seal

Protect from
dust

Storage areas should be covered or air tight if possible. Uncovered storage allows dust to settle on the ivory objects as well as the velvet padding, and such accumulations of dust may cause damage.

Eliminate
unnecessary
moves

Move ivory objects as seldom as possible. Eliminate all unnecessary moves. Ancient ivory is extremely fragile. In order to maintain it in its original state as nearly as possible, those entrusted with the care of ivory should know the nature of the medium and the possibilities and causes of breakage and damages. A careful evaluation of an ivory object should be made before it is moved. Many ivories have unique details which are not seen from the front.

Know the
characteristics
of ivory

Do not wear
gloves

Hands must be clean before touching ivory. The use of gloves to handle ivories is not recommended. Glove fabrics could be damaging to an ivory carving, and with gloves there is danger of the object slipping from one's grasp.

Protect from
light

Ivory loses its natural color if continuously exposed to sunlight. Storage and display should be arranged so that natural light does not strike the pieces. Old ivory often has a yellowish color, but this is natural patination which enhances the appearance.

Wash the surface of ivory with mild soap and water *only* when

180

in good condition. *If* washing is attempted, the object should be dried immediately. Do not allow the soap and water solution to be in contact with the ivory any longer than necessary. Linen is excellent for drying, because it absorbs moisture readily and does not have lint. Do not use a material which is linty. *Do not soak ivory*. Applications of water should be kept to a minimum as ivory is likely to warp and crack. A mild detergent may be used, followed by careful drying. *Wash with mild soap and dry immediately with linen* *Do not soak*

When ivory is in good condition, it is possible to preserve and maintain it by observing a few simple precautions. If it is in a fragmentary or fossilized condition, it should be cleaned, strengthened or stabilized only by an expert. Ivory buried in the ground for a long time becomes damaged by the action of salts and water. Salt encrusted and semifossilized ivory tends to split and warp when put into water or dampened with water. Do not wash salt-encrusted, fossilized or semifossilized ivory objects. All ivory becomes brittle with age. *Only experts can clean difficult pieces* *Do not wash salt-encrusted or fossilized ivory*

Regardless of age, all ivory is easily and quickly damaged by warpage if it is exposed to heat, dampness, or both. Ivory reacts quickly to sudden changes in temperature and humidity. Sudden atmospheric changes cause ivory to warp and crack. This can occur so quickly that it can be observed with the naked eye. *Avoid heat, dampness, and sudden changes in temperature*

Never lift an ivory object by any projecting part, rims or edges. Even slight stress and strain on small areas of brittle ivory can result in breakage. Flat, finely carved pieces may be moved by inserting a thin, flat piece of smooth cardboard under the object; however, extreme care must be exercised if this method is used. Repeated caution must be drawn to the fact that the condition and strength of an object dictates all handling methods and procedures. *Do not lift ivory by rims or edges* *Insert cardboard underneath to move* *Condition dictates procedure*

Do not allow any part of an ivory object to protrude beyond the carrying box, tray, or storage shelf. Each object should have its own individual carrying box, properly identified with number and brief description on the outside. If individual boxes are not provided, cover ivory in storage with clean cloth. *Do not allow objects to protrude* *Carry and store in separate boxes*

Unpack objects on padded tables. If possible, pad tables with velvet; remnants can be purchased at a nominal cost and are a good investment. Do not pad tables with any material which is rough or inclined to have lint. *Unpack on padded tables*

Save all packing materials for later examination in the event

Examine
packing
materials for
fragments
Maintain high
relative
humidity

fragments have become detached from pieces. Broken ivory cannot be successfully restored unless the fragments are recovered.

Ivory must be kept in a rather high relative humidity. The humidity must be constant. About 55% is recommended.

BIBLIOGRAPHY

Ashton, Sir Leigh. *Masterpieces in the Victoria and Albert Museum.* London, Her Majesty's Stationery Office, 1952.

Beckwith, John. *Caskets from Cordova.* 8 vols. London, Her Majesty's Stationery Office, 1960.

Beihoff, Norbert J. *Ivory Sculpture Through the Ages.* Milwaukee, Milwaukee Public Museum, 1961; distributed through the American Association of Museums, Washington, D.C.

"Cleaning and Preserving Ivories," *The Museums Journal,* Technical Notes, January, 1932.

Cnotliwy, Eugeniusz. *Studies on the Techniques of Working Bone and Horn in Western Pomerania in the Early Middle Ages.* IIC Abstract No. 2820, 1960-1961.

Cott, Perry B. *Siculo-Arabic Ivories.* Princeton, New Jersey, Princeton University Press, 1939.

Cox, Warren E. *Chinese Ivory Sculpture.* New York, World Publishing Co., 1968.

Crawford, Vaughn E. "Ivories from the Earth," *Bulletin of the Metropolitan Museum of Art,* Vol. 21 (1962), pp. 141-148.

Cust, A. M. *Ivory Workers of the Middle Ages.* 1902.

Gairola, T. R. *Preservation of a Bone Object.* IIC Abstract No. 2636, 1960-1961.

Kantorowicz, Ernst. "Ivories and Litanies," *Journal of the Warburg Institute,* Vol. V (1942), pp. 70-71.

Koechlin, Raymond. *Les Ivoires Gothiques Français.* Paris, 1924.

Longhurst, Margaret H. *English Ivories.* London, 1926.

Maskell, Alfred. *Ivories.* Rutland, Vermont, Charles E. Tuttle, 1966.

Todd, William. "A Vacuum Process for the Preservation of Bone and Similar Materials," *Technical Studies in the Field of Fine Arts,* Vol. IX, no. 3 (1940), pp. 160-164; *The Museum News,* Vol. XXI, no. 13 (January 1, 1944), pp. 7-8.

Webster, R. "Ivory, Bone and Horns: Vegetable Ivory and Tortoiseshell," *Gemmologist,* Vol. 27, nos. 322-323 (1958), pp. 91-98.

Wills, Geoffrey. *Ivory.* Cranbury, New Jersey, A. S. Barnes Co., 1969.

11

Glass Objects

Glass is one of man's most beautiful and versatile media. As a plastic substance, it offers a tremendous scope for the creative artist. In its liquid state it can be shaped, and in its solid state it can be cut, engraved, sandblasted and etched. Basically, glass is a combination of silica with some alkali or alkaline earth, such as lime. Generally, it is a silicate of soda, or a combination of silica of soda, or a combination of silica or flint with one or more of the salts of sodium, to which are added certain metallic oxides.

The first furnaces which produced glass were volcanoes. When man first used glass he took it from the ground. It was already fused and cooled. The glass which is formed naturally by volcanic action is called obsidian. It is found in many parts of the world. Usually dark, or black, and translucent, it can be chipped and flaked to make arrow points, spear heads, knives and razors. Man probably began to use naturally fused glass tools for hunting as long ago as Paleolithic times.

The origin of glass in its artificial state (that is, man-made) is obscure, and the honor of its discovery is contested by several nations. It was probably the Syrians, whose imagination was first fired by its jewel-like beauty some 4500 years ago. Excavations in the Tigris-Euphrates region have revealed remnants of the glass-furnaces which these ancient artisans worked; the earliest known piece of table glass—a light blue cylinder remarkably free of flaws—was found near Baghdad.

It was not until about 1500 B.C. that the Egyptians began to make simple drinking vessels, but the inhabitants of the Nile valley soon brought the craft to a high degree of perfection, founding an industry which made the glass-houses of Alexandria world-famous in Ptolemaic times. A particularly beautiful form called *millefiori* (thousand flowers), made from slices of varicolored threads, persisted well into the Christian era.

The sand-core method was used by the early Egyptian glassmen to fashion the glass bowls and bottles in which food and wine were left for the dead. It involved building up a core of sand on a wooden or metal rod around which the molten glass was modeled. With this laborious method, they manufactured thousands of unguent containers in which they exported cosmetics across the Mediterranean.

Although an Egyptian slave is credited with the invention of hollow-ware in one operation by pressing molten glass into open molds, it was the Phoenicians who made the most significant discovery about a thousand years later, when they began blowing plastic glass into hollow shapes on the end of metal blowpipes, using incised molds to form the inflated material into decorative shapes. The news was quickly absorbed by the Egyptian glassmakers (around 50 B.C.) and developed to such a degree that after Egypt fell to Imperial Rome, a major portion of the tribute exacted from the conquered nation was in the form of glass.

Egyptian glassmen were lured with prizes to establish what was to become a thriving industry on the Tiber. Exquisite articles of fragile glass brought fantastic sums, while sturdy glass goblets went for a copper coin in the Roman market. Nothing new was evolved by the Romans, but their elaborate luxury glass captured the trade of the entire western world. Though unintentional, the domestic glass of Rome had a greenish cast which was lighter or deeper according to the quantity of iron

184

in the sand. As displayed in museum cases today, the beautiful iridescence of much Greco-Roman glass is due to the partial decomposition of its surface and the formation of innumerable thin scales, a condition resulting normally from its long burial in the ground.

From Rome, glassblowing radiated to the Roman colonies, spreading northward into the valleys of the Rhone and the Rhine and across the seas. During the Roman occupation, several furnaces were operating in Britain, and, after the Roman withdrawal, the Britons continued producing a bluish green ware for Anglo-Saxon bowl-shaped cups, tumblers ornamented with a raised pattern in glass thread-work, and deep beakers with projecting claws. Chiddingfold was the center of English glass manufacture at the time and continued to make window glass and a coarse ware for domestic use during the next 1000 years.

In a sense, Islam took the place of Rome as the unifying force in Mediterranean culture. Early Islamic glass continued the tradition of the late Antique but gradually acquired an individual freedom of style in the wheel-engraved and relief-cut wares of Egypt and Iran, which is in marked contrast to the geometric regularity of their prototypes. The greatest contribution of the Moslem glassworkers to the development of glass was in the enamelled wares of the thirteenth and fourteenth centuries; polychrome enamelling and gilding on large bowls, mosque lamps, and bottles attained unprecedented splendor.

The role that Islamic enamelled glass played in the brilliant flowering of the Venetian glass industry during the fifteenth and sixteenth centuries is undisputed. The great achievement of Venice was a fragile, light weight glass displaying a smoothness and clarity never before reached. It also took color well, and soon gorgeous vessels of Venetian *cristallo*, decorated with gilding and filigree, graced every royal table in Europe and was eagerly sought wherever costly glass could be afforded.

There was such a demand for Venetian glass that the glass

furnaces were moved to the island of Murano the better to guard their secrets, and glassmakers were stringently governed by law. Masters of the art of glassmaking were forbidden to leave under penalties which ranged from a term in the galley to death. The law further prohibited their teaching their craft to outsiders.

Some did manage to leave and set up glassworks in other countries. Factories were established in England, Portugal, Spain, France, Austria, and Germany, all inspired by the *façon de Venise* but with national characteristics of their own. In northern Europe, where changes came about more slowly, glassmakers developed distinct forms such as the *Humpen*, a tall, cylindrical beaker, and the *Römer*, a goblet with a prunted, hollow stem. This latter form became a classic German shape of the period and with modification continues today. The prunts add intriguing optical accents to the sober Waldglas (forest-green) color produced by the potash from burning forest vegetation.

In the sixteenth century, some Venetian glassmakers were persuaded to set up glasshouses in England, and in 1575 Queen Elizabeth granted Verzelini the right to make glass in the *façon de Venise* and train British glassworkers, thus founding the modern glass industry in England. Since lack of wood to heat the furnaces was always a problem with Verzelini and his contemporaries, experiments with coal were performed, and in the early seventeenth century a coal-burning furnace was patented by Sir William Slingsby. However, it was the melting furnace invented in 1635 by Captain Thornese Franke that transformed glassmaking.

The second major advance in the late seventeenth century was the perfection of a good lead glass by George Ravenscroft, who, in cooperation with The Glass Sellers' Company of London, experimented with native raw materials to free the English market from foreign domination in ingredients and production. The cumulative result was a glass that was stable and soft enough to cut without chipping and with a refractive brilliance never before seen. Ravenscroft's high-content lead glass was so successful and popular abroad that the term *crystal* came to mean lead glass rather than the Venetian soda-lime *cristallo*.

Glassmaking was the first industry brought to the New World from Europe. As early as 1535 glass was being made in Mexico. The first glass house in the American colonies was established in Jamestown, Virginia, in 1608, by a London company attracted to the abundant supply of sand near virgin forests. It failed in 1609. In fact, the history of American glassmaking is a constant sequence of struggles, failures, and fresh starts. Most of the factories changed hands and names rapidly, losing craftsmen to rival enterprises and operating only for a few years.

The earliest successful glass factory was established in 1739 by Caspar Wistar near Allowaystown, New Jersey, and a splinter group, the Stanger brothers, left him to found their own glass factory at nearby Glassboro in 1781. The tradition begun by these two factories is known today as South Jersey; the type was generally free-blown and subsequently tooled into pitchers, bowls, and bottles of simple beauty.

In 1765 another glass house was founded in Manheim, Pennsylvania, by a German immigrant, Henry William Stiegel. His aim was to compete with expensive European ware; he produced glass of such fine quality that many of his pieces were indistinguishable from the Continental imports. This venture failed because of the American Revolution, rising costs, and Stiegel's personal extravagance, but he produced an enormous amount of beautiful glass.

Another German, John Frederick Amelung, founded the New Bremen Glassmanufactury in Maryland, which set a high standard in its clear glass decanters, glasses, and goblets during its short existence of one decade.

Following the population trend westward, glassworkers moved also to New Geneva and Pittsburgh in western Pennsylvania and then into Ohio, where Stiegel-type glass continued to be made. By 1800 a dozen glassworks were working in

187

ART OBJECTS

New Jersey, including the Olive Glass Works, which eventually became part of the Owens Bottle Company and today is part of what became Owens-Illinois.

In the late 1820's American glassmakers revolutionized the glass industry. They invented a way to press glass mechanically. This was the first major advance in glassmaking since the blowpipe. The process was very simple. Molten glass was dropped into a patterned mold and forced into every part by a tightly fitting plunger. Pressed glass can be made clear, opalescent or colored. It is unusually heavy and often has many flaws. It lacked brilliance because it could not be reheated. A "lacy" (stippled) background was devised to give it sparkle. It was actually a "poor man's cut glass." Competition between pressed glass products and cut glass led to the pressed glass process of fire polishing which gave it a surface almost as smooth as blown glass. Most well known and successful of the products is a lacy pressed glass referred to as Sandwich glass. It derived its name from the little Cape Cod town of Sandwich where a factory was started in 1825. Its lovely designs and glowing colors are part of its attraction. In the "fancy glass" category, the glass products of Louis Comfort Tiffany (1848-1933) achieved a new high in color, shapes and pattern, displaying an elegant style known as *Art Nouveau*.

Very little original work came from Sweden until the time of World War I. In the 1920's a sudden development of modern Swedish glass came about as a result of the Swedish Arts and Crafts Society's endeavor to encourage employment of painters at the famous Orrefors Glassworks. At the same time, other beautiful works were produced in Denmark, Norway, Finland, and particularly at the Leerdam Glassworks in Holland.

The technique of glass production has actually changed very little during the past 4000 years. Electricity and other methods of controlling heat have expedited the manufacture, but its quality and beauty still depend on the skill, vision and artistry of the glassmaker, just as it did ages ago.

The distinctive quality of modern glass can be traced back

188

to the efforts of three or four men in glassworks in Sweden and Holland earlier this century. These artist-designers wanted to produce something appropriate for their own time with the wonderful medium of glass. In the past decade and a half there has been a revolution of thought, experiment and achievement. Manufacturers of glass, led by visionary European leaders, have begun to look at glass and its uses with fresh minds directed to modern needs. In experimental research there has on the whole been a large ratio of success along with a wide expansion of vision in the intriguing production of glass objects.

Types of Glass

Soda-Lime Glass is made from inexpensive materials which are relatively easy to melt and shape. The earliest man-made glass, it is the least expensive to make and purchase.

Borosilicate Glass is used extensively in the home because of its resistance to breakage, corrosion and thermal shock. It is also used extensively in science and industry. It can withstand temperature changes that would break soda-lime glass. Its dimensions change very little with temperature variations.

Lead Glass has a high index of refraction which gives it many optical applications in the manufacture of lenses and prisms. It is used to shield against atomic radiation and is desirable for electronic purposes. It is easily worked and has exceptional sparkle and luster. This type is identified with fine crystal, such as the famous Steuben glass and Waterford crystal.

96% Silica Glass is made by removing almost all of the elements except silica from a borosilicate glass after it has been formed by the conventional technique. Its valuable properties include exceptional thermal endurance, chemical resistance, and electrical characteristics. It can be heated cherry red and plunged directly into ice water without damage. It transmits ultraviolet and near infrared rays and therefore has a value in heating applications.

189

Aluminosilicate Glass combines good electrical and chemical properties with outstanding thermal shock resistance and unusually high softening temperatures. It does not require special processing and is made by traditional techniques. It is used for high temperature thermometers, combustion tubes, stove-top cookware and for space-vehicle windows.

Fused Silica Glass is the simplest both physically and chemically and highest in performance. It is made directly from silica without other constituents. Fused silica glass has outstanding electrical and acoustical properties and a high melting point. With minimal thermal expansion, it can be formed in a wide range of shapes and sizes. It has many flight-vehicle applications.

Methods of Working Glass

Engraving is done mostly with a stone or carborundum wheel which rotates on a spindle using an abrasive such as emery powder in oil. Usually, there is a large collection of wheels to choose from, varying from 1/8″ to 3″ or 4″ in diameter. They can quickly be interchanged on the rotating spindle. Diamond point is another method of engraving but it is seldom used today because it lacks the flexibility that the skilled glassworker requires. The most recent form of engraving tool resembles a dentist's drill on a flexible drive which provides the pleasures of the practice without the expense of the traditional tools.

Cutting is similar to engraving because a turning wheel is used to bite into the surface of the glass. The wheel, made of stone or cast iron, is larger and abrasive. Water is used with it instead of oil. Most of the methods of decorating glass are a means of attacking the glass object and removing a part of the glass.

Sandblasting is a way of cutting away glass by directing an abrasive sand into a stream of compressed air, controlled to enable the worker to produce effects similar to engraving. Sandblasting lends itself especially to bold sculptural effects.

Figure 101. CHANDELIER. English or Irish, ca. 1800. Crystal. This handsome ceiling fixture with its complex structure and fragile material requires handling and cleaning by an expert. The cut-glass central pillar is in vase form with pendant bell-form and drops. The metal mounts are modern. *Courtesy, Museum of Fine Arts, Boston.*

Figure 102. CINERARY URN. Roman, 1st century B.C. to 1st century A.D. Aquamarine blown glass. This urn was unearthed in southern Italy in the town of Paestum, 22 miles southwest of Salerno, in 1870. Burial in the ground for nearly 2000 years caused disintegration of the surface of the glass. Roughness from erosion causes the glass to refract light, giving it a brilliant iridescence. The flaky surface particles are easily disturbed. Any movement of the flakes always results in losses. *Do not touch flaky, disintegrated glass objects with bare hands. Courtesy, Los Angeles County Museum of Art.*

Figure 103. VASE. Louis Comfort Tiffany, American, 1848-1933. In the "fancy glass" category, the products of this great American designer achieved a new high in color, shape, and pattern. Typical is the free flowing iridescent green and lava black of the peacock-feather design. *Courtesy, Museum of Fine Arts, Boston.*

Figure 104. JEWEL CASKETS. American, 1830-1850.
American glassmakers revolutionized the glass
industry by inventing a way to press glass me-
chanically. A most distinctive form is the lacy
Sandwich glass illustrated. *Courtesy, Museum of
Fine Arts, Boston.*

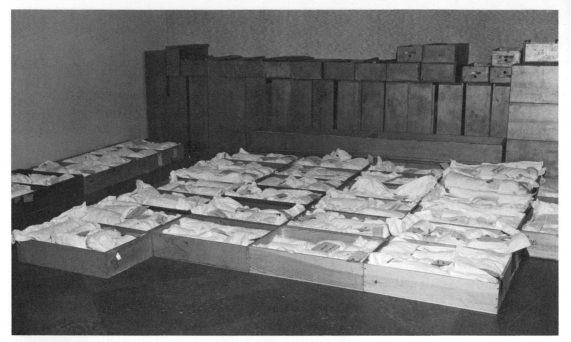

Figure 105. These carrying boxes, 16″ x 24″ x 5″ deep, were used to pack small glass objects for transfer to the new facility of the Los Angeles County Museum of Art. (They were also used for small ceramics, small metal and wooden pieces.) *Courtesy, Los Angeles County Museum of Art.*

Figure 107. DIAGONALS. Lloyd Atkins, designer, contemporary. Smooth crystal block with rounded sides, the front and back each cut diagonally, in opposite directions. Top and bottom surfaces repeat the tapering outline. The crystal rests on a circular revolving stand.

Figure 106. ROTATING SQUARE. Paul Schulze, designer, contemporary. Engraved block of solid crystal, cut to suggest a square form rotating through space. *Courtesy, Steuben Glass, New York.*

Figure 108. GAZELLE BOWL. Sidney Waugh, designer, contemporary. Blown-crystal bowl (resting on a solid crystal base, and engraved with a decorative frieze) embodies three techniques of hand glass-making—blowing, cutting, and engraving.

Figure 109. HUMPEN. German, 1700.
This enamelled glass is adorned with
scene of papermaking.

Figure 110. BOTTLE. German, 1572. Enamelled glass with a gilt top. *Courtesy, Los Angeles County Museum of Art.*

Acid Etching is another way of treating the surface of glass and can be used to leave a varying degree of matt surface.

Glass has been used as an art medium throughout its history. Until the last quarter of the nineteenth century, all glass was formed by hand. In a world where machines have almost replaced the artistry of individuals and the skill of a man's hands is becoming less and less appreciated, it is remarkable that more glass is being hand-made than ever before. The versatile medium of glass effectively combines the sensitive talents of the artist with the careful precision of the craftsman.

RULES FOR CARE AND HANDLING

Never lift or carry a glass object by handles, rim, or any project- *Do not carry*
ing part. Always support it at the bottom with one hand and at one *by projection*
side with the other hand. Rims, lips, handles and other projecting
parts are vulnerable to damage. Many museum objects have had
these areas repaired or restored.

Ancient glass is subject to chipping and flaking. For this reason, *Gloves may be*
hands should never come in contact with it. Clean white gloves are *worn, but not*
recommended for handling some glass objects but *gloves can cause* *with ancient*
extensive damage to ancient glass. Ancient glass which has been *glass*
buried in the ground usually has an uneven surface. Erosion of the
surface by chemicals in the soil causes a brilliant iridescence which
appears to be pigment but actually is refraction of light. Just one *Touch and*
finger placed on such a surface will remove slivers of the colored, *move ancient*
disintegrating material. Ancient glass should not be moved unless *glass with*
absolutely necessary. Smooth tissue paper is advisable as a buffer *caution*
between the fingers and the object. Tape several thicknesses to
thumb and forefinger so the edges of the paper will not disturb
flaky surfaces and cause losses. The weave of a glove can dislodge
flakes.

Never move more than one piece of glass at a time. Do not put *Move one piece*
ancient glass in a carrying device to transport it. Never let it come in *at a time*
contact with cotton, fabrics, excelsior or plastics.

All glass except ancient glass should be carefully padded when *Pad glass*
transferring it within the premises. Padding and separating pieces *(except ancient*
with a soft, resilient material will prevent damage during move- *specimens)*
ment. Abrasions, chipping and breakage can be avoided if padding *during transfer*
is carefully arranged within the carrying device and if the carrying
device itself is padded or lined with a soft material. Cotton should
not be allowed in contact with glass pieces having a rough surface. *Do not*
Small particles of it may cling to the object and on removal damage *overcrowd*
the surface. *carrying boxes*

Never overcrowd a carrying box with pieces of glass. It is prefer- *Do not allow*
able to have too much padding than to overcrowd a box. *objects to*

Do not allow a glass object to protrude beyond the edges of its *protrude*

199

carrying device, regardless of how short the distance of the transfer.

Collect fragments if object is broken

If a piece becomes chipped or broken in handling, collect all fragments, no matter how small, and preserve them for future restoration.

Move pieces of same size together

When moving several glass objects, move together those which are approximately the same size. It is unwise to mix large and small objects in or on the same moving device.

Unpack on padded counter

Unpack glass objects on a padded table. Even healthy, stable pieces can become scratched unless the table on which they are placed is padded with a nonabrasive material.

Inspect packing materials

When unpacking a shipment of glass objects, save all packing materials until the pieces have been inspected for condition. Minute fragments may be lodged in packing material.

Label in storage

To eliminate unnecessary handling, bins, shelves, or containers should have a brief description of each piece and its identifying number.

Report in writing

As soon as they are known, conditions of glass objects should be reported and recorded. A verbal report of a damage is meaningless; written reports and photographs of damage are valuable.

Desired RH

A constant relative humidity of about 40% is best for glass.

BIBLIOGRAPHY

Abdurazakov, A. A. and Bezborodov, M. A. "Chemical Investigation of Medieval Glasses of Central Asia," *Uzbekskii Khimicheskii Zhurnal* (Russia), Vol. 6, no. 3 (1962).

Belknap, E. McCamly. *Milk Glass.* New York, Crown Publishers, Inc., 1959.

Buckley, Wilfred. *The Art of Glass.* New York, 1939.

Burton, John. *Glass.* Philadelphia, Chilton Books, 1968.

Caley, Earle R. *Analyses of Ancient Glasses, 1790-1957, A Comprehensive and Critical Survey.* Corning, New York, The Corning Museum of Glass Monographs, Vol. 1 (1962).

Eisen, Gustavus A. *Glass: Its Origin, History, Chronology.* New York, 1927.

Frothingham, Alice Wilson. *Spanish Glass.* New York, Thomas Yoseloff, 1964.

Haynes, E. Barrington. *Glass Through the Ages.* Baltimore, Md., Penguin Books, Inc., 1964.

Honey, William Bowyer. *Glass: A Handbook for the Study of Glass*

200

Vessels of all Periods and Countries and a Guide to the Museum Collection. London, Victoria & Albert Museum, 1946.

Kampfer, Fritz and Beyer, Klaus G. *Glass: A World History.* Greenwich, Conn., New York Graphic Society, 1967.

McKearin, Helen, and George S. *Two Hundred Years of American Blown Glass.* New York, Crown Publishers, Inc., 1958.

Morey, G. W. *Properties of Glass.* New York, Reinhold Publishing Corp., 1953.

Neuberg, Frederic. *Ancient Glass.* London, Barrie & Rockliff, 1963.

Ritchie, Patrick D. "Spectrographic Studies on Ancient Glass—Chinese Glass from Pre-Han to T'ang Times," *Technical Studies in the Field of Fine Arts,* Vol. V, no. 3 (January, 1937), pp. 209-220.

Savage, George. *Glass.* New York, Putnam Publishing Co. 1965.

Seligman, C. G. and Beck, H. C. "Far Eastern Glass: Some Western Origins," *Bulletin of the Museum of Far Eastern Antiquities* (Stockholm), No. 10 (1935), pp. 1-64.

This is Glass. Corning, New York, The Corning Glass Works, 1957.

Werner, A. E. "The Care of Glass in Museums," *Museum News,* Vol. 44, no. 10 (June, 1966), Technical Supplement No. 13, pp. 45-49.

Wilkinson, O. N. *Old Glass—Manufacture, Styles, Uses.* London, Ernest Benn, Ltd., 1968.

Wills, Geoffrey. *The Country Life Book of Glass.* London, Country Life, 1966.

———. *English and Irish Glass.* London, Guinness Superlatives, Ltd., 1968.

Winchester, Alice (Ed.). *The Antiques Book.* New York, A. A. Wyn, Inc., 1950.

12

Textiles and Costumes

The collecting and study of textiles, costumes and costume accessories is a rather recent museum function. Widespread interest in textiles, giving impetus to systematic and intensive research, has developed only since the last half of the nineteenth century. After ancient Chinese silks were unearthed in 1914 by Sir Aurel Stein in the Lop Desert of Chinese Turkestan, on the route opened by the Chinese for silk trade with western Asia in the second century B.C., scholarly investigation of textiles accelerated.

Stein's discovery stimulated individuals and museums to examine critically, as well as to collect, textile specimens in order to gain greater knowledge of the historical, artistic and technological achievements of earlier cultures. Now many costume and textile museums are fully operative, such as The Textile Museum in Washington, D.C., and the Cooper-Hewitt Museum of Design in New York; a great number of museums have added costume institutes and textile departments.

This chapter is dedicated to Stefania P. Holt and in fond memory of the late Eugene I. Holt. Mr. and Mrs. Holt, distinguished scholars in their field, were Curators of Costumes and Textiles, Los Angeles County Museum of Art, from 1953 until their retirement in July, 1966. Their knowledge, dedication and enthusiastic interest in the subject generated for the author a finer appreciation and greater interest in the fascinating study of textiles and the history of costume.

The study of textiles and costume designs has proved to be a valuable guide in archaeological, anthropological and sociological research and has added a great deal to the study of art history, especially in pinpointing the dates of paintings and the identification of the sitters by the costume worn.

The word *textile* denotes all woven fabrics, including tapestries and carpets. For effects of luster, delicacy and softness, in combination with strength, durability and usefulness, textiles have been woven from protein fibers from the animal kingdom (wool, hair, fur, etc.) and from the vegetable kingdom (cotton, flax, hemp, etc.). Because of the perishable nature of both vegetable and animal fibers under certain conditions, few weaves have been preserved from ancient times.

Up until recent times, all colors were extracted from natural substances. Particularly during antiquity, the choice of color for a fabric depended to a great extent on the rank of the prospective purchaser. Some colors were restricted to the exclusive wear of government dignitaries. For example, one of the most important ancient dyes was Tyrian purple, which derived its name from the city of Tyre, situated on the Phoenician coast. It was extracted from a small gland in the body of the mollusks, Murex Brandaris and Mures Trunculus. It was this color that the Roman emperors favored for their togas, which gave rise to the expression "born to the purple."

Another dye, red madder, was extracted from the roots of the plant Rubia Tinctorum. It probably originated in India but was also used extensively in Egypt, Greece and Rome throughout antiquity. Madder was the principal red dye, but the shade and beauty of color is complicated by the use of mordants; the same dye can vary from pink to lavendar to orange, depending on the mordant. (A mordant is a substance like acetic acid or cream of tartar, with which a fiber is treated to make the dye fast.) Madder was popular until the middle of the nineteenth century when alizarine, the chief component of madder, was produced synthetically. Also known to the early Egyptians was the red dye Kermes, extracted from the bodies

203

of the insect Coccus Arborum. It was replaced by cochineal, which was introduced to the Old World from Mexico.

When the Roman army invaded England, they found the aboriginal natives covered their bodies with a blue coloring matter extracted from the leaves of the woad plant. Woad was used as an important textile dye until it was replaced by the brighter blue dye, indigo, in the fourteenth century. A rich yellow dye, saffron, obtained from the stigma of the Crocus Sativus plant, was used by the ancients along with safflower, which was cultivated in China, Egypt, and India.

The art of weaving, along with pottery, is probably one of the oldest inventions. Some researchers maintain that weaving is the earliest craft practiced by primitive man. Whether its practice goes back to the nomadic era has not been ascertained. However, the craft does appear sporadically among primitive peoples. There seems to be little doubt that the Chinese unraveled silk cocoons and put the raw material to practical use more than five thousand years ago.

The art of weaving is so ancient and widespread that determining its origin is impossible. Possibly the weaving of baskets suggested the construction of a rudimentary loom for the weaving of useful articles such as rugs, mats and clothing. Weaving on a frame was practiced in the Stone Age. Later other appliances were conceived when wool and linen thread came into use and shuttle weaving, the most rudimentary form, evolved.

What is known as the tapestry weave is more advanced, but in both types there is a warp and a woof, with vertical and horizontal threads usually crossing at right angles. There is evidence that tapestry weaving was practiced throughout the world by peoples so geographically remote from one another that there seems to be no possibility that one communicated the art to another. For example, some claim that ancient Egyptians could not have passed on their craft to ancient Peru, but this is not certain, since the voyage of the Ra and recent archaeological investigations into similarity in writing indicate some contact between primitive tribes.

Extant examples of early Egyptian weaving are of linen. The Egyptians were probably the most skillful weavers in ancient times. The Copts, their lineal descendents, continued the craft of weaving and attained great proficiency in wall hangings and garments for the dead. Many of the dyes used by the Copts have retained their original color, freshness, and brilliance for over twelve hundred years. Fortunately, the hot, dry climate has preserved many fine examples. The most beautiful woven products of Egypt were exported to the Roman Empire.

The best Persian textile masterpieces challenge Persian accomplishment in other media. The products of Persian looms serve today to document cultural history and illuminate the interchange of national influences in successive eras. The earliest extant example of Persian weavers, dating from the Sassanian period (224-642 A.D.), were justly famous in both East and West. With the Islamic invasion in the seventh century, new motifs in woven fabrics were introduced. The Seljuk rulers loved luxury. It was their support of arts and crafts of the conquered country that brought about a new refinement in design as well as virtuosity in technique.

The Mongol invasion of Persia initiated further changes in the style of Persian weaving. With the rise of the Safavid rulers at the beginning of the sixteenth century, the golden age of Persian textiles began. The luxurious court life made great demands for the sumptuous costumes of princes and nobles, which the splendid organization of royal looms facilitated. Of particular magnificence are the sixteenth century Persian velvets with lustrous silk pile enhanced by brocading. Foreign weavers learned their trade in Persian workshops, and itinerant Persian weavers spread the craft to other countries.

The Greek and early Roman weavers used wool and linen threads. Silk was not known to the Romans until the Christian era. Not until several centuries later were silkworms cultivated in Europe. After the Saracens conquered Spain in the eighth century, silkworms were cultivated and the production of silks began to develop. Before then China, Persia and other east-

205

ern countries had a monopoly on the weaving of silk fabrics.

During the Middle Ages and the Renaissance, the Italians achieved great prominence in silk weaving. From the thirteenth century on silk was woven in Italy. Lucca, Florence, Bologna, Milan, Genoa and Venice were the chief centers for silk weaving between the thirteenth and seventeenth centuries. A demand for fine fabrics—velvets, brocades, silks and tapestries —kept the weavers' looms busy. The materials produced were for secular and ecclesiastical costumes as well as for wall hangings. Meanwhile, Saracen weavers wandered as far as Germany, France and Britain.

In France the early centers for silk manufacture were initially in the hands of Italians; a truly French style did not appear until the seventeenth century. In England silk weaving was also done mostly by foreigners. Not until the beginning of the seventeenth century were English products noticed, but in the eighteenth century British silk fabrics were competing with French production.

In every country the early weavers eventually formed guilds to protect their interests from second-rate competitors and unqualified apprentices. These guilds became the forerunners of our present workers' unions. In Italy, as far back as the tenth century, members of the weavers' guild regulated the practice of their trade. They enjoyed privileges and a unique degree of protection from the state through special legislation.

The early history of Peru is obscure, but undoubtedly the art of weaving developed there in ancient times. Certainly its practice was entirely independent from that of the Old World or the Orient. Surviving examples of Peruvian weaving, however, often reveal a remarkable similarity to Coptic tapestry weaving, although the patterns are curiously stylized, often geometric abstractions of grotesque animals and human figures.

In New England during the Colonial Period the manufacture of textiles was highly developed. The Puritans were well experienced in the craft of weaving. Determined to produce commodities for their own needs, the colonists set up looms in their

Figure 111. Garment Decoration. Egyptian, 7th to 9th century. Tapestry, polychrome wool with natural linen. Symmetrical composition shows warrior and prisoners skillfully balanced. Superb quality attests to the luxury of apparel worn by nobles at the Islamic courts. *Courtesy, Cooper-Hewitt Museum of Design, Smithsonian Institution.*

Figure 112. PAIR OF MITTS. Ehinca, Ch'an-Sha. 3rd century B.C.
Silk. Part of a set, including fragments of a kerchief and a
bonnet. Though faded and stained after some two thousand
years of burial, these ancient silk textiles are rare examples of
the extraordinary skill of early Chinese silk weavers. The fine
warp-face weave still retains a glimmer of the original brown,
vermilion, yellow, and honey colors, and the subtle geometric
design (probably symbolic) gives evidence of ancient culture.
*Courtesy, Cooper-Hewitt Museum of Design, Smithsonian Insti-
tution.*

Figure 113. Silk reversible cloth. Persian, 12th century. *Courtesy, Los Angeles County Museum of Art.*

Figure 114. COSTUME STORAGE. Costumes are better cared for and preserved if they are stored on mannequins but few museums can afford to have mannequins for storage purposes. Garments in the style of these eighteenth-century gowns require special handling and storage to avoid creases and folds which weaken fiber structure, causing eventual deterioration of the fabric. 1 (upper left). One-piece dress of mauve taffeta, multicolored flowers on a striped ground; Watteau pleat and draw-cord pannier skirt. English, third quarter of the 18th century. 2 (upper right). Dress of white brocaded silk enriched with gold thread; multicolored floral design, gilt lace and embroidered linen stomacher. French, about 1760. *Courtesy, Los Angeles County Museum of Art.*

These costume dollies were designed and constructed for the transfer of wearing apparel. Each costume is contained in a separate pliofilm hanging garment bag with zippered opening. The bags have a see-through quality which eliminates unnecessary handling. Throughout the process of moving, garments are kept in a hanging position, not folded and boxed. The moving devices have ball-bearing casters for ease in movement. Each dolly is equipped with a metal label holder (figure at lower right) to hold a brief description and identifying numbers of the garments. *Courtesy, Los Angeles County Museum of Art.*

Figure 115. SPECIAL HANGERS FOR STORING WOMEN'S GOWNS. The top device supports the shoulders, sleeves and neckline of the garment. The weight of very wide, long skirts and petticoats is supported at the waistline with farthingale-like hanger which is adjustable up and down. The upper part is also adjustable. Before these hangers are used they are padded or upholstered. *Courtesy, Colonial Williamsburg Foundation.*

Figure 116. Example of a double-cloth cotton textile. Peruvian, 1200-1400. Flat textiles and fragmentary specimens are protected when they are sealed between sheets of plexiglass. This method makes specimens accessible for study without the fabrics being subjected to handling and permits the study of both sides of weaves. *Courtesy, Los Angeles County Museum of Art.*

homes. Soon they were able to depend on their own products for such necessities as fabrics for clothing, bedding, etc.

Today many synthetic materials and specialized machinery have replaced the product of the silkworm and the art of the weaver. Only history will tell whether the brilliance and colors of synthetics will last as long as the products of ancient weavers.

RULES FOR CARE AND HANDLING

Light damages textiles

Exposure to natural light damages textiles. The fibers become weakened, dyes fade and lose their natural colors. The rate of deterioration depends on the composition of the light, the temperature and the humidity. Almost all types of illumination cause varying degrees of damage, but the ultraviolet rays of sunlight are the prime cause of weakening of the fibers of textiles. Never subject a textile or a costume to sunlight or reflected light from the sun. When costumes and textiles are on exhibition, the exposure to sunlight, its reflected rays, or any artificial illumination should be kept at a minimum. Lights in galleries should be turned off as soon as the visiting hours have ended. Costumes and textiles should be stored in darkness.

Sunlight

Artificial light

Store in darkness

A casual examination does not always reveal a deterioration of threads in a fabric. Sometimes a garment may appear to be in good condition until it is moved, adjusted, or folded. Some curators excuse the folding of textiles and costumes because of lack of space, but they should *never* be folded. Every crease in a garment or textile specimen weakens the threads.

Do not fold

The age of a specimen and the period of its exposure to adverse atmospheric conditions all determine the longevity of its life. Any period of exposure to dry heat or sunshine deprives a fabric of its original resilience; the longer the exposure, the quicker the threads rot and the fabric deteriorates.

Dry heat destroys resilience

Dust is a major problem with all textiles. Never use a duster to clean, particularly a feather duster. It does not solve the problem; it only rearranges the dirt. Unless the fabric is extremely fragile, use a hand vacuum with a slow-action suction for removing dust.

Dust is a major problem

Use hand vacuum with slow-action suction

Textiles are subject to attack by insects and should be isolated from any possibility of damage from the action of insect pests. Textiles of animal origin, such as wool and silk, are more liable to an attack by insects. Fabrics are especially vulnerable to larvae eggs, fungus and mold. If the exhibition and storage areas are kept clean and dry, there is little chance that damage will occur. If mold, fungus, or larvae eggs appear, remove with a soft brush and fumigate immediately. If the condition is not extensive, a good airing may arrest

Insects attack textiles

Brush and fumigate to eliminate larvae eggs or fungus

214

the growth. If the sturdiness of the material permits, some fabrics may be washed in a mild soapy water without any damage or further deterioration. A non-toxic detergent should be used. No fabrics should be washed unless all dyes have been tested for fastness in the washing solution. The surest solution is to fumigate regularly.

Laundering

Silverfish are often thought to attack only paper products but they also damage fabrics. There are many effective commercial sprays and dusting powders on the market to control silverfish. They should be used in storage areas, not on the specimens. Professional fumigation, however, is preferable to any household product to prevent damage by pests.

Use commercial sprays and dusting powders for silverfish

Thymol vapor may be used to sterilize textiles, if a professional fumigation service is not available. Thymol crystals in a saucer placed over a 40-watt light bulb will produce thymol vapor. The articles to be fumigated should be put in an airtight compartment with the crystals and light bulb and should remain subjected to the vapor for at least forty-eight hours. After that the door should not be opened for at least another twenty-four hours. This is a simple yet effective method which even the smallest museum may undertake. Thymol vapor usually kills any live insects or larvae in fabrics or fur. The use of paradichlorobenzene crystals in storage boxes, drawers, or garment bags lessens the chance of mildew or mold.

Professional fumigation is preferred

Thymol vapor is effective and inexpensive

Paradichlorobenzene protects from mildew and mold

Stains allowed to remain on a fabric cause it to undergo a chemical change. Stains should be removed immediately. Those of long standing are usually very difficult to remove. Before experimenting with a "household hint," it is well to remember that the preservation of an historically, esthetically important textile *with stains* is more desirable than to remove the stains with a product which might damage the fabric. Valuable textiles and costumes should be cleaned and stains removed by a professional textile conservator.

Remove stains as soon as possible

Costumes and textiles should never be folded for long. Every fold weakens fiber structure. Creasing of a fabric is a fold pressed tight and is more damaging than folding. A pressed crease causes threads to weaken and break. Broken threads endanger the entire specimen. When it is absolutely necessary to fold, several layers of acid-free tissue paper should be wadded in such a way that the tissue is in the inner part of the fold. Crumpled tissue is more effective than uncrumpled. Acid-free tissue paper should be used invariably.

Avoid folding: creases break threads

Acid-free tissue paper

215

ART OBJECTS

When preparing unmounted textiles or costumes for exhibition, make certain that any unavoidable folding is not repeated on older creases. Repeated folding of a material compounds the damage.

Search packing materials before discarding Lost parts

When unpacking costumes, always unfold and uncrumple all tissue paper and other packing materials and search through them before discarding. Otherwise, buttons and other detached pieces may be lost. The historical and esthetic importance of a costume is significantly spoiled if buttons or buckles are lost. Replacements are poor substitutes as a rule.

Pack loosely for storage or shipment

Put similar fabrics and costumes together when they are packaged or stored. Never pack the materials tightly. Store so loosely in a container that they actually float. When it is necessary to fold for shipment, bear in mind that tight packing is in reality creasing and creasing breaks threads.

Remove pins and dress shields

Do not allow pins to remain in or on fabrics, including costume articles. Unless they are rustproof, pins leave stains and attempts to remove rust stain often damage the fabric. Always remove all pins and dress shields before storing.

Keep sharp objects away

Keep sharp objects and writing pens away from textiles and costumes. Never use a sharp or pointed object to open a box containing fabric specimens or costumes. Felt-tipped pens and ball-points contain a fluid that is virtually impossible to remove from fabrics without noticeable damage.

Clean hands

Always have clean hands when handling textiles, costumes, and accessories, Museum collections include representative examples of historic and artistic significance, whether of recent origin or ancient. Soiled, damp hands cause serious damage to any fabric.

Roll on tubes longer than specimens

Some textiles may be successfully rolled for storage or shipment. Some are usually better rolled than flat. Rolling should be done on drums or tubes of sturdy cardboard, and the tubes should be as wide in diameter as possible. Care must be exercised so that creases are not rolled in. Acid-free tissue paper should be used. Drums or tubes should be longer by several inches than the width or length of the textile. The edges of a textile should be at least one inch away from the ends of the tube.

Seal between plexiglass for study and storage

Small textiles, fragments, or pieces in poor condition are easier to study if sealed between sheets of plexiglass. This allows the study of both sides of the textile without handling. Net cases sewn around fragile fabrics are also helpful. These methods allow identifying labels to be placed on the outer surfaces. If flat pieces must be wrapped in tissue paper, moth crystals (paradichlorobenzene) should be placed in the container, drawer, or bin.

Unmounted fabrics which are not rolled or sealed between sheets of plexiglass should be handled, carried, moved or stored in a flat position, unless their extreme size will not permit. Smaller textiles can be stored in a map cabinet or any cabinet with shallow drawers. A dust cover should be kept on top of each drawer of specimens. If more than one piece is stored in a single drawer, separate each fabric with sheets of acid-free tissue paper. Ideally, one textile specimen to a drawer would eliminate handling. *Unmounted textiles*

Store small textiles in shallow drawers

When shifting small framed or mounted specimens, a piece of heavy cardboard should be placed under the frame or mount. The board should be the same size as the frame or mount. This procedure will lessen vibrations. In any handling of framed and mounted textiles, observe the same precautions as for framed paintings, prints, or drawings. Textiles mounted on stretchers should be handled only by the stretchers, as is recommended for the handling of paintings on stretchers. *Transfer framed and mounted textiles as recommended for paintings*

If costumes are stored on mannequins, they should be completely covered to prevent dust accumulating. Mannequins stored without costumes on them should also be covered. A soft, pliable plastic sheet is recommended. Neither muslin nor any other cloth is recommended. In time, dust permeates this material and eventually settles on the costume or undraped mannequin. *Cover costumes and mannequins with plastic sheets*

Always lift a mannequin by its framework. Its extremities are not intended to support the weight of the framework. Most mannequins have detachable arms, legs, and sometimes head. These elements should be detached and moved separately. *Lift mannequins by framework*

Not all museums can afford mannequins for storage purposes. Many museums cannot even afford them for exhibition areas. Nevertheless, hanging a costume, rather than storing it in a box or drawer, increases the life of it *if* other precautions are also taken. In lieu of mannequins in storage areas, padded hangers serve the purpose and are recommended provided they are padded correctly and with a material which will not be injurious to the costume and further provided that the hangers themselves will not have adverse effects on the garment. Hangers made of synthetic resins (plastic), if sealed up in a case containing paradichlorobenzene, will soften and damage materials. *Hang costumes*

Store costumes on mannequins

Avoid plastic hangers

All garments on hangers must be protected from accumulating

Transparent garment bags dust. Ordinary transparent garment bags are useful. Care must be taken not to catch the materials of garments in the zippers. Transparent garment bags enable immediate recognition. All garment storage coverings should have at least a see-through area to eliminate unnecessary handling.

Previous use of fabrics A good part of the textile specimens and costumes found in museums have already been subjected to the uses for which they were intended when they were created. Usually costumes have been worn and in some cases have suffered from wear and exposure to climatic conditions. Often foreign substances and microrganisms have already contributed to deterioration to some degree before the

Ancient textiles demand great care pieces enter a museum. The preservation, restoration, and prevention of further deterioration is the responsibility of the museum or collector. Most ancient textiles need special treatment to prevent further deterioration.

Do not use tar paper Never use tar-lined paper with or near costumes or textiles. Warm, humid atmospheric conditions cause tar paper to melt or dissolve. If the soft tar reaches the fabric, serious damage ensues. Even the vapor from insect repellents will make the tar lining of paper soften and dissolve.

Desired RH All textiles and costume materials should be stored in well-ventilated rooms and exhibited in well-ventilated galleries. If total air-conditioning and humidity control are not possible, some ventilation must be provided. For maximum protection, strive for a relative humidity of about 40%.

Effects of moisture When exposed to an atmosphere saturated with moisture, linen absorbs 13% of its weight, cotton 21% and wool and silk 30%. Studies are being made to establish the degree of humidity at which various fibers may be dried. When cotton is drying, each little fiber moves. Cotton is a flat fiber with twists in it; it cannot be made into a smooth thread, as can linen. All vegetable fibers move as they dry. When linen fibers have been wet or damp, the drying process rotates in the direction of the center part of the letter S. Wool is elastic and weakens when wet.

Do not use any tapes except cloth Transparent adhesive tapes should never be used for mending, restoration, or conservation of fabrics. The removal of any tape from a fabric is difficult and often aggravates adverse conditions.

Solvents are detrimental The use of solvents to remove adhesive tape is detrimental to fabric structure and dyes. In certain research laboratories, it has been found that fixing ancient textiles either to a rigid or a flexible support with adhesives may be accomplished successfully only if the adhesives satisfy certain conditions. They must be completely transparent and colorless. They must have sufficient adhesive qualities, even after exposure to atmospheric conditions over a long period of time. They must not be subject to any kind of change in color caused by light or atmospheric conditions. They must be completely free of anything which harms or changes fibers or dyes. Acceptable adhesives must be applied at room temperature. They must not in any way change or alter the quality or properties of the textile. They should be easily removed, if the fabric has been received with tapes and removal is necessary. They must not interfere with carbon-dating of textile materials.

Fixing ancient textiles is a special procedure

Tapes and carbon dating

If restoration of a textile is thought of as treatment in order to restore the textile to its former or better condition, then of course preservation and conservation is for the purpose of maintaining it in a healthy state. During a period of disintegration a fabric undergoes chemical changes. Most of them are irreversible. Those who restore, repair, or handle textiles should know a great deal about the physical and chemical properties of ancient fibers as well as recent ones. Much has been written in professional periodicals about the conservation of recent fibers but there is much to be learned about the conservation and restoration of ancient textiles.

Restoration requires knowledge of ancient and recent fibers

BIBLIOGRAPHY

Beek, H. C. A. van and Heertjes, P. M. "Fading by Light of Organic Dyes on Textiles and Other Materials," *Studies in Conservation*, Vol. 11 (1966), pp. 123-132.

Boucher, François, *20,000 Years of Fashion: The History of Costume and Personal Adornment*. New York, Harry N. Abrams, Inc., 1967.

Demeny, L. "Degradation of Cotton Yarns by Light From Fluorescent Lamps," *IIC Conference on Museum Climatology*, London (1968), pp. 53-64.

Fleming, E. R. *Encyclopedia of Textiles*. New York, Frederick A. Praeger, 1958.

Hope, Thomas. *Costume of the Ancients*. London, William Miller, 1968.

Huenefeld, Irene Pennington. *International Directory of Historical*

Clothing. Metuchen, New Jersey, Scarecrow Press, 1967.

International Institute for Conservation of Historic and Artistic Works: 1964 Delft Conference on the Conservation of Textiles. London, International Institute for Conservation, 1965.

Köhler, Carl. *A History of Costume*. Emma von Sichart, Ed. New York, Dover Publications, Inc., 1963.

Laver, James. *The Concise History of Costume and Fashion*. New York, Harry N. Abrams, Inc., 1969.

McClellan, E. *History of American Costume*. New York, Marlboro Books, 1969.

Padfield, T. and Landi, S. "The Light-Fastness of the Natural Dyes," *Studies in Conservation*, Vol. 11 (1966), pp. 92-107.

Pritchard, M. E. *A Short Dictionary of Weaving*. New York, Studio Publications, Inc., Thomas Y. Crowell, 1955.

Reath, Nancy Andrews and Sachs, Eleanor B. *Persian Textiles and Their Technique from the Sixth to the Eighteenth Centuries, Including A System for General Textile Classification*. New Haven, Conn., Yale University Press, 1937.

Robinson, H. M. and Reeves, W. A. "A Study of the Effect of Light on Cotton and Other Cellulose Fabrics," *American Dyestuff Report*, No. 50 (1961), pp. 17-31.

Rozmarin, G. N. "Progress in the Study of Aging of Fibrous Cellulosic Materials," *Russian Chemical Review*, Vol. 34 (1965), pp. 835-867.

Strömberg, Elisabeth. "Dyes and Light," *ICOM News*, Vol. 3, no. 3 (June, 1950), Appendix, pp. 1-4.

Textile Institute, The. *Identification of Textile Materials*. 4th ed. Manchester, England, The Textile Institute, 1958; reprinted 1961.

Textile Museum Staff. *Principles of Practical Cleaning for Old and Fragile Textiles*. Workshop Notes No. 14. Washington, D.C., The Textile Museum, 1957; *Museum News*, Vol. 43, no. 6 (February, 1965), Technical Supplement No. 6, Part II, pp. 50-52.

Weibel, Adèle Coulin. *2,000 Years of Textiles*. New York, Pantheon Books, 1952.

13

Tapestries and Rugs

TAPESTRIES

A tapestry is a heavy handwoven fabric, usually pictorial in design. It is made on a loom by threading the design of weft threads into the warp with the fingers or a bobbin. This process allows the weaver to pack the fine weft (wool, silk, or metal) so closely that it completely conceals the coarser warp (wool, cotton, or linen). The latter is evident only as ribs. Each area of color is built up separately, in blocks or patches, and the slits between the adjacent sections of design subsequently sewn up.

The history of tapestry weaving is continuous. True tapestries were made in ancient China, Egypt, Greece, and pre-Columbian Peru. Their earliest function was undoubtedly utilitarian, just as in Medieval and Renaissance Europe, when they were used as wall hangings to afford warmth as well as color to the cold stone walls of chateaux and cathedrals. They also provided coverings for chairs, tables, benches, cushions, canopies, and even horses.

At the height of their popularity five hundred years ago, there were over 150,000 tapestry weavers at work in the vari-

221

ous centers throughout France and Flanders. Today approximately one tenth of this number are at work in France, with about 200 at Aubusson, 40 in the government atelier of Gobelins, and fewer still in the government's establishment at Beauvais.

According to legend, French tapestry weaving started in Aubusson around 711 A.D., a legacy from the Saracens. Wherever it began, these early works have disappeared. The earliest tapestries of any significance extant are the Gothic examples from the fourteenth century, the greatest of which is a series on the Apocalypse in Angers. It was commissioned in 1379 by the Duc D'Anjou from merchant-weaver Nicolas Bataille after designs by Jean de Bondol. Despite its great age, it is in sufficiently good state of preservation to have had a profound influence on the father of modern tapestry, Jean Lurçat.

In fact, the rudimentary techniques and limited range of colors (integral to the two-dimensional Gothic vision) are responsible for the superior state of preservation of earlier works compared with later examples. During the Baroque period, in particular, when detailed imitation of paintings became fashionable, and the number of dyes multiplied to imitate the tonal gradations of the painter, the new dyes employed were often unstable as well as harmful to the fibers. That is why many of these later tapestries are more faded and fragmented than examples executed two or three centuries earlier.

The Florentine Renaissance painter Raphael exerted a great influence in this trend towards pictorialism. In the Acts of the Apostles, a series which he executed for production in Brussels, he adapted the medium he knew to the unfamiliar medium of tapestry with no concessions for the silhouette exigencies of the woven surface. Nevertheless, his finished work had such success that for 150 years Brussels was given over to stereotyped reproductions. This practice of transposing the genius of one art to another was continued as subsequent generations utilized the cartoons of Rubens in the seventeenth century, Boucher in the eighteenth, and Goya in the nineteenth.

Great impetus was given to the craft by the French prime

222

minister Colbert, who in 1662 cast a shrewd eye on the profitable enterprise and took over, in the name of Louis XIV, the Gobelins tapestry workshops and then Beauvais. They were placed under the art dictatorship of Charles LeBrun, who had 800 weavers in his charge. His successor Oudry mobilized the best painters in the kingdom to cater to the decorative commands of Louis XV's mistress, Mme. de Pompadour. Next in line to head up the royal works was Boucher, who completely converted the esthetic of tapestry to painting with a bobbin, adding hundreds of new dyes—and new problems—for the weaver in silk and wool.

In extant examples, the detrimental effect of this trend to reproduce the painter's palette is unhappily demonstrated. Attempts to increase the number of colors for three-dimensional representation were encouraged by the spirit of experimentation in the air. The poor light-fastness of nearly all vegetable and animal dyes is established beyond question and their preservation, in the presence of light, is not yet possible. Those which have survived the best, as is evidenced by Medieval tapestries hanging in museums, are those where the dominant colors are browns, blacks, heavy reds, and indigo blues in wool (except for browns and blacks produced by oxidation of iron). In contrast, 50 years of permanent exhibition in the dimmest tolerable conditions would destroy yellow natural dyes and would impair the brilliance of madder and cochineal red, and indigo blue on cotton. In general, natural dyes in older tapestries have faded in hue, preserving color harmonies, whereas a synthetic dye can change radically, from orange to pink for example.

Another reason for the poorer condition of later tapestries is the increased use of silk from the end of the seventeenth century through the eighteenth century. Originally coarse silk was used only for highlights, but then the use of fine silk was expanded to represent entire skies. Today, large sections of silk weft which have been left unsupported are in such bad condition that the pressure of a needle will reduce them to fine powder.

Science too has contributed to the super-complexity and

ultimate dissolution of tapestry weaving. For a number of years, around 1840, the chemist Michel Chevreul headed Gobelins. He devised a palette of 10 circles of clear colors, each divided into 72 scales and each with a number of tones, for the enormous total of 14,000. By twisting two threads of different colors together to make a third, the possible combinations were raised to almost 200 million. As a result of this color expansion, the time it took a skilled weaver to produce a yard lengthened from a month to a year. It also raised the labor costs twelve-fold and shrank the output in reverse ratio.

There are three basic methods of repair, 1. re-weaving, done primarily by dealers interested in resale; 2. stitching to a backing, the method particularly suitable for museums, where the aim is to show the repair and not substitute the lost portions; and 3. use of synthetic resins for impregnation and adhesion to a woven support.

Tapestries must be cleaned before they are restored. Modern methods, including adhesives and impregnants, must be carried out on a grease-free, dust-free surface. After vacuuming, if washing is recommended, dyes should be checked for color-fastness. Dyes of European tapestries woven before 1750 are usually fast in water. However, a sample thread can be tested by soaking in a detergent solution overnight and pressing between white blotting papers. Dry cleaning is feasible only for small pieces in a volatile solvent like perchlorethylene.

RUGS

Fine rugs are art objects of the highest order. Their use as floor coverings or wall hangings goes back to remote antiquity in the Orient. In the dim dawn of civilization, shepherd tribes probably spread them on beaten earth floors to seal off the cold.

Felt is probably the most ancient material used for carpets, originating as bark felt as early as the Upper Paleolithic period, about 25,000 to 30,000 years ago. Such an example was found in the tomb of Pasyrk in the Altai mountains and is now in the Hermitage Museum, Leningrad. It is a rectangular piece of black wool, or hair, about three and a half feet by five on which there is appliqué work. Plaited rushes for floor coverings were also used during the Upper Paleolithic period.

Although no actual specimens have survived, we know from reliefs and literary documents that rugs were known in ancient Egypt, Assyria, and Babylonia. Excavations in the early twentieth century by Sir Aurel Stein in Central Asia have revealed important fragments of woolen pile rugs from the second century B.C. through the third century A.D. They were found in dwellings, refuse heaps, and grave pits of Lou-Lan, on the Chinese trade route. Another fragment of a pile rug of the fifth or sixth century A.D., found by Le Coq at Kyzil, near Kutcha, shows a technique in which the knot encircles only one warp thread, a characteristic of Spanish rugs. The oldest rug extant is a Coptic fragment (about 400 A.D.) in The Metropolitan Museum of Art, woven in Egypt by methods familiar from Persian rugs and still in use by modern craftsmen. It provides the first decisive evidence that pile rugs were made in the Near East in the first millenium A.D. Since Egypt was part of the Byzantine Empire, we can assume that other provinces also were manufacturing such rugs at this time.

The practice of rug knotting was a skilled craft in Persia under the Sassanian kings (226-637 A.D.). Their splendid palaces were enhanced with silk fabrics and rugs for divan and floor, products of the court looms. Carpets of this period were of wool or silk, embroidered, pile woven or tapestry woven. Literary sources describe the most sumptuous of the time, a famous garden carpet known as the "Spring of Chosroes." The report that it bore innumerable precious stones and was worked with gold threads is strong proof against its having been a pile carpet. Reputedly, it was made for the vast hall of the palace of Ctesiphon near Baghdad and was part of the booty taken by the Arabs when they defeated the Persians in 635 A.D. According to legend, it was then cut up into small pieces and one-fifth went to the Caliph Omar, one piece to his son-in-law, Ali, and the rest to 60,000 Arab soldiers for about $3,000 each. Calculating the drachma at about 25 cents, the original value of this fabulous carpet can be estimated at more than $200,000,000.

Rug knotting was a highly developed craft in the Muhammadan era, which began in 622 with Muhammad's flight from Mecca. As the caliphs' armies invaded Syria, Mesopotamia, Persia, Egypt, and North Africa, they adopted the art of weaving from the conquered nations who had civilizations superior to their own.

Although the weaving of rugs had existed in Persia from ancient times as a nomad and village craft, it was under the royal patronage of the Timurid dynasty (1392-1502) that the zenith of Persian design was reached. Plant ornament, arabesques, scrolls, and various Chinese motifs prevail, the medallions became more varied and fanciful, cartouches with floral and animal compositions were introduced, and broad rug borders became heavier and richer than ever before.

The most avid patrons of the rug industry in Persia were the Shahs of the Safavid dynasty (1502-1736). It was probably at the command of Tamasp I (1526-76) that the famous mosque rugs were woven at Ardabil. One is in the Victoria and Albert Museum, London, and another is in the Los Angeles County Museum of Art, gift of J. Paul Getty. At this time, dyes and wools were of the finest quality, and the medallion carpets were distinguished by their majestic size, brilliant color, and perfection of detail.

A superb type of seventeenth century Persian rug has long been called Polonaise, because such rugs were favorites in the courts of Poland and it was assumed that they had been made there. However, recent research has confirmed the fact that they were made in Persia in the court factories of Isfahan and Kashan. These brocaded rugs are of two types—the more spectacular one with a ground of gold or silver thread against which delicate patterns are knotted in silk.

As the Muhammadan armies penetrated India, establishing

226

the Mughal Empire, a brilliant regime carried the impetus of Persian culture, tempered by the older culture of the Hindus. The result was the manifestation of some very beautiful art, among which were exquisite rugs. Deftly woven after Persian originals but with different color schemes and a distinct type of floral composition, they resemble in form and feeling the decorative panels of the Taj Mahal.

The court rugs of Turkey seem like stylized versions of the elaborate Persian carpets but lack the exuberance of Persian design in medallions and corners. The elaborate floral scrolls have an individuality of their own, and some of the court prayer rugs are still among the finest examples in existence. The type most familiar to the collector was woven in the villages during the eighteenth century. They are the well known prayer rugs of Ghiordes, Kula, and Ladik, close relatives in pattern but woven at different centers in Anatolia, Asiatic Turkey.

The rugs of Caucasus have a savage grandeur with great appeal and originality, which cannot be confused with the other national types. The earliest known dragon carpets date from the sixteenth century. In the later examples, the zoomorphic forms become almost pure design, the formalized geometric bird and beast motifs appearing in brilliant colors with strong contrasts.

Like all tent dwellers, the wandering tribes of Turkestan used rugs constantly as required articles for everyday life. Their mobile dwellings may be regarded as roving rug factories. The majority of their production is known as Bukhara by the trade and bear small geometric patterns against backgrounds of rich red. As they were meant for hard daily use, they were sturdily woven. Probably those extant do not date from before the nineteenth century since the earlier examples were eventually worn out.

In the Occident, during Medieval times and even later, the commonest form of floor coverings was coarse tapestries and ingrains. Hand-knotted rugs were produced by the Saracens in southern Spain as early as the thirteenth century. The Flem-

227

ish art of hand-knotting rugs, which we know from six-teenth-century examples, was imitated in England at Wilton in the eighteenth century in an attempt to duplicate the beauty of Brussels floor tapestries. Hand-knotted rugs are made today at Wilton but called Axminsters after the little town in Devon-shire where the factory was first established. In France, a very fine type of hand-knotted pile rug called Savonnerie was made in distinctly French patterns. Its name is derived from the fac-tory founded by Pierre Dupont in 1627 in the ancient soap works (savonnerie) at Chaillot. Manufacture was transferred in 1827 to Gobelins, where it is still active. The name has been extended to hand-knotted pile French rugs made at Aubusson and elsewhere in France.

In America, the history of rugs begins in Colonial days when every village had its weaver to whom housewives brought their balls of rags sewn together in long strips. As late as 1890, there were 854 rug-carpet factories still in operation. W. P. Sprague started the first factory to manufacture yarn carpets in Phila-delphia in 1791. An important technical advance was made by Erastus Bigelow, a medical student of Boston, who har-nessed an ingrain loom to steam power, increasing the yardage possible on the hand loom. He also patented a power loom for weaving Brussels and Wilton carpeting. By 1930, there were almost a thousand carpet looms in the United States.

The quality of a rug is measured by the fineness of the weave. This estimate is based on the number of knots to the square inch, which generally runs from 80 to 400. However, there are some rare examples with over 2000 knots to the square inch. Rug weaving may be divided into four main types. Two are knotted, leaving a pile which varies from loose to tight, long to short. These are the Ghiordes and Sehna knots. The other types, which have no knots and no pile, are obviously less wear-resistant and suitable only for furniture and wall coverings.

For the most part, time has not dealt kindly with rugs. They are subject to deterioration from dirt and wear; even

228

Figure 117. Courtiers With Roses. 15th century, Arras or Tournai, ca. 1435-1440. Wool. Tapestries, now used purely to decorate the contemporary interior, were once a necessity for brightening and warming the medieval wall. In this example, the forms of the fashionably garbed courtiers describe graceful arabesques against the all-over pattern of this typical Franco-Flemish work. Modern heating systems with their drying properties must be guarded against, since many fabrics, which survived for centuries in cold barren castles, are now in an advanced stage of dry rot. *Courtesy, Metropolitan Museum of Art.*

Figure 118. DAVID AND BATHSHEBA. Flemish (Brussels), ca. 1520.
Uneven hanging causes undue, uneven stress on the threads of
the fabric. This condition was recorded before permanent installation. Note the uneven rippling at top and bottom. *Courtesy,
Los Angeles County Museum of Art.*

Figure 119. ARMORIAL TAPESTRY (one of a pair). French, early 16th century. *Courtesy, Los Angeles County Museum of Art.*

Figure 120.

Figure 121.

Figure 122.

Figure 121. A Scene in the Levant. French, 18th century. Tapestry (Royal Beauvais). *Courtesy, Los Angeles County Museum of Art.*

Figure 122. The Ardabil Carpet, 1535. Persian, Safavid Dynasty, 1502-1736. *Courtesy, Los Angeles County Museum of Art.*

Figure 120. Textile Panel. Hispano-Islamic, Spain, late 13th-early 14th century. Tapestry woven in colors and gold. Motif of "The Drinking Ladies" is enclosed in roundel. *Courtesy, Cooper-Hewitt Museum of Design, Smithsonian Institution.*

Figure 123. COORDINATED ACTION INSURES SAFETY IN RUG ROLL-
ING. *Courtesy, Los Angeles County Museum of Art.*

Figure 124. STORAGE ROOM AT COLONIAL WILLIAMSBURG. Rugs
are rolled on to wooden poles, which have cardboard sleeves.
Courtesy, Colonial Williamsburg Foundation.

Figure 125. SILK TAPESTRY. Chinese, Ch'ing Dynasty (1644-1912). *Courtesy, Los Angeles County Museum of Art.*

Figure 126.

Figure 126. TEXTILE FRAGMENT. Dutch or German, early 18th century. Block printed cotton. This fragment of coarse cotton is a very early example of block printing in fast colors, although only black and red are developed. The overly ambitious character of the design may be noted in the right section, where block marks show inaccurate joining. The "picotage" ground, a finely dotted effect, is achieved by means of many small nails driven into the block, here printed in red and black. *Courtesy, Cooper-Hewitt Museum of Design, Smithsonian Institution.*

Figure 127. TEXTILE DETAIL. English, ca. 1780. Black printed cotton. Powerful studies of birds dominate the flowering-tree motif in this English block print. The colors are shades of red, blue, brown, violet (now faded), and dark purple; blue and yellow were added by pencil. *Courtesy, Cooper-Hewitt Museum of Design, Smithsonian Institution.*

their normal conditions expose them to the tread of shoes, which has worn away the lustrous pile in many cases. The bare or slippered feet of Oriental custom were naturally less destructive than the heavy boots of European use, but unfortunately most of the fine examples which we know are those which have come into the possession of Western collections as spoils of war or gifts to kings and ambassadors. However dimmed in color, design, and texture, a glimmer of the former magnificence remains to enchant Western eyes.

RULES FOR CARE AND HANDLING

Protect tapestries and rugs from strong light. Strong artificial illumination and sunlight cause colors to fade and threads to deteriorate. The rate of deterioration depends upon the intensity of light, how long the exposure, and upon temperature and humidity. Any artificial lamplight in time will damage the dye colors and threads of any textile, but the ultraviolet rays from the sun and from ultraviolet lamps result in the most rapid fading of colors and weakening of fibers. Tapestries and rugs on exhibition should be kept in darkness when galleries are not open to the public. They should be given "rest periods" from exhibition. Always store tapestries and rugs in total darkness. *Protect from strong light*

Remove for rest periods in darkness

The age of a rug or tapestry, the use to which it has been put, and its past exposure to adverse atmospheric conditions determine its condition. To prolong the longevity of tapestries and rugs in a condition at least as good as when received, do not subject them to dry heat. Dry heat deprives the fibers of their original resilience and results in the rotting of threads. Exposure to direct sunlight or the reflected rays of the sun causes exactly the same damage. *Dry heat causes threads to rot*

Deterioration of threads cannot always be noticed if the specimen is examined while it is hanging on a wall or laid on a floor. Weakened threads often go unnoticed until the condition has progressed so far as to reveal an actual lesion in the fabric. If held to the light and carefuly examined, square foot by square foot, or square inch by square inch, holes and thin areas can be detected more easily. *Deterioration of threads is not easily detected*

Experts can repair broken threads, places worn thin, and even large holes. All repairs and restorations, including lesions caused by cutting or burning, should be done by a competent conservator who is specialized in this unique field of restoration. Unfortunately, there are few such specialists. As soon as damage is discovered, have the repair done immediately. The longer the condition exists, the more serious it becomes. Broken threads deteriorate rapidly and progressively, especially if the tapestry or rug is hanging or is handled frequently. *Restore only by expert*

Repair immediately

Most tapestries and rugs which enter a museum's collection have

239

already been exposed to adverse conditions—climatic conditions, wear and tear from usage and handling, or a combination of adversities—at some time in the past. Dampness, foreign substances, insect pests, or incorrect handling usually have contributed to deterioration before a museum receives a tapestry or rug. Dampness and moths are the two greatest enemies.

Dampness and moths are the greatest menace

Too often repairs made in the past have been poorly done by amateurs. This compounds the problem for a conservator or restorer. Preservation, restoration, and prevention of further deterioration are the responsibility of the collector. Regular, careful inspections should be made. Regular fumigation should be a rule in every museum. Thorough examinations should be made no less than once a year. Inspections should be repeated throughout the year. Fumigation should take place at least every two months. Records of inspections and fumigation should be maintained.

Make frequent inspections and fumigate on a regular basis

Attack by insects

As with all textile fabrics, rugs and tapestries are subject to attacks by insect pests. Any fabric of animal origin (wool, silk, etc.) is likely to be food for insects. All textiles are susceptible to larvae eggs, fungus, and mold. If they are kept clean, checked at regular intervals, kept in a dry atmosphere at all times, and fumigated on a regular basis, there is little chance that damage will occur. If fungus appears, or insects are discovered, fumigate immediately and direct attention to atmospheric conditions. If the condition is not extensive, a good airing will sometimes control the condition so that fumigation may be delayed for a few days or even a week. The best protection is preventive regular fumigation. Only neglected tapestries and rugs are damaged by fungus and insects.

Periodic fumigation prevents larvae eggs, fungus, and mold

Remove dust with a slow-action vacuum unless piece is fragile

Always vacuum both sides

Dust accumulates even under the most ideal conditions. There are dust accumulations in air-conditioned buildings. Do not use a duster to remove dust; dusters only rearrange the accumulation. If the rug or tapestry is in good condition—if there are no broken threads, it is not frayed, the edges are intact, and it has not been extensively restored—the best method to remove dust is with a hand type, slow-action, suction vacuum cleaner. Even with a slow-action vacuum, care must be taken in using it on a piece in good condition. Use it with even strokes always in the same direction, either vertically or horizontally, repeating the strokes in the opposite direction. Never use the vacuum on a fragile or frayed piece or on one which has been extensively restored. Regular removal of dust accumulations is recommended. Always vacuum both sides.

Stains which have been allowed to remain for a long time are difficult to remove. This should be done only by an expert. Some conservators specialize in the conservation and restoration of textiles, tapestries, and rugs. The preservation of an historically important rug or tapestry *with stains* is better than risking damage which might occur with the use of some "household hint" formula by an inexperienced amateur. Always consult a conservator. Any kind of stain causes the fabric to undergo chemical changes. Advice and guidance may be secured from the National Institute of Cleaning and Dyeing or the National Institute of Rug Cleaning at Silver Springs, Maryland. *Experts should remove stains*

Chemical changes from stains

Rugs and tapestries should never be folded but sometimes it is unavoidable. If size or lack of space make it impossible to store them flat, then roll them instead of folding them. Always roll rugs against the pile, right side inward. Roll them on a pole or tube. Never use a metal pole or pipe. Metals oxidize; rust causes serious damage by staining. Use poles of light-weight wood which has been thoroughly seasoned. If the rug or tapestry is not too heavy, a cardboard tube may be used. Cover it first with acid-free tissue paper or glassine paper. *Avoid folding*

Roll right side inward
Do not roll on metal pipes or poles

Cover cardboard tubes with acid-free tissue

When rolling a rug or a tapestry, the tube or pole should be two or more inches longer than the roll and at least three inches in diameter. It is very important that the pole or tube extend beyond the rolled piece to prevent the edges from becoming soiled or damaged from contact with other objects or from handling. During the rolling process, take care that creases are not rolled in. It has been proved that a crease will sometimes hang out, if it has not been rolled for very long and is given enough time to hang, but it is better to eliminate creasing than take the chance. A crease, actually a fold pressed tight, weakens threads and causes them to break. Any broken or weakened thread endangers the entire structure. When folding is necessary, never fold on the earlier creases. This compounds the danger of weakening the woven structure and of threads breaking or becoming weakened. *Size of poles or tubes*

Do not roll in creases

Do not repeat creases

If folding is unavoidable, the first folds should be parallel to the warp threads. When the piece is later rehung, these folds will then be horizontal, and the weight of the tapestry or rug will usually take them out within a few days. Vertical folds seldom completely "hang out" of any kind of fabric. Do not leave a rug or tapestry folded indefinitely.

241

Storage for rolled rugs and tapestries should be arranged so that as many pieces as possible may be easily accessible for identification or removal without having to disturb or move others. Rug racks are convenient for handlers and are easily constructed. Arms, or pegs, of well-seasoned wood or heavy doweling can be attached to a wall at two-, three-, or four-foot intervals to accommodate various sizes and lengths. The racks should be set at a slightly upward angle to prevent movement of the rolls. Do not place one rolled tapestry or rug on top of another. Separate racks should be provided for each rolled specimen. Ideally, rug and tapestry storage racks should be enclosed in a cabinet or closet to minimize dust accumulation, even if the building is air-conditioned. In any case, sheets of polyethylene film or glassine paper should be laid over the racked rolls to protect them from dust.

Small examples and fragmentary specimens should always be moved, stored, or carried in a flat position. A flat position is more protective, but often size will prohibit this. Small fragments can be protected by sealing them between sheets of plexiglass. This has the added advantage of allowing the study of both sides without actually handling the fragment. This method also makes it possible to place identifying labels on the plexiglass sheets.

Small specimens may be conveniently stored in map cases or any cabinet with shallow drawers. If the fragments are sealed between sheets or plexiglass, several can be safely stored in a single drawer. If plexiglass protection is not provided, use one drawer for each piece, if possible; if not possible, separate specimens with sheets of acid-free tissue paper.

Do not use tar-lined paper near a tapestry or a rug. Atmospheric changes cause tar paper to melt and result in serious damage, particularly to fabrics. If insect repellents are used, even the vapor from them will cause the tar lining on paper to ooze, causing damage difficult to eradicate.

Do not use transparent tape, masking tape, or any other kind on tapestries or rugs for "mending," identification, or any other reason. The adhesives on all commercial tapes are harmful to both the structure of the textile and the dyes in it. Attempts to remove tapes are usually difficult and invariably aggravate conditions by losing a part of the fabric with the tape. The area from which tape has been removed will be found to have undergone a change in color,

Store individually on racks

Do not stack

Store with protective covers

Keep in a flat position

Seal with plexiglass

Store small specimens in shallow drawers

Do not use tar paper

Never use tape

Tapes discolor and scar

leaving a scar. This diminishes historic and intrinsic qualities as well as value. It is not advisable to embroider identifying marks on a tapestry or rug. *Identifying marks*

Small, framed or mounted tapestries or fragments should be handled in the same way as a framed painting, print or drawing. Do not carry framed examples by the top or by any one side. Always carry frames with one hand at the bottom and one hand at one side. This allows a more secure grasp and balances the frame. There is less chance of its slipping if carried in this way. Never carry more than one frame at a time. Remove screw eyes, wires, and hooks from frames before storing or shipping. *Carry framed pieces with two hands* *Remove screw eyes, wires, and hooks*

Air-conditioning and humidity control help tapestries and rugs. If air-conditioning is not provided, specimens should be stored and exhibited in well-ventilated rooms or galleries. Periodic movement allows a circulation of air. If a building is not air-conditioned, stored tapestries and rugs should be regularly unrolled to allow air to circulate. *Air-conditioning and humidity control*

Avoid dampness at all times. Strive for a relative humidity between 40% and 65%. Humidity should never be allowed to exceed 70%. Most authorities agree that a range between 40% and 70% is generally safe but recommend that relative humidity should be kept below 65%. *Desired RH*

A conservator who restores, mends, repairs, or cleans a rug or tapestry should be a specialist. He must know a great deal about the physical and chemical properties of both ancient and recent structures, materials, and dyes. Only knowledgeable and experienced conservators should attempt the restoration or cleaning of valuable tapestries and rugs. More harm than good results from the work of inexperienced repairers or cleaners. *Cleaning and mending require specialists*

BIBLIOGRAPHY

Ackerman, Phyllis. *Tapestry: Mirror of Civilization.* New York. Oxford University Press, 1933.

Back, E. A. "Carpet Beetles and Their Control," *United States Department of Agriculture Farmers' Bulletin,* Washington, D.C., United States Government Printing Office, 1923.

Beger, O. "Die Restaurierung von Wandteppichen," (The Restoration of Tapestries), *Speculum Artis* (Zurich), Vol. 14, no. 5 (1962), pp. 40-46.

Bode, Wilhelm von and Kühnel, Ernst. *Antique Rugs from the Near East*. Braunschweig, Klinkhardt & Biermann, 1958.

Brown, J. C., Stephens, C. B., and Whewell, C. S. "Assessment of Modification of Wool During Wet-processing," *CIBA Review*, No. 6 (1962), pp. 2-27.

Calatchi, Robert de. *Oriental Carpets: History, Aesthetics, Symbolism*. New York, World Publishing Co., 1968.

Campana, P. Michele. *Oriental Carpets*. New York, Marlboro Books, 1969.

Cavallo, Adolph S. *European and Peruvian Tapestries in the Museum of Fine Arts*, Boston. 2 vols. New York, October House, 1967.

Collingwood, Peter. *The Techniques of Rug Weaving*. New York, Watson-Guptill Publications, Inc., 1968.

D'Hulst, Roger A. *Flemish Tapestries—From 15th to 18th Century*. New York, World Publishing Co., 1968.

Greene, Francina S. "The Cleaning and Mounting of a Large Wool Tapestry," *Studies in Conservation*, Vol. II (1955), pp. 11-16.

Juvet-Michel, A. "Pile Carpets of the Ancient Orient: The Dyeing and Knotting of Oriental Carpets," *CIBA Review*, No. 15 (November, 1938), pp. 512-516; "Symbolism in the Oriental Carpet," pp. 525-526.

Kendrick, A. F. and Tattersall, C. E. C. *Guide to the Collection of Carpets in the Victoria and Albert Museum*. London, Victoria and Albert Museum, 1931.

Mumford, John Kimberley. *Oriental Rugs*. New York, Scribner's Sons, 1900.

Myers, George Hewitt. "Rugs: Preservation, Display and Storage," *Museum News*, Vol. 43; Technical Supplement No. 6, Part I (February, 1965), pp. 45-49.

Tattersall, C. E. C. *Handwoven Carpets, Oriental and European*. New York, Charles Scribner's Sons, 1924.

Thompson, W. G. *A History of Tapestry from the Earliest Times to the Present*. London, Hadder & Stoughton, Ltd., 1930.

Turkham, Kudret H. *Islamic Rugs*. New York, Frederick A. Praeger, 1969.

Weibel, Adèle Coulin. *Two Thousand Years of Textiles*. New York, Pantheon Books, 1952.

14

Furniture

Of all the decorative arts, furniture is the most utilitarian. Its history began when primitive man realized that his bed of leaves felt better when raised off the ground with sticks and logs. Undoubtedly the first chair was a rock pulled up to the fire. The next step was decorating these useful forms with carvings and paintings and embellishing them with contrasting materials. The oldest surviving chairs, as we know them, are Egyptian. Especially famous is the gold furniture, including a carrying chair, which belonged to Queen Hetepheres, widow of the great pharoah Sneferu, founder of the IVth dynasty (ca. 2650 B.C.). It was excavated from her tomb on the east side of the Great Pyramid by the Museum of Fine Arts–Harvard University expedition in 1925.

Other superb articles of furniture dating from around 1350 B.C. were found in the tomb of Tutankhamen, who ruled during the XVIIIth dynasty. His chairs were splendidly carved and gilded, inlaid with ebony and ivory, and often covered with rich materials. Some of this opulent furniture appears to have been used in the household before it was sealed into burial tombs to provide the deceased in his "after life" with the same comforts he had enjoyed in the real world. All of it illustrates

245

functional excellence and a high degree of esthetic refinement. That it has survived for thousands of years attests to the preservative conditions of burial in the hot dry climate of Egypt.

Throughout antiquity, chairs were reserved for dignitaries; they were not items for ordinary household use. The word *chair* is still used as an emblem of authority in parliamentary use. Gradually, the concept of chairs as a privilege, monopolized by rulers and ecclesiastical personages, disappeared, and it became a normal article of furniture during the Elizabethan age in England (1558-1603).

Like the early people who preceded them, the ancient Greeks and Romans used little furniture, but whatever records we have indicate that it was splendidly constructed and exquisitely finished. Unfortunately, the climate was less preservative than in Egypt. It is mostly from the vase paintings, murals, and stone reliefs that we derive any information.

From them we learn that the couch or bed was the most important piece of furniture in the classical household. It served not only for sleeping but also for reclining while eating. At meal time, a low table was conveniently provided; mattresses and pillows added to the general comfort of the occupant. Legs and feet were turned to replace the carved animal ones of Egypt; in the fifth century B.C. backs of chairs assumed more graceful lines to allow greater freedom of posture while sitting. Roman furniture, based on Greek prototypes, became increasingly elaborate and was often enriched with carving, inlay, engraving, damascening, and veneer.

During the Middle Ages in Europe domestic life was insecure. The residences of the rich were usually fortressed strongholds, protected by moats; their halls were comparatively bare and empty. As they traveled about from castle to castle, with their furniture in wagons, their pieces had to be easily dismantled for transport. Dining tables, for example, were of trestle construction, consisting of a long board resting on two or more supports so that they could be taken apart. When not in use the dismantled parts were propped against the wall.

The most showy piece of furniture in the homes of fifteenth century dignitaries was the four-poster bed, which possessed a ceremonial significance right up to Georgian times in England. It stood in a place of honor in the principal living room. Although no complete example survives prior to 1500, contemporary inventories and miniatures show that in a house of any pretension, it was invariably draped and upholstered with rich fabrics. During the Renaissance when Italy was the pacesetter of the rest of Europe, the most important single item was the *cassone* or ornamented chest. It served as a clothes closet, storage area, seat, bed, table, and trunk. It was often rich, not only with carving but also with gesso, gold and inlay. Sometimes there was a handsome painted panel on the front, executed by a leading artist of the time. Many of these were stripped from the chests and are now museum treasures hanging on walls. The upholstered armchair of the Italian Renaissance has also survived in museums and mansions. The seats are covered with leather, velvet or embroidery, often trimmed with a valance that boxes them in, and decorated with round-headed nails and fringes.

However, it was France that produced the earliest comfortable chairs in the widest variety and made the greatest strides in making furniture generally more comfortable. By 1700, most of the familiar forms had appeared. A notable addition was the *fauteuil*, with carved arms and upholstered seat; its counterpart has been variously named in every country. The sumptuous formality of Louis XIV (1661-1715) eased into the graceful fluidity of the Régence and Louis XV styles (1715-1774) as life became gayer and more frivolous. About this time springs were invented, which greatly changed the upholstery principle.

As a series of economic and political revolutions throughout Europe in the eighteenth and nineteenth centuries endorsed the right of every man to life, liberty, and happiness, domestic life became more secure and refinements and distinctions between furniture forms multipled. By 1750, when France's international influence reached its zenith, the repertoire of home furnishings had expanded to cater to a new class of rich and cultivated commoners with leisure as well as money.

New types were created, oriented toward comfort and convenience. There were small tables for different purposes—tea, cards, and other pleasures. Wing chairs became popular to shut off drafts. The common chest developed into a chest of drawers. Cabinets, which evolved from the Gothic box into the dominant piece of furniture in the 1700's, became more elegant and lavish as time went on. Specialized types were invented, such as the desk cabinet, the jewel cabinet, and the sewing cabinet. Most significant was the curio cabinet which emerged in response to the eighteenth century mania for collecting. Multiplicity of shapes was accompanied by variety of materials. Gilding of wood continued in favor but numerous varnishes, such as *vernis Martin*, freely employed in imitation of Chinese lacquer, gained popularity. Design and execution were exquisite, but the gulf widened between function and form; there was a growing lack of relationship between ornament and the space it covered.

A reaction to the curvilinear excesses of the Rococo style took place in the time of Louis XVI as a result of the excavations of classical interiors and furniture at Pompeii and Herculaneum. The subsequent return to the straight line and the right-angle rule in both structure and ornament had a purifying effect which was soon reversed by the splendor of the Empire.

Contemporary designers have developed further in the direction of functional simplicity and are groping toward new principles expressed in new materials. The use of machinery has introduced cheaper, time-saving factory methods, and transportation by railroad has facilitated the distribution of orders for a rapidly expanding furniture market. The craft skills of cabinetmakers have, in fact, given way to mass production, but little true advance has been made except in novelty of line. Marcel Breuer's bent-tubing chair, probably the most radical

248

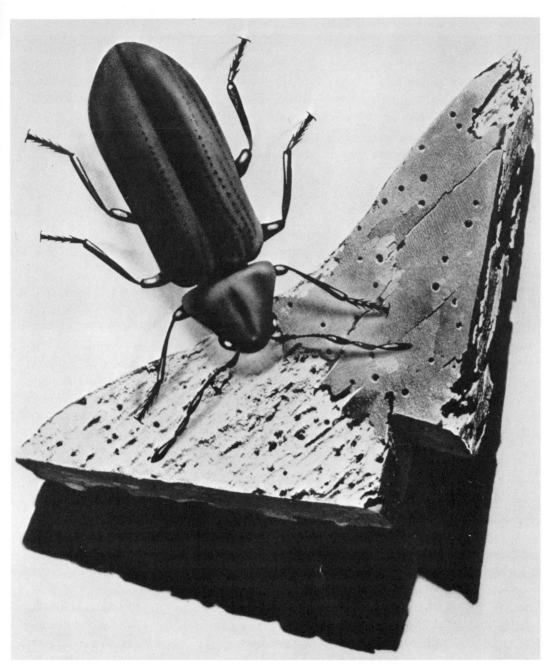

Figure 128. WOOD-BORING INSECT. An enlarged photograph of a beetle has been superimposed on infested wood in actual scale to demonstrate its destructive action on wood sculpture and furniture. Insects constitute the greatest menace to wood and, if not controlled at an early state, a wood piece may literally disintegrate. *Courtesy, Research Laboratory, Museum of Fine Arts, Boston.*

Figure 129.

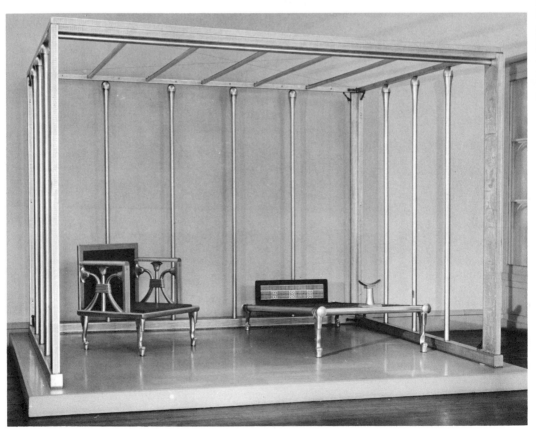

Figure 129. REPRODUCTION OF THE FURNITURE
OF QUEEN HETEP-HERES. Egyptian, Dynasty
IV, Old Kingdom. Part of the amazing treasure of gold-covered furniture unearthed from
the bottom of the secret burial shaft in front
of the Great Pyramid in the new cemetery
at Giza by the Harvard-Boston Expedition in
1906. Originals in Cairo Museum. Reconstruction made by Ahmad Youssof Moustafa. 1. is
a painting by Joseph Lindon Smith of the
tomb chamber showing condition in which
fragments were found; 2. shows present installation in gallery. *Courtesy, Museum of Fine
Arts, Boston.*

Figure 130. CUBICULUM (BEDROOM) FROM THE
VILLA NEAR BOSCOREALE. Roman, ca. 40-30 B.C.
Room contains a couch and footstool, with
bone carvings and glass inlay. *Courtesy, Metropolitan Museum of Art.*

Figure 131.

2.

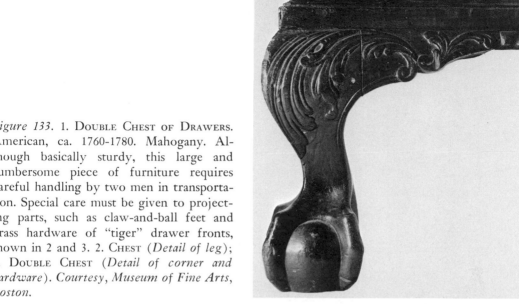

Figure 133. 1. DOUBLE CHEST OF DRAWERS. American, ca. 1760-1780. Mahogany. Although basically sturdy, this large and cumbersome piece of furniture requires careful handling by two men in transportation. Special care must be given to projecting parts, such as claw-and-ball feet and brass hardware of "tiger" drawer fronts, shown in 2 and 3. 2. CHEST (*Detail of leg*); 3. DOUBLE CHEST (*Detail of corner and hardware*). *Courtesy, Museum of Fine Arts, Boston.*

3.

Figure 134. Four Post Bed. Derby-Rogers House, American, early 19th century. 1. shows delicate carving and gilding of this imposing piece of furniture, which demands slow and deliberate maintenance; 2. reveals faded portion of toile valance. Ultraviolet absorbing filters should be used over fluorescent and daylight sources of light to retard fading of textures. *Courtesy, Museum of Fine Arts, Boston.*

step forward, is almost the only basic change in furniture design. Alvar Aalto of Finland has adapted the same theme to bent plywood. Undoubtedly, any future trailblazing will result, as in other twentieth century fields, from the collaboration of artist and engineer.

RULES FOR CARE AND HANDLING

The display of furniture is a major museum problem. If it is exhibited in galleries, the risk of damage by the visiting public is compounded. Ideally, furniture should be shown in a period room, complete with other objects of the same era. However, unless the room is glass-enclosed, there are distinct disadvantages to this method which allows visitors to roam about the room. Objects displayed without barriers invite the public to use the furniture.

Even with maximum guarding, visitors will open drawers and doors, touch wood and fabrics, and help themselves to small, easily-concealed objects or parts of furniture, such as keys. They will place objects on the furniture and sit on tables, chests, and chairs unless tapes are stretched from the back to the front of the seat. Tapes—and even barriers—are ignored by weary museum goers.

Yet a piece of furniture does not show to advantage in a glass case. Furniture presentations are more effective if the pieces are shown together as a suite to recreate a period ensemble complete with carpets, tapestries, paintings, porcelain objects, wallpaper and other objects which reflect the era when they were created. If visitors could be trusted to respect museum objects, they might experience more enjoyment with access to period-room arrangements. If they were free to move about, they would certainly gain more knowledge from being able to observe objects at close range.

Unfortunately, visitors must be controlled. Restrictions must be imposed; if not, there is an invitation to touch, to use, and even to steal. It is a pity that the "unwritten contract" every museum wishes it had with every visitor is observed by such a small percentage of the museum visiting public.

Unless furniture is shown in an enclosed room, it must be put into galleries and decorative objects exhibited in cases or on walls out of the reach of people. "Do Not Touch" signs are not observed by everyone. Because people relate to furniture, it is probably subject to more abuse by them than any other kind of museum collection.

Furniture usually consists of more than one kind of material;

many pieces are composed of a variety. A single item may be subject to damage or deterioration from several causes. A wood chair may have metal embellishments or fittings, decoration with paint or gold leaf, a seat of fabric and cushioning of yet another material. Because there can be so many kinds of material in a single piece of furniture, additional care and handling suggestions may be found in other chapters.

Examine carefully before moving — Examine carefully a piece of furniture before moving. Most objects which have found their ways into a museum have undergone some restoration of elements or replacement of parts or surfaces. If records of past repairs do not exist, try to determine the extent and nature of what may have weakened the structure of the piece. Compensate for structural weaknesses when handling.

Record findings — Look for conditions. If a damage or weakness appears to be new or progressive, consult a conservator before moving. Record observations and report them so they may become a part of permanent records.

Move pieces singly with two men — Move only one piece of furniture at a time. Never stack one piece on top of another when moving furniture or storing it. All furniture should be carried by two men. Large, heavy pieces may require more than two men when they are to be lifted but the smallest chair or table should never be carried by one man. Never

Do not push — push a piece of furniture across the floor, even if it is equipped with rollers or casters.

Never lift by projecting part or decorative element — Never lift a chair by its arms or by its back. Two men are necessary to lift chairs by their seats so that weight will be evenly distributed. Never lift a piece of furniture by a projecting part, the overhang of a table, drawers, galleries or finials. Projections and decorative elements were never intended to bear the weight of the piece. Always lift furniture by its lower members or seats so that the greater weight is above the grasps.

Do not rest on top — Do not turn a piece of furniture over so that it rests on its top side unless a conservator or antique furniture expert has advised the position because of weakened or missing legs or some other precarious condition.

Secure doors and drawers — To prevent movement and possible damage in transit, tie unlocked doors and drawers in place before transfer. Move drawers separately if the furniture is heavy, in poor condition, or if joints are loose. Never use harsh, coarse rope or twine. A soft cloth tape

260

will not damage surface finishes, but ropes and twines scar surfaces, *Use soft*
cause abrasions, and can cause dents in some woods and surface *cloth tape*
finishes.

Do not allow hands to come in contact with upholstered areas. *No hands on*
Fabrics used for upholstering are easily soiled by damp, grimy *upholstery*
hands. Deposits from hands are difficult to remove. To clean a
piece of upholstery, ideally it should be removed from the furniture. This is often a tedious, precarious job. The textile may be
the original upholstery and impossible to replace.

Remove marble and other removable tops, such as protective *Move tops*
glass, from tables, cabinets and other furniture before moving. *separately*
Tops should be moved separately. Protect them from scratches by
cushioning them on a hand truck with furniture pads. When lifting
a top off, tilt it on edge.

Remove finials and all other removable decorative elements if *Remove and*
detachable. If not removed, they may otherwise fall off, get broken, *wrap*
become scratched or lost. Wrap them in soft cotton cloth or some *detachable*
other unabrasive material for separating. Do not put them in drawers, *elements*
where they may become scarred or broken during movement.

Extend extra care to those decorative ornaments which cannot *Pad attached*
be detached. Pad them carefully before moving the piece. Decora- *ornaments*
tive areas and ornamentations are subject to damage from applied
pressure or sudden shocks.

Abnormal pressure and weight stresses should be avoided. Much
depends on age and condition, but some parts of furniture cannot
withstand unnatural positions and pressures. Feet and bases of *Compensate*
cabinets, chests and tables, legs and arms of chairs and tables *for structural*
should be guarded particularly. Even if repairs or replacements are *weaknesses*
known, compensate for natural structural weaknesses in the design.
If all such parts are regarded as potentially dangerous, much grief
can be avoided.

If damage occurs during the transfer or cleaning of furniture, *Preserve*
report it immediately and follow up with a written report. If parts *detached parts*
or fragments become detached, preserve them carefully for future *and report*
repair.

A flat-bedded truck or dolly is suitable for moving most sizes *Avoid*
and shapes of furniture within the museum. Never allow a piece *extension*
to extend beyond the edges of the conveyance. *beyond truck*

It is sometimes safer to lash furniture to a hand truck. If so,

Secure furniture to truck use soft cloth tape. If it is a small piece, one man can move the hand truck safely, if the floor is level. Generally, it is a better rule to have two men accompany it, especially if the furniture piece is heavy and unwieldly, the floor not level, or if it involves loading onto an elevator.

Keep stored furniture covered Objects exposed to dirt require frequent housekeeping. When upholstered furniture is not on exhibition, keep upholstered areas protected with dust covers. Use clean cloth, acid-free tissue paper or glassine paper. Actually the entire piece of furniture should be covered for maximum protection. Dust also damages the surface of wood, but too frequent dusting and cleaning are potentially *Do not use plastic covers on lacquer* harmful. Do not use plastics on lacquered surfaces.

An unhealthy atmosphere fosters damage by wood-feeding insects. Insects can damage furniture extensively in a short period of time if atmospheric conditions are not corrected and insects not *Inspect regularly for insects* eliminated. Inspect furniture regularly: back, underneath, drawers, crevices, interiors and plywood backboards. The presence of a light colored powder may be the first indication of attack by wood-feeding insects. To guard against insects and dry rot in wood exposed to outside elements, a fungicide such as Cuprinol may be used. Termites are the most devastating of the pests and work fastest. Furniture beetles are almost as damaging: their life *Fumigate regularly* cycle may run two years. The only way to control insect activity and prevent their destruction of wood is to fumigate regularly.

Haphazard cleaning and polishing damage patina Cleaning and restoration of antique furniture must be done gently to avoid damaging the patina. Consult an authority. Unless there is a thorough knowledge of the material, more harm than good can come from haphazard methods of polishing and cleaning.

Do not wax oiled woods Wax should not be applied to oiled woods. If applied to an oiled surface, it becomes sticky. Unless the wood is stripped of its coatings, it is impossible to return to an oil-treatment care.

Apply oil sparingly Do not use heavy oil on oil finished furniture. After an oil application, remove all excess to prevent a sticky buildup. Some authorities recommend a light furniture oil without wax. Apply it once a month and clean surfaces once a year with a mild detergent followed by a sparse application of light oil with "rotten stone." Rub it well into the surface of the wood, let stand for an hour or two and then remove excess oil with a soft, clean cloth.

The care of teak and walnut is about the same. Teak is almost

262

indestructible and walnut is also quite durable and tough. Both are relatively porous. Oak is the sturdiest of all woods. *Teak and walnut are durable*

Oak is sturdy

Rosewood demands special care, since it is denser and will not absorb as much oil. Even with a lacquer surface, it can be protected with a light coat of furniture oil. This is comparable to putting wax over the paint on an automobile. Oiled rosewood should have all excess oil wiped away to prevent a buildup of film which is damaging to the surface when dust accumulates. *Rosewood demands special care*

Lost drawer pulls and other hardware should be replaced with duplications of the originals if possible. Hardware substitutions decrease the value of antique furniture, but quite authentic-looking substitutes are available. The date of manufacture is obvious to the trained eye. Damaged, dented original hardware is preferable. *Replace lost hardware*

Old hardware is preferable

Loose spindles on chairs and other pieces of furniture should be reglued immediately to prevent breakage or loss. Replacements of spindles can be made by skilled cabinetmakers or woodworkers. The same kind of wood should be used and the finish should be matched. The value of an antique piece is reduced in proportion to the number of spindles, rungs, legs, or other elements which have been replaced with newly fashioned substitutes. *Spindles*

Keep replacements to minimum

Loose legs and rungs should be reglued immediately. Consult a conservator about the kind of glue to use. If a turned piece does not fit into its joint easily, do not force it. Rungs and legs and other similar parts are usually solid wood. If a solid piece is forced into a weaker area, there will be damage or breakage. Excessive dryness causes members to become loose. If legs, rungs or spindles loosen, check atmospheric conditions, temperature and humidity. *Reglue turned parts*

Check temperature

Surface scratches on oiled pieces can be removed by rubbing a recommended oil into the surface with a cloth pad. Always rub *with* the grain. A finishing application of oil and a goodly amount of "elbow grease" will usually bring back the wood's patina. If wood is veneered, use extreme caution. It is easy to go through veneering by rubbing too hard or too long in one area. Deep gouges and dents should be referred to an expert. *How to remove scratches*

Do not attempt to repair or minimize damages on wood which has a lacquered finish. Lacquer is easily scratched. Unsuccessful attempts to deal with scratches on lacquered finishes often result in the entire surface having to be refinished. It is safer and less expensive to have a conservator do the work. *Consult an expert on lacquer*

Skilled furniture restorers can remove dents from veneered wood by using steam to bring the soft wood core under the veneer back into position. An expert can remove a dent so successfully one would never know it existed. If it is not done well, the color can be pulled out and the grain of the wood raised.

Burns present special problems. A scorch usually can be handled by rubbing it down with fine steel wool and oil and then restoring the wood tone with oil polish. If the surface is veneered, there is the chance that the burn has penetrated the veneering. An expert restorer can lift the burned section of veneer and replace it so skillfully that the patch is not visible.

Acid stains bleach color out of wood. Restoration of acid damages should be referred to experienced furniture restorers. Refer all major chair repairs to an expert who is experienced in this kind of repair work. Major repairs to chairs include restoration or replacement of seats, stretchers, legs, arms, arm supports, and crest rails. Beware of major repairs to veneered drawer fronts. These major repairs should never be attempted by an amateur.

It is important to determine if a piece has a lacquered finish before any repair work is done. The difference between a lacquered finish and a hand-rubbed, oil finish is sometimes difficult to determine. Teak rarely has a lacquer finish; walnut is sometimes lacquered. Rosewood, being very hard and dense and subject to expansion and contraction, is often given a flat lacquer finish. Any lacquer finish will scratch more easily than an oiled finish; treat it gently.

When wood remains in the wrong atmospheric condition, it dries out. Excessive dryness causes wood to crack and causes joints, rungs, spindles and legs to loosen. Dry wood deteriorates and causes desiccation of glue. This can always be attributed to atmospheric conditions or changes in temperature. Furniture decorated with marquetry or inlay is quickly damaged by dryness.

The most common form of wood deterioration due to atmospheric conditions is dimensional changes resulting from repeated or sudden changes in the atmosphere and relative humidity. Atmospheric changes cause wood to alternately absorb and give up moisture. Expansion and contraction across the grain cause wood to warp. If storage facilities are not air-conditioned, furniture should be kept in well-ventilated areas. Avoid direct drafts on all furniture

Restorers remove dents from veneer

Burns present problems

Refer acid stains and major chair repairs to expert

Before repair or cleaning, determine if surface is lacquered

Cracks, warping, and loosening of joints

Store furniture in air-conditioned rooms or well-ventilated areas

and all woods. A circulation of air is desirable, but direct drafts can be almost as harmful as excessive dryness. Strive for a relative humidity of about 55% for wood objects. *Desired RH*

If a drawer sticks, it should be eased out slowly, if possible. If it does not glide easily, there has been some expansion of the wood. This may be in the wood of the drawer itself, or the furniture into which it fits, or both. Drawers stick because of atmospheric conditions or changes in atmosphere. If the atmosphere is corrected in time, a drawer which would not glide will return to its norm and can be opened easily; do not force it. Once the drawer has been removed, a little beeswax on the runners helps it to glide. *Do not force drawers* *Beeswax helps drawers glide*

Many old rocking chairs were once straight chairs. Rockers were an afterthought when it was found that rockers would work on chairs as well as cradles. Those which have been added to a straight chair are seldom the same kind of wood as the chair. If the chair is a painted one, it is difficult to determine if the rockers were added. If rockers are replaced, they should be made of the same kind of wood as the chair. *Replace rockers with same wood as chair*

A painted chair no older than seventy-five years is almost certain to show signs of use and wear and be received in a dirty condition, especially if it is one of those sturdy seats which were made for use in a kitchen. It may have several coats of paint on it. In the process of cleaning and refinishing, many or all of the coats of paint may have to be removed. If the wood is found to be a fine hard wood, the chair should be restored with fresh paint so that it will be in its original condition, or as nearly so as possible, including stencil decorations, if any. An expert restorer can do this successfully if he is familiar with this type of chair. Sometimes complete stripping of the paint is not necessary even if stencil decorations are worn away. *Maintain original character in repairs*

BIBLIOGRAPHY

Albers, Vernon M. *The Repair and Reupholstering of Old Furniture.* Cranbury, New Jersey, A. S. Barnes Co., 1969.

Baker, Hollis S. *Furniture in the Ancient World: Origins and Evolutions, 3100-475 B.C.,* New York, The MacMillan Co., 1966.

Becker, G. "On the Examination and Estimation of the Natural Resistance of Wood to Termites," *Holz Roh-u. Werkstoff*, Vol. 19 (1961), pp. 278-290.

Bjerkoe, Ethel Hall. *The Cabinet Makers of America*. Garden City, New Jersey, Doubleday & Co., Inc., 1957.

Cescinsky, Herbert. *English Furniture from Gothic to Sheraton*. New York, Dover Publications, 1968.

Chippendale, Thomas. *The Gentleman and Cabinet-Maker's* Dictionary. London, 1754; revised eds., 1755, 1762.

Comstock, Helen. *American Furniture*. New York, The Viking Press, 1962.

Edwards, Ralph. *The Shorter Dictionary of English Furniture*. London, Country Life, 1964.

Grandjean, Serge. *Empire Furniture*. London, Faber & Faber, 1966.

Hayward, Helen (Ed.). *World Furniture: An Illustrated History*. New York, McGraw-Hill Book Co., 1965, 1967.

Hepplewhite, George. *The Cabinet-Maker and Upholsterer's Guide*. London, 1788.

Herberts, K. *Oriental Lacquer: Art and Technique*. New York, Harry N. Abrams, Inc., 1966.

Hughes, Therle. *Old English Furniture*, New York, Frederick A. Praeger, 1969.

Joy, Edward T. *The Book of English Furniture*. Cranbury, New Jersey, A. S. Barnes Co., 1966.

Lockwood, Luke Vincent. *The Furniture Collectors' Glossary*, reprint of the Walpole Society publication of 1913, Da Capo Press Series in *Architecture and Decorative Art*, Vol. 8, New York, Da Capo Press, 1968.

Margon, Lester. *Masterpieces of American Furniture*. New York, Architectural Book Publishing Co., Inc., 1965; New York, Hastings House Publishers, Inc., 1968.

Ormsbee, Thomas Hamilton. *The Story of American Furniture*. New York, The Macmillan Co., 1934.

Prax, Mario. *An Illustrated History of Furnishings from the Renaissance to the Twentieth Century*. New York, George Braziller, 1964.

Ramsey, L. G. G. and Comstock, Helen (Eds.). *Antique Furniture: The Guide for Collectors, Investors and Dealers*. New York, Hawthorn Books, Inc., 1969.

Richter, Gisela. *The Furniture of the Greeks, Etruscans and Romans*. New York, Frederick A. Praeger, 1969.

Sheraton, Thomas. *The Cabinet-Maker and Upholsterer's Drawing Book*. London, 1791-1794; New York, Frederick A. Praeger, 1969.

Verlet, Pierre. *The Eighteenth Century in France: Society, Decoration, Furniture*. New Haven, Conn., Yale University Press, 1967.

Winchester, Alice (Ed.). *Antiques Magazine*, and the staff of *Antiques Magazine*. *The Antiques Treasury of Furniture and Other Decora-*

tive Arts at Winterthur, Williamsburg, Sturbridge, Ford Museum, Cooperstown, Deerfield, and Shelburne. New York, E. P. Dutton & Co., Inc., 1959.

Wolsey, S. W. and Luff, R. W. P. *Furniture in England: The Age of the Joiner.* New York, Frederick A. Praeger, 1969.

15

Jewelry

Jewelry is unique among the decorative arts in that it must be handled and worn to be best appreciated. In a museum case, where most precious jewels are exhibited, they lose much of their intrinsic value, for jewels were designed to heighten the wearer's appearance; only on the human form can their fitness and splendor be displayed.

Whether they have survived as burial accoutrements interred with their owners as in ancient times, or as personal possessions which have come to our attention through pure chance, family sentiment, or recognition of their outstanding value, they reveal the customs of a people more intimately than any other craft.

The character of ornaments throughout their history has depended in great part on the supply of minerals, metals, and gems, but changes in style and taste may be attributed to religious beliefs, customs, and modes of dress. Although they give delight as objects of art, our emphasis is on their relation to costume and trends of fashion since these factors have so often determined their popularity and disappearance.

The wearing of personal adornments dates from the Stone Age, when the first cavewoman stuck a bright feather in her

268

hair. In primitive antiquity, adornments consisted of a tooth or a stone strung about the neck in the belief that it would ensure some magical power of protection. Such ornaments of shell and bone from the Neolithic period have been preserved. As proof of an advanced Chaldean civilization, the jewelry of Queen Shubad, who ruled in Mesopotamia around 3000 B.C., has been excavated by the University Museum, Philadelphia. Her elaborate headdress of gold leaves, lapis lazuli beads, and double-loop earrings still have sufficient appeal for contemporary women to want them copied in less costly materials.

The ancient Egyptians developed a high degree of skill in chasing and engraving precious metals to be used independently or as settings for gems. Gold and silver were both used in predynastic times, but silver ores occurred only in small quantities. Many handsome pieces, retrieved from long burial in tombs, feature gold open-work (a test of the craftsman's ability) and inlays of semi-precious stones, such as amethyst, onyx, chalcedony, carnelian, garnet, quartz, turquoise, and rock crystal. They were incorporated into settings of gold and other materials for rings, necklaces and broad collars, bracelets and anklets, which were worn by both men and women.

Faience (glazed earthenware) was also a favorite for beads because of its texture and color. ("Egyptian blue" has never been duplicated exactly by subsequent generations.) Indeed, even precious stones were prized mostly for their color and luminosity and were left unfaceted and often unpolished, sometimes retaining the irregularities of the pebble. With a wide choice of stones and advanced techniques, jewelry making reached its zenith in Egypt during the ninth to twelfth dynasties of the Middle Kingdom. At this time the magical quality of jewelry was particularly stressed. The wearer's superstition led to the production of amulets and ornaments of a religious nature, initiating a trend which became part of our European heritage. We can trace its progress through the Egyptian scarab beetle, the Mithraic emblem worn by Roman soldiers, the rosary of Christianity, and the modern traveler's Saint Christopher.

269

A link between the jewelers of the East and the emerging Aegean and European civilizations was the use of electrum, an alloy of gold and silver, which was used for jewelry and metalwork in Egypt and also in northern Asia Minor as early as 2000 B.C. Evidence is provided by the excavations at Troy of the "Treasure of Priam," which contained elaborate diadems, bracelets, earrings and pectorals. Naturalistic ornaments, such as open-work flowers set with lapis-lazuli and rock crystal, exercised great influence on fifth-century Greek jewelry and were ultimately the ancestor of much Italian Renaissance design. Granulated goldwork was also found in some of the Trojan treasures. This complicated technique was perfected by the Greeks, who were rivaled in this art only by the Etruscans. In its simplest form, it involves pouring molten gold into water to form small spheres of the metal as the liquid drops cool. Two thousand years later it reappeared as a popular feature of much Victorian jewelry.

Under the Roman Empire, gems as distinct from jewelry gained importance. Emeralds, pearls, and sapphires were held in particular esteem. Through trade with the Eastern Empire, Rome came into contact with the fabled wealth of the Orient, and the refined designs, originally derived from Greeks and Etruscans, became lavish and ostentatious. Rings were a popular item in Roman life. Under the Emperor Tiberius they were regarded as a sign of rank which only men descended from three generations of freemen were permitted to wear.

With the establishment of Byzantium as the capital of the Christian Church and the inheritor of civilized crafts, jewelry came increasingly under ecclesiastical dominance, and many treasures have been preserved because of this religious patronage. During this time and later in the so-called Dark Ages, the Teutonic and Celtic races that overran Europe after the destruction of the Roman Empire developed jewelry in zoomorphic patterns with a lapidary skill of an extremely high order.

As the European communities prospered, inevitably the desire for jewelled adornment increased. The growth of the

270

guild system with its rigorous enforcement of apprenticeship raised the craft to a high degree of technical efficiency. The great demand as well as the rise of individualism liberated the craft from the overriding dominance of the Church.

So universal was the vogue for jewelry as a status symbol in the late Middle Ages and Renaissance that sumptuary laws had to be passed regulating the amount of jewelry with which even the baker's wife could adorn her person. The Ordonnances of 1283 in France forbade the bourgeoisie from wearing precious stones, belts of gold or pearls, and coronets of gold or silver. Nevertheless, portraits of the period reveal that not only were necks, heads, ears, and arms heavily laden with every conceivable type of jewelry, but garments themselves were embroidered with pearls, precious stones, and metals. Moreover, the low-cut bodices and wide loose sleeves which came into style made a pendant or a necklace a decorative necessity in the mid-fifteenth century.

During the Renaissance, which is usually considered the fountainhead of modern jewelry, the revival of the antique gave the principal stimulus to late fifteenth- and sixteenth-century jewelers, who were particularly excited by antique cameos and intaglios. The art of cutting precious stones was spurred on in Florence by the Medici, who had a great fondness for intaglios. In the mid-fifteenth century, stones were usually cabochon-cut, but with improvement in the lapidary's art, faceted gems became more common. The four stones considered precious were the same as today—ruby, emerald, diamond, and sapphire, but not in the same order of preference.

Rings continued to be of primary importance to denote wealth and position. Throughout the High Renaissance thumbs were embellished with rings, often of very elaborate design. The second, third, and index fingers, upper as well as middle joints, were covered with rings. Since they were made in such great profusion, rings provide the major source for public and private collecting today.

In the intervening centuries before the French Revolution,

jewelry remained almost exclusively the prerogative of the very rich, but by the time of Queen Victoria's death quantities of jewelry in the most and least costly metals abounded. No woman was so poor that she could not afford a ring or a brooch. Actually, vast quantities of jewels, produced for less than grand occasions throughout the eighteenth and nineteenth centuries, have survived because of their lack of intrinsic value. Still, they are of interest to the collector because they were usually more sensitive to changes in fashion than the costly pieces.

Throughout the nineteenth century, France maintained its role as the most important country for the manufacture of jewelry, although ideas may have originated in Italy, England or Germany. In fact, English jewelry is usually better made than French, and English technical innovations were copied in France. The Art Workers' Guild (1884) and the Arts and Crafts Exhibition Society (1886) fostered a new kind of jewelry based on pre-Raphaelite doctrine.

Rapid changes of fashion, possibly artificially promoted, have marked the last half of the nineteenth century as well as the twentieth. In the 1860's, costume jewelry attained a popularity which it has never lost. Cheap ornaments with "pearls," "rhinestones," and "diamonds" were machine-made rather than hand-made, reflecting the growing industrialization and a less discriminating clientele.

The technique of mounting jewels on springs, perfected by the French jeweler Oscar Massin in this decade, coincided with the preference for those stones which showed off best in such invisible mountings, namely, diamonds. Another reason for the popularity of diamonds during this era was the opening up of the South African diamond mines, some of whose vast reseources were first offered on the Paris market in 1868. By their very nature they were destined to commercialize fine jewelry. With the introduction of the first mechanically made collet, an element of mass production replaced the artist's personal contact with his material.

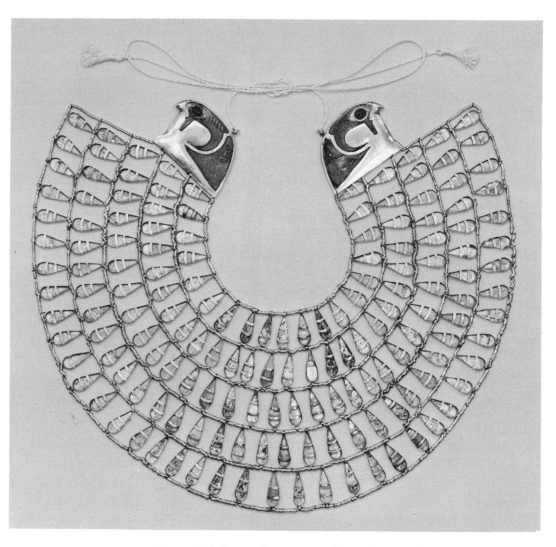

Figure 135. BROAD COLLAR WITH HAWK HEADS. Egyptian, XVIII
Dynasty. Gold. This dazzling gold collar is inlaid with carnelian,
lapis lazuli, and other precious stones. It was found with a great
treasure of jewelry, gold, and silver tableware, and exquisite
cosmetic equipment in the Tomb of the Three Princesses, minor
wives of Thutmosis III (Dynasty XVIII). *Courtesy, Metropolitan Museum of Art.*

Figure 136. NIKE EARRING. Greek, 4th century B.C. Gold. This
dramatic enlargement of a ¾ view of this rare and precious
jewel (which fits into the palm of one's hand) reveals the high
degree of perfection realized by the classical goldsmith. Every
minute detail—from the feathers on the goddess' wings to the
reins guiding the horse and chariot—are treated with infinite
precision. The museum is fortunate in possessing such a jewel,
which probably adorned a statue made of ivory and gold
thousands of years ago. *Courtesy, Museum of Fine Arts, Boston.*

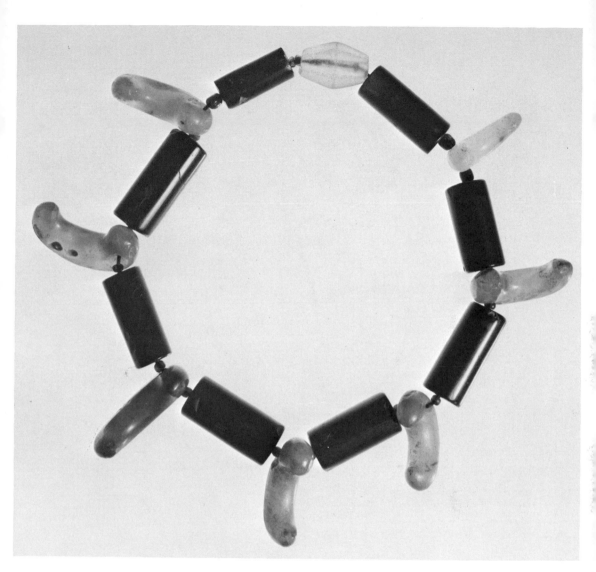

Figure 137. Necklace. Japanese, Tumulus Period, ca. 250-550
A.D. Jasper, crystal and glass.

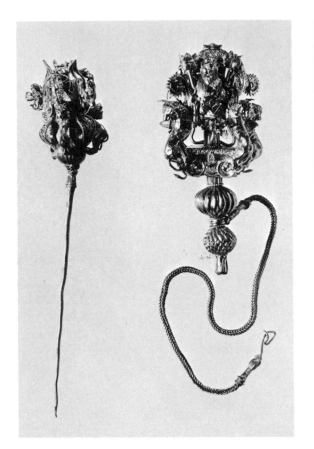

Figure 138. Two Pin Heads. Greek, 5th century
B.C. Gold. Enlarged drawing (right) by Suzanne
Chapman of pin head showing intricacy of work-
manship in classical Greece. *Courtesy, Research
Laboratory, Museum of Fine Arts, Boston.*

Figure 139. GOLD PINS. Etruscan, 6th century B.C. Gold. 1. shows pins in actual size; 2. which is a magnification (10 times actual size) of pin on left demonstrates proficiency of the early Etruscan goldsmith in the art of granulation. *Courtesy, Research Laboratory, Museum of Fine Arts, Boston.*

Figure 140. MEDALLION. Greek, Hellenistic, ca. 2000 B.C. Gold.
Courtesy, Los Angeles County Museum of Art.

Figure 141. A YOUNG LADY OF FASHION. Paolo Uccello, Florentine, 1397-1475. Tempera and oil on wood panel. Renaissance
jewelry was an integral part of the dress. Note sleeves embroidered with gold, pearl choker, shaved forehead, and hair
caught up in a jeweled headdress embroidered with pearls and
stones. *Courtesy, Isabella Stewart Gardner Museum, Boston.*

Figure 141.

Th'admired Empresse through the worlde applauded, Unto the eares of every forraigne Nation.
For supreme Virtues rares t Imitation :   Cannopey'd under powreful Angells winges
Whose Scepters rule fames lowde-voyc'd trumpet lawdeth, To her Immortall praise sweete Science singes
Are to be sould in Popes head Alley by Io Sudbury and Geor Humble.

Figure 142. QUEEN ELIZABETH. William Rogers after Isaac
Oliver, English, 1589-1604. Engraving. The fashion of completely covering body, costume, hair, etc., with jewels in the
Renaissance is well demonstrated in this royal portrait. Such
lavish display was obviously limited to the rich. *Courtesy, Museum of Fine Arts, Boston.*

Although the middle-class values of nineteenth century society did not provide a favorable atmosphere for precious jewelry, its manufacture continued in cheaper materials in larger and larger quantities. The quality is generally inferior to that of earlier work although there are certain notable exceptions.

The exquisite pieces of René-Jules Lalique (1860-1917) set the tone for a new mode of Gallic elegance. It bore the stamp of the current Art Nouveau style which preferred the irregularity of handcrafted pieces to the high finish associated with machine work. This international style, which allowed the greatest freedom to the artist's spirit, was also mastered by the firm of Fabergé in Saint Petersburg and by Louis Comfort Tiffany (1848-1933) in America. Unpolished metals, stones *en cabochon*, and encrustations of patina proclaim the surface unviolated by artificial means.

Between World Wars I and II, the focus of the jeweled arts moved from Paris to New York, as many European jewelers emigrated to the United States. One dominant factor which evolved was the use of platinum as a setting in place of gold. Indeed, the mass production of costume jewelry and the development of diamond-cutting constitute the major contribution of the United States, giving it a place with the great jewelry centers in Europe.

Just as we have learned a great deal about personal adornments of the ancients from vase paintings, illuminated manuscripts, and oil paintings, the future dating of articles of jewelry may well depend on fashion magazines and fashion designers' sketches. Informal clothes and a casual way of life has reduced the scope of the jeweler's craft. Certainly what is being produced today cannot compare with the magnificent examples of jewelry's finest hours in the past.

RULES FOR CARE AND HANDLING

Do not use cotton for storage or shipment

Do not package jewelry with packing or wadding cotton. Cotton particles adhere to the interstices and delicate surfaces of earrings, brooches, pins, pendants, necklaces, chains, and other articles of jewelry with open areas, moving parts, etc. Gem settings, for example, may be caught in cotton, loosened, and eventually be lost.

Wrap first in acid-free tissue or cloth

Wrap jewelry pieces in acid-free tissue paper, mulberry paper, or soft cloth, then in cotton padding for protection against travel shock.

Examine packing materials

Always carefully examine trays, boxes, and all packing material to make sure that no stones have become dislodged from their mountings or parts of jewelry detached. If time does not permit this, set the whole aside for later examination. Jewelry can be repaired or restored only if all parts are preserved. Replacement is a

Lost elements reduce value

poor substitute for the original, particularly in ancient pieces. It depreciates the historic and artistic value.

Unpack on padded tables

Unpack jewelry on padded tables. If any parts have become detached, they can be retrieved without damage if the unpacking area is padded. Jewelers often display items on velvet pads or in

Velvet table covers

velvet trays or boxes. Aside from the fact that the color and richness of the fabric shows jewels to advantage, the pile of velvet is protective. The cost of velvet table covers is well worth the investment. Velvet lasts a long time, even with much use. It takes years to wear the pile of velvet down to bare threads.

Store jewelry in closed areas

Solid pollutants suspended in the air—dust, dirt, lint, and dirt particles—are abrasive and can damage jewelry. Keep jewelry in closed cases or drawers in padded, individual bags.

Repair by expert

Do not attempt to repair or mend jewelry unless you are an expert. This is a specialized endeavor and should be entrusted only to reputable experts. Be sure your repair man is experienced and will not substitute gem stones of lesser value or quality. Conservators who themselves are not equipped to make repairs to jewelry should be consulted when repairs are done by someone outside the museum.

Items worthy of being in a museum collection usually are not of recent origin. Ancient jewelry should not be subjected to needless handling. Do not open and close containers unnecessarily or adjust the fastenings of jewelry. They must be protected against undue stress and strain. Never try on rings or other items of jewelry. With handsome or valuable pieces the temptation must be resisted, especially by females.

Never wear gloves when handling jewelry. The grasp is less secure for such small objects and threads from gloves may cause breakage or loosening of parts and stones.

Wrap and store separately each piece of jewelry even if it is a part of a set. A matching necklace, earrings, and bracelet should be kept together but not allowed to touch each other, for abrasions will result.

Carry only one piece of jewelry at a time. When moving specimens short distances, the piece should be gently lifted to a sturdy velvet-covered board or to its own storage box. The board should be large enough so that the piece is not near the edge. Pinning certain pieces such as a necklace to the board with noncorrosive T-shaped headed pins ensures their safety during movement.

Silver jewelry and jewelry pieces with silver parts should be stored in containers lined with tarnish-resistant cloth to inhibit the discoloration caused by reaction with sulphur compounds. Camphor placed in a container inside a storage or exhibition case will give some protection. Plastic bags protect silver from oxidation to a degree. Every effort should be made to prevent oxidation so that polishing is seldom necessary. With each polishing a bit of the surface is lost.

Bronze jewelry should be inspected regularly for "bronze disease." Pieces which have developed bronze disease should be removed and treated by an expert conservator. Bronze disease does not usually develop if the atmosphere is dry. Exposure to dampness should always be avoided with all metal jewelry.

Never attach tape or gummed labels to pieces of jewelry. These leave a foreign residue which is damaging to metals. Also, there is a chance that in removing a tape or label, an element of the jewelry will come away from the piece and adhere to the adhesive.

Identifying museum numbers must not be directly applied to jewelry pieces. No matter how small, they mar the beauty of jewelry and are often difficult to remove.

For example, affixing an identifying number to the back of a

Tags brooch is an unhappy procedure, for the backs of valuable jewels are often as intricately wrought and interesting as the faces. The only logical solution is small jewelers' tags equipped with a fine but strong thread for tying. Extreme caution must be exercised in attaching or removing them. This method has the disadvantage that tags may be lost from the pieces, but if records are complete, there should be no difficulty in identifying pieces. With or without tags,

Storage each piece of jewelry should have its own storage compartment within a storage case bearing the museum number.

Desired RH Maintain about 40% relative humidity for jewelry. High humidity fosters tarnish.

BIBLIOGRAPHY

Bradford, E. D. C. *Four Centuries of European Jewellery*. London and New York, 1953.

———. *English Victorian Jewellery*. London, Country Life, 1959.

Davis, Mary L., and Pack, Greta. *Mexican Jewelry*. Austin, Texas, University of Texas Press, 1969.

Evans, Joan. *A History of Jewellery, 1100-1870*. New York, Pitman Publishing Corp., 1953.

———. *Magical Jewels of the Middle Ages and the Renaissance, Particularly in England*. London, Oxford University Press, 1922.

Flower, Margaret. *Victorian Jewellery*. New Haven, Yale University Press, 1966.

Grancsay, Stephen V. "The Art of the Jeweler: A Special Exhibition," *Bulletin of The Metropolitan Museum of Art*, Vol. XXXV, no. 12 (December, 1940), pp. 211-220.

Hansford, S. Howard. *Chinese Carved Jades*. Greenwich, Conn., New York Graphic Society, 1968.

Hartman, Joan M. *Chinese Jade of Five Centuries*. Rutland, Vermont, Charles E. Tuttle Co., 1969.

Hoffmann, Herbert, and Davidson, Patricia F. *Greek Gold: Jewelry from the Age of Alexander*. (exhibition catalogue) Boston, Museum of Fine Arts, 1968.

Hornung, Clarence P. *A Sourcebook of Antiques and Jewelry*. New York, George Braziller, 1968.

Lesley, Parker. *Renaissance Jewels and Jewelled Objects in the Melvin Gutman Collection at the Baltimore Museum of Art*. Greenwich, Conn., New York Graphic Society, 1969.

284

Marshall, F. H. *Greek, Roman and Etruscan Jewellery.* (catalogue) London, The British Museum, 1911.

Pack, Greta. *Jewelry and Enamelling.* Princeton, New Jersey, D. van Nostrand & Co., Inc., 1961.

Rorimer, James J. *Medieval Jewelry—A Picture Book.* New York, The Metropolitan Museum of Art, 1944.

Rossi, Filippo, *Italian Jeweled Arts.* New York, Harry N. Abrams, Inc., 1957.

Steingraber, Erich. *Antique Jewelry.* New York, Frederick A. Praeger, 1957.

———. *Antique Jewellery: Its History in Europe from 800-1900.* London, Thames & Hudson, 1957.

Wood, R. W. "The Purple Gold of Tutankhamun," *The Journal of Egyptian Archaeology*, Vol. XX (1934), pp. 62-65.

16

Books

The aim of the first scribes was to give their writings permanent form. Accordingly, they chose to inscribe their messages on durable materials such as stone, metal, or baked clay. The earliest records we have are the inscriptions which the Chaldeans incised with a stylus into wet clay before baking. During excavations in Lower Mesopotamia, Dr. John Peters unearthed tablets in the ruins of the Temple of Nippur dating from around 6000 B.C.

A closer ancestor of the printed book is the Egyptian papyrus scroll of the Old Kingdom (about 3000 B.C.). Wound on one or two sticks, usually round, it replaced the more laborious method of writing on stone. The pith of the stems of reeds was cut into thin strips and laid in a criss-cross fashion, one layer horizontally and one layer vertically, pressed and let dry. Although papyrus had to be handled carefully and was quite absorbent, it proved to be a receptive surface for ink applied with a reed pen. During the second century B.C., improvements were made in the preparation of sheepskins and calfskins in the form of a roll for writings, but until the fall of Rome, papyrus was the common material for books.

Early books consisted of single sheets. The first separate

286

sheets were vellum and later, paper. They were folded once and gathered together by sewing through the central fold and were held together by sewing them onto flexible bands. To keep the sheets flat and protect them, early books were placed between thin boards. Later it was found simpler and more convenient to join the boards and the book.

The date of the first codices is unknown, but bookmaking came into general use in the ninth century with the advent of paper making. The Chinese claim the honor of discovering how to make paper by teasing out silk or vegetable fiber under water at the beginning of the second century A.D. The earliest examples which have come down to us date from within fifty years of this time and were discovered by Sir Aurel Stein in the Great Wall of China. Some of the paper was examined and found to be made of rags. It took almost a thousand years for knowledge of this invention to penetrate Europe; its progress through the Persian trade route can be traced via Korea (600 A.D.), Japan (610-625), Samarkand (751), Baghdad (791), Spain (1151), Italy (1216), France and Germany (fourteenth century), England (1494), Mexico (1575), and Philadelphia (1690).

The binding of separate sheets was a radical but convenient change from the earlier roll. By the time attractive coverings were added to the outer boards of books for protection, all essential principles of modern bookbinding had been established. The only important improvement is that, instead of single sheets folded once, large single sheets were folded many times, with the outer edges trimmed. Many different materials are now used for both text and binding, but the construction remains the same. Today, with modern bookbinding on a mass production scale, machinery performs all the operations formerly accomplished by hand.

The production and decoration of books was a dominant Medieval art. Bookmaking and the decoration of books flourished in France, especially during the thirteenth century; the University of Paris extended the art beyond the production of monasteries. The illumination of sacred texts, formerly done entirely by monks, became a lay craft during this time. Those who practiced the art were called *enlumineurs*, from which the modern word *illumination* originated.

Neverthless, interest in religious books did not wane. The following century realized the epitome of fine book decoration in Gothic manuscript illumination, from which we derive a great deal of our knowledge of the art of the epoch as well as the customs and dress of the peoples.

About the middle of the fifteenth century, the printing-press appeared in central Europe, eclipsing the art of illumination. As far as we know, printing with movable type was invented by Gutenberg of Mainz, Germany, independent of the Asian craft which had been practiced for hundreds of years. The number of books produced increased enormously. This rise in the production of texts caused a demand for more book-binders. Until this time, almost all bookbinding and a large percent of the texts and decorations had been done in monasteries. With the machine printing of books, the craft of book production was transferred to the establishments of commercial printers and binders, eventually causing a change in the entire character of the book in the following centuries.

For hundreds of years animal skins—vellum, leather—were virtually the sole material used for book covers. Their texture lent itself to decoration and ornamentation. Some were lavishly embellished with carved ivory and enamelling, encrusted with various metals or studded with precious jewels. Such elaborate bindings were usually for royal personages or were destined for religious documents. Unfortunately, many of these sumptuous coverings were later destroyed to reclaim their valuable metals and jewels, but some of them do remain in the safe-keeping of museums and churches. One of the earliest surviving examples is the seventh century Gospel of Theolinda in Monza, Italy. Gold tooling of leather was introduced via Venice from the East, where it had been practiced for hundreds of years. The new art spread to other European countries, where the

288

Italian designs were emulated. Designs in cut leather, stamping and repoussé were also popular.

During the last two centuries, the increasing demand for copies of works has caused speedier methods for the multiplication of books, and leather has become virtually obsolete for book covers, since the individuality of the animal skin does not lend itself to a large-scale automatic process. Thus, leather has been replaced by cloth, which can be produced in rolls for use on web-fed casemaking machinery.

In the past two decades of this century, mechanical bookbinding has improved. Technological developments in automation have enabled the mass production of books to meet the ever-growing demand for reading matter. Furthermore, from the nineteenth century on, wherever leather has persisted for bindings, its decoration could be done by machinery. However, an encouraging trend has been a recent renewal of interest in handcrafted bindings. For example, French bookbinding and cover embellishments became even more technically accomplished and elegant. In England, interest in bookbinding was revived, and its new techniques subsequently influenced the art on the continent and in the United States.

Precious bindings of recent origin, however, are few. Fortunately, an interest in fine binding and hand decorations has been encouraged by local, regional, and national crafts organizations. Outstanding examples of hand-bound, hand-decorated books are usually included in competitive crafts exhibitions throughout the country. Many of these displays are circulated nationally to other museums and similar institutions.

It is unfortunate that most modern books are not durable. According to one expert, new books are dying prematurely, while books published before the Civil War are still strong and healthy. Many books published since 1870 have become so brittle that they actually crumble when touched. It is said that the Library of Congress alone has over 50,000 decaying volumes despite the fact that it has a conservation department.

Experts trace the sad fate of modern books to cheap paper

and the public demand for inexpensive books. Formerly, a nonchemical rag paper was used. Today, paper is largely made by combining a chemical with ground wood fiber. This method results in the formation of sulphuric acid within the paper, making it almost self-destructive. William J. Barrow, a recognized expert on book restoration, maintains that almost every sheet of paper made in the United States since about 1850 is eating itself away at a rapid rate. He estimates the life expectancy of 99 percent of the books manufactured in this country between 1900 and 1930 is no more than twenty-five to forty years. This indicates that only 1 percent of the books printed during that period could survive the beginning of the next century.

Decaying, brittle books may be microfilmed for posterity. Many are being preserved thus by the Association of Research Libraries. The Association has received several grants for its work in investigating methods of preserving modern books. The appraisal of a book, as well as the reasons for preserving it, depends on its content as well as its form. However, the value of special limited editions, inscriptions inside books, the history of former owners and collectors, handsome bindings and decorations cannot be transferred to microfilm.

It is hoped that widespread attention will be directed to the serious matter of the preservation of books for future archives and that the importance of rectifying the present situation will stimulate publishers and paper manufacturers. One hope lies in fairly recent industrial experimentation in the manufacture of paper, which will make available a product with a life span of at least 2000 years. In the meantime, every care must be accorded books now in existence. All possible precautions must be taken for their preservation.

Figure 143. LINDAU GOSPEL (front cover). St. Gall, Switzerland, 9th century. Gold and precious stones. The illuminated manuscript of the four gospels, which this lavishly ornamented cover encloses, was written on firm vellum by several scribes in the Swiss monastery. The most beautiful book cover in existence, its safety and preservation is insured by being kept locked in a case in a vault. It is rarely on view to the public. *Courtesy, Pierpont Morgan Library.*

Figure 144. BREAKFRONT. English, ca. 1740. Mahogany. An attractive means of displaying as well as protecting precious volumes is this magnificent piece of furniture. To treat leather bindings, the British Museum has developed a leather dressing that is highly recommended. *Courtesy, Museum of Fine Arts, Boston.*

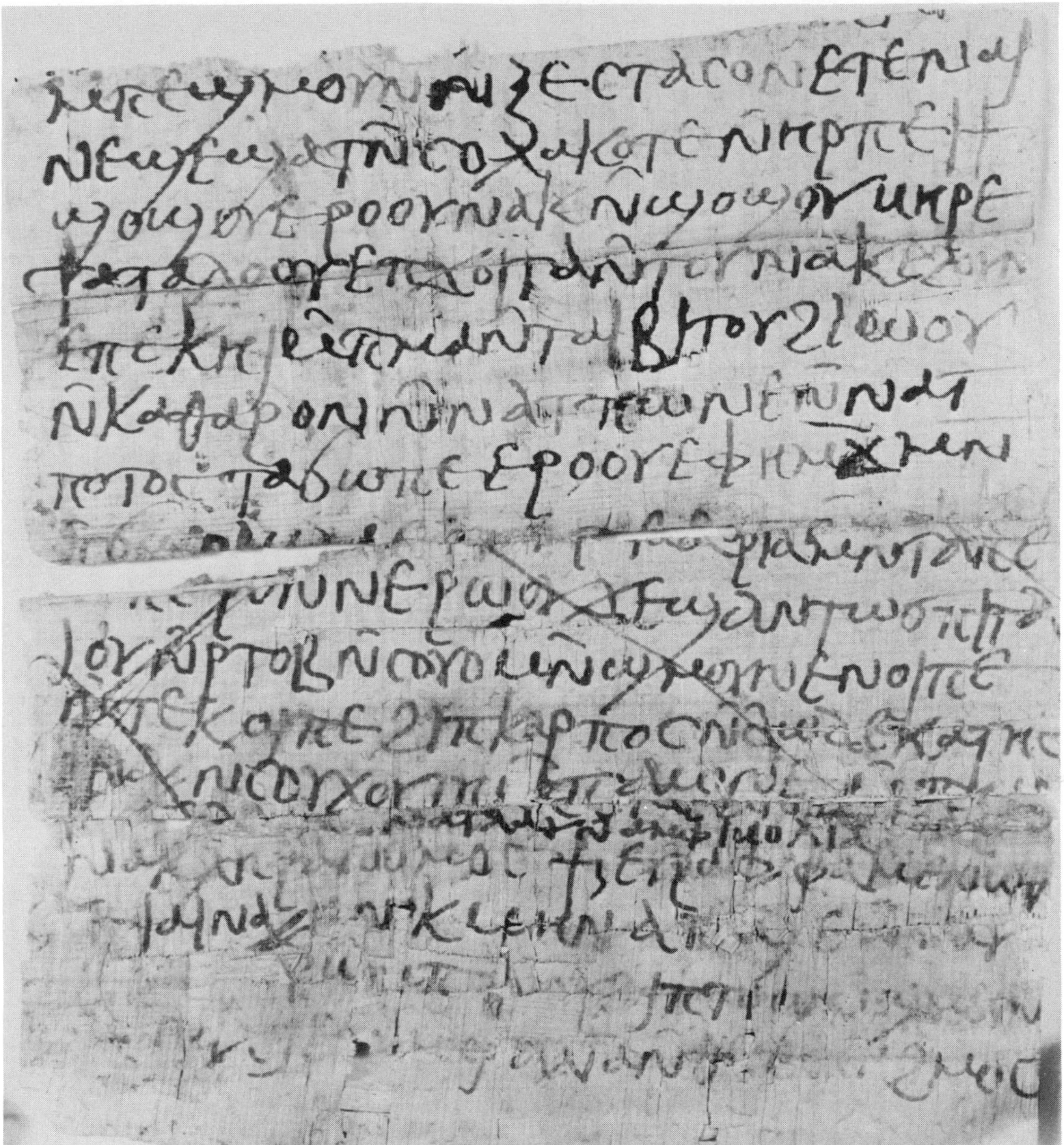

Figure 145. PAGE FROM A COPTIC MANUSCRIPT. Egyptian, 4th-5th century. Ink on papyrus. *Courtesy, Los Angeles County Museum of Art.*

Figure 146. PAGES FROM A PSALTER. The Netherlands, mid-15th century. Tempera and gold leaf on vellum. Hidden away in monasteries, such illuminated manuscripts have survived for centuries. *Courtesy, Los Angeles County Museum of Art.*

RULES FOR CARE AND HANDLING

*Circulation
of specialized
books should
be limited*

*Give
instructions
on handling*

*Extend the
same care as to
other museum
objects*

Most museum libraries are specialized in their collections. Circulation of books should be limited to staff members, qualified students, lecturers and scholars who are supposed to know how to handle them. Those who do not know correct handling and have access to fine museum volumes should be cautioned and be required to receive instructions from the librarian. Museum staff members should be offered periodic instruction courses.

When using or handling a museum library book, extend the same respect and care accorded to other museum objects. Many books in a museum's library are rare volumes; many have high values and are irreplaceable. All books have certain values; none of them should be abused.

Museums should adopt and enforce rules regulating the use, care and distribution of their library books. These ordinances should be rigidly and consistently enforced. This places the responsibility and burden on the head librarian.

*Handle like
unbound
works
on paper*

*Keep rare
books under
lock and key*

*Responsible
library
supervision*

Improper handling and use of a book can be as hazardous for its life and condition as other causes of deterioration. The treatment and care recommended for unbound works of art on paper should be demanded for the handling and use of books, rare volumes in particular. Rare ancient books are sometimes subjected to unnecessary handling out of curiosity. Valuable books should be kept under lock and key.

The best insurance against damage from human handling is responsible supervision, rigidly enforced rules and librarians who respect books and their preservation so much that they are not reticent about speaking up when they see a book mishandled. Librarians should be required, when necessary, to call attention to basic handling rules. This helps to prolong the life of books in a reasonably good condition.

It is curious that many museum people who know a great deal about safe handling of art objects and respect them do not know, or ignore, the correct way to open a book or how to care for it.

Basic rules are elementary, yet many people mistreat their own books.

Do not "crack" bindings. Never stack open books, one on top of the other. Do not place open books face down. Never stand books on their front edges; this causes the book to be forced open by its own weight, spreads the covers, crushes leaves and breaks bindings. *Do not stack open books*

When reading or thumbing through a book, turn the pages by the upper, outer corners. This prolongs its life. Never moisten fingers to turn a page. This dampens the paper and leaves a residue which stains any paper. Abuse and incorrect handling of books is unforgivable. *How to turn pages*

Do not attach paper clips, staples or pins to pages, covers or dust jackets. If books are received with paper clips or other metal devices attached to pages, remove them immediately before they cause further damage. Rust and corrosion of metals stain paper and contribute to deterioration, not to mention the unsightliness of rust stains on the leaves of a book. *Corrosion of metal stains paper*

Brown stains frequently appear on the pages of books, especially along the edges. Sometimes these spots of discoloration appear because of defects in the process of the manufacture of the paper, but more often they appear because temperature and humidity have been allowed to go beyond the safety limit. As with works of art on paper, this condition is referred to as *foxing*. Pulp paper develops discoloration more easily and quickly than rag-content paper but any quality of paper will develop foxing if temperature and humidity are not controlled. *Atmosphere causes foxing*

Never repair a tear with scotch tape, rubber cement, water soluble tape or pressure sensitive tape. The only safe way to mend a tear is with Japanese paper or Chinese rice paper, using rice or wheat flour for the adhesive. *Never repair with tape or cement*

Paper by its very nature is susceptible to damage from many causes. Pulp paper, the cheapest and lowest grade, is the most vulnerable. In the case of books, human handling ranks highest in causes of damage. The second greatest hazard is attacks by insects. Other causes are mold, mildew, extreme heat, dampness, water, sudden changes in temperature and relative humidity, strong light, sunlight and dust. Books should be kept dry and well aired, preferably in an air-conditioned atmosphere. *Paper is subject to deterioration for many reasons*

Keep books dry and well aired

297

ART OBJECTS

Mildew and mold

Dampness is food for mildew and mold growth. If relative humidity is high, the moisture content of paper rises, the paper swells and mildew and mold develops. Mold growth in or on books may be recognized as a grey, dusty substance, called *bloom*. Its color makes it easily recognized on dark bindings.

Paradichloro-benzene prevents mold growth

Paradichlorobenzine crystals in containers on book shelves helps prevent mold growth. If relative humidity is kept well below 68%, preferably below 65%, mold growth can be prevented. The relative humidity safety limit is about 50%; if allowed to drop as low as 45%, no serious harm will result unless this low range continues over a long period of time. Over dryness can be counteracted by reducing heat and increasing ventilation. Old, valuable, leather bound

Desired RH

books should be kept at 55% RH with a moderate circulation of air but no direct drafts.

Dampness and darkness cause fungi growth

Mold and mildew are fungi growths caused by dampness, warmth and darkness. If fungi growth appears on or in books it should be removed by professional book conservators. Mold can be removed with a fine camel's hair brush. This should not be

Isolate infected volumes

done in the presence of unaffected books. Infected volumes should be moved to another room before the mold is disturbed. The spores of the fluffy growth are easily scattered and difficult to control. In the process of removing mold, it is sometimes difficult for conservators to avoid rubbing spores into the tissues of paper or binding.

Fumigate books regularly except leather bound

Books should be regularly fumigated by a professional exterminator, experienced in fumigating libraries. When an entire library is fumigated, it must be remembered that parchment, vellum and leather, all protein materials, should not be present. These materials tend to harden during the action of some fumigants. Gaseous fumigation to sterilize a room containing mold-infested books is effective

Seal room

only if the room is thoroughly sealed.

Sulphur dioxide causes rot

The rotting of paper can often be traced to the action of sulphuric acid over a period of time. Sulphur dioxide in industrial areas is eventually converted into sulphuric acid which attacks a wide variety of materials. It can be partially eliminated with air-

air-conditioning helps

conditioning but even air-conditioned buildings should be fumigated. All sulphur in the air is from the burning of fuel. The powdery, decayed condition of some ancient book bindings can be traced directly to the action of sulphuric acid.

298

Unless the building is air-conditioned, do not store books in basements or establish libraries in basement areas. This is only asking for trouble. Any subterranean area tends to be damp, and dampness is harmful to books, affecting paper and bindings as well as the glue and thread which hold them together. *Do not store in basement*

Glues used in the binding of books become desiccated if books are kept near a heating outlet or in an atmosphere which is too warm. Sunlight causes the same condition. When glue becomes desiccated, bindings give way and the book soon becomes dilapidated. If the text paper also has been affected, rebinding may be tenuous or impossible. *Avoid heat and sunlight*

Leather bindings stain easily, particularly from moist hands. The older and drier the leather, the more subject to staining. Hands should be clean before handling books. To reduce damage, protect valuable volumes with dust jackets. *Hands stain bindings* *Protect with dust jackets*

When moving library books on a book truck or hand truck, fragile volumes and all volumes with delicate leather bindings should be wrapped with acid-free tissue paper. Limp, unstable books may require a piece of rag matboard to act as a stiffening before wrapping. *Moving*

Arrange books on book trucks so that there is no movement during transfer. Wadded, crumpled tissue paper can be used to fill in spaces and eliminate shifting. Padded, heavy bookends are even better. They can be used again and again. Do not "pack" books on book trucks. *Arrange transfers to minimize movement*

Damaged, deteriorated books are very special problems. The restoration of them is a highly scientific, technical process. Like a human patient, book ailments must be diagnosed to determine the exact nature of them and how serious or progressive the disease is. In Rome, half a block from St. Peter's Square, the Institute for the Restoration of Books, Churches and Paintings is operated by its founder, Father Pinzuiti, and has gained world wide fame for restoring rotting, molded, disintegrated books, manuscripts and documents. Combining a knowledge of chemistry with a love of art and the desire to preserve old documents, Father Pinzuiti has achieved amazing results by grafting thin linen or silk sheets, interweaving them with old fibers so skillfully that they can scarcely be seen. A Montreal woman, Mrs. Liseotte Stern, who learned her profession of "master bookbinder" in her native Germany more than thirty-five years ago, gives new life to books which look *Consult a specialist for restoration* hopelessly beyond restoration. Mrs. Stern does most of her work for McGill University's Osler and Redpath Libraries.

Master book doctors are few in number. Their services are costly but justifiable. Knowledge, care and respect for books by those who use them would all but eliminate the need for book restorers.

BIBLIOGRAPHY

Archer, John and Lydenberg, H. M. *The Care and Repair of Books.* 4th rev. ed. New York, R. R. Bowker Co., 1960.

Armitage, F. D. *Atlas of Paper-Making Fibres.* Epsom, England, Guidhall Publishing Co.

Barrow, William J., Research Laboratory. *Permanence/Durability of the Book—V: Strength and Other Characteristics of Book Papers, 1800-1899.* Richmond, Va., W. J. Barrow, 1967.

———, and Church, R. W. *The Manufacture and Testing of Durable Book Papers.* Richmond, Va., Virginia State Library Publication No. 13, 1960.

Bookbindings. London, Victoria & Albert Museum, 1963.

Church, Randolph W. (Ed.). *Deterioration of Book Stock—Causes and Remedies: Two Studies on the Permanence of Book Paper.* Richmond, Va., Virginia State Library Publication No. 10, 1959.

Cunha, George Daniel Martin. *Conservation of Library Material: A Manual and Bibliography on the Care, Repair and Restoration of Library Materials.* Metuchen, New Jersey, Scarecrow Press, 1967

Gawrecki, Drahoslav. *Compact Library Shelving.* Chicago, American Library Association, 1968.

Grant, Julius. *Books and Documents: Dating, Permanence and Preservation.* London, Grafton & Co., 1937; New York, Chemical Publishing Co., 1938.

The History of Bookbinding. Baltimore, Baltimore Museum of Art, 1957.

Horton, Carolyn. *Cleaning and Preserving Bindings and Related Materials.* Chicago, American Library Association, 1967, 1969.

Hunter, Dard. *Paper-making.* 2nd ed. New York, Alfred A. Knopf, 1947.

Kimberly, Arthur E. and Emley, Adelaide L. *A Study of the Removal of Sulphur Dioxide from Library Air.* National Bureau of Standards, Miscellaneous Publication No. 142, Washington, D.C., United States Government Printing Office, 1933.

Langwell, W. H. *The Conservation of Books and Documents.* London, Pitman Publishers, 1957.

Lee, Marshall. *Bookmaking: The Illustrated Guide to Design and Production*. New York, R. R. Bowker Co., 1965.

Orcutt, William Dana. *The Book in Italy During the Fifteenth and Sixteenth Centuries*. New York, Harper & Brothers, 1928.

Plenderleith, H. J. *The Preservation of Leather Bookbindings*. London, The British Museum, 1947.

Plumbe, Wilfred J. *The Preservation of Books in Tropical and Subtropical Countries*. Kuala Lumpur, Oxford University Press, 1964.

Putnam, G. H. *Books and Their Makers During the Middle Ages*. New York, Hillary House, 1962.

Tribolet, Harold W. *All the King's Horses*. Chicago. The Lakeside Press, R. R. Donnelley & Sons Co., 1954.

Watson, James. *The History of the Art of Printing*. New York, Gregg Press, Inc.; reprint, including a translation of Jean de la Caillé's *Histoire de l'Imprimerie*.

Weiss, H. B. and Carruthers, R. H. *Insect Enemies of Books*. New York, New York Public Library, 1937.

Wilson, William K. *Preservation of Documents by Lamination*. National Bureau of Standards, Monograph No. 5, Washington, D.C., United States Government Printing Office, 1959.

References

GENERAL BIBLIOGRAPHY

American Association of Museums Committee, Report of. "Packing and Handling of Art Objects," *Museum News*, Vol. 26, no. 5 (September 1, 1948), pp. 1-8.

American Federation of Arts Quarterly., Vol. 1, no. 4 (1963). (Entire issue devoted to the care and preservation of works of art and the problems of traveling exhibitions.)

Arnason, H. H. *History of Modern Art: Painting, Sculpture, Architecture.* New York, Harry N. Abrams, Inc., 1968.

Barail, L. C. *Packaging Engineering.* New York, Reinhold Publishing Corp., 1954.

Basic Museum Management. Ottawa, The Canadian Museums Association, 1969.

Bazin, Germain. *The Museum Age.* New York, World Publishing Co., 1968.

Boger, Louise Ade. *The Dictionary of Antiques and Decorative Arts.* New York, Scribner's Sons, 1957.

Bostick, William A. "What is the State of Museum Security?" *Museum News*, Vol. 46, no. 5 (January, 1969), pp. 13-19.

Braude, Felix. *Adhesives.* Brooklyn, New York, Chemical Publishing Co., 1943.

Brawne, Michael. *The New Museum: Architecture and Display.* New York, Frederick A. Praeger, 1965.

Bredius, Abraham and Roerich, N. "Des Dangers de Transport des Oeuvres d'Art," *Mouseion*, Vol. 15, no. 3 (1931).

302

Brown, A. W. *Insect Control by Chemicals.* New York, Wiley & Sons, 1951.

Burgess, E. Martin. "An Inexpensive Vacuum for Impregnating Small Friable Objects," *The Museums Journal,* Vol. 54, no. 5 (August, 1954), pp. 125-127.

Burr, Nelson E., compiled by. *Safeguarding Our Cultural Heritage.* Washington, D. C., Library of Congress, 1952.

Cameron, Duncan F. *Are Art Galleries Obsolete.* Toronto, Peter Martin Associates, 1969.

Carmel, James H. *Exhibition Techniques.* New York, Reinhold Publishing Corp., 1962.

Coleman, Laurence Vail. *Museum Buildings.* Washington, D. C., American Association of Museums, 1950.

Constable, W. G. "Curatorial Problems in Relation to Conservation," *Museum News,* Vol. 24, no. 9 (November 1, 1946), pp. 6-8.

———. "Curators and Conservation," *Studies in Conservation,* Vol. I, no. 3 (April, 1954), pp. 97-102.

Cox, Trenchard. *Pictures, Handbook for Museum Curators.* London, The Museums Association, 1956.

Daifuku, H. "Collections: Their Care and Storage," *The Organization of Museums,* Paris, UNESCO, 1960.

Dudley, Dorothy H., Wilkinson, Irma Bezold, and others. *Museum Registration Methods,* revised edition. Washington, D. C., American Association of Museums and The Smithsonian Institution, 1968.

Fall, Frieda Kay. "New Industrial Packing Materials: Their Possible Uses for Museums," *Museum News,* Vol. 44, no. 4, Technical Supplement No. 10 (December, 1965), pp. 47-52.

Florian, M. L. *Investigation of Mold Material.* Special Report No. E 544, Ottawa, The National Gallery of Canada, October 7, 1960.

Gardner, Helen. *Art Through the Ages.* Revised by Horst de la Croix and Richard G. Tansey. New York, Harcourt, Brace & World, Inc., 1969.

Gettens, Rutherford J. "Polymerized Vinyl Acetate and Related Compounds in the Restoration of Objects of Art," *Technical Studies in the Field of Fine Arts,* Vol. IV, no. 1 (July, 1935), pp. 15-17.

Graham, John, II and The Curatorial Department of Colonial Williamsburg. "Solving Storage Problems," *Museum News,* Vol. 41, no. 4 (December, 1962), pp. 24-29.

Greathouse, G. A. and Wessel, C. J. *Deterioration of Materials.* New York, Reinhold Publishing Corp., 1954.

Guthe, Carl E. *So You Want A Good Museum.* Washington, D. C., American Association of Museums, New Series No. 17, 1957, reprinted 1964.

Hodes, Scott. *The Law of Art and Antiques: A Primer for Artists and Collectors.* Dobbs Ferry, New York, Oceana Publications, 1966.

Horwitz, Minna H. and Stout, George L. "Experiments with Adhesives for Paper," *Technical Studies in the Field of Fine Arts*, Vol. III (1934), pp. 38-46.

Janson, H. W. *History of Art.* 2nd edition. Englewood Cliffs, New Jersey, Prentice-Hall, Inc., 1970.

Keck, Caroline K. and others. *A Primer on Museum Security.* Cooperstown, New York, The New York Historical Association, 1966.

Lanier, Mildred B. "Storage Facilities at Colonial Williamsburg," *Museum News,* Vol. 45, no. 6 (February, 1967), pp. 31-33.

Little, David B. "Safeguarding Works of Art: Transportation, Records and Insurance," Technical Leaflet 9, *History News* (American Association for State and Local History, Madison, Wisconsin), Vol. 18, no. 8 (May, 1963).

Longaker, Jon D. *Art, Style and History.* Palo Alto, Calif., Scott, Foresman, 1969.

Lucas, Alfred. *Antiques: Their Restoration and Preservation.* London, Edward Arnold & Co., 1924; 2nd ed. revised, 1932.

Mayer, Ralph. *The Artist's Handbook of Materials and Techniques.* New York, The Viking Press, 1946.

Mills, John Fitzmaurice. *The Care of Antiques.* London, Arlington Books, 1964.

Moore, Alma Chestnut. *How To Clean Everything: An Encyclopedia of What to Use and How to Use It.* New York, Simon & Schuster, 1961.

Mori, H. and Kumagat, M. "Damage to Antiquities Caused by Fumigants," *Scientific Papers of Japanese Antiques and Art Crafts*, Vol. 8 (1954).

Moss, A. A. "The Application of X-ray, Gamma Rays, Ultra-Violet and Infra-Red Rays to the Study of Antiquities," *Handbook for Museum Curators,* Part B, Section 4, London, The Museums Association, 1954.

Offner, Richard. "Restoration and Conservation," *Studies in Western Art, Problems of the 19th and 20th Centuries,* Vol. IV (1963), pp. 152-162.

Organ, Robert M. *Design for Scientific Conservation of Antiquities.* Washington, D. C., the Smithsonian Institution Press, 1969; distributed by Random House, New York.

Osborn, Elodie Courter. *Manual of Traveling Exhibitions.* Museums and Monuments Publication No. 5, Paris, UNESCO.

Padfield, T. "The Design of Museum Show Cases," *London Conference on Museum Climatology.* London, International Institute for Conservation of Historic and Artistic Works, 1967.

Pease, Murray. "An Institute for Museum Conservation," *Museum News,* Vol. 27, no. 6 (September 15, 1949), pp. 7-8.

Plenderleith, H. J. *The Conservation of Antiquities and Works of Art.* London, Oxford University Press, 1956.

———. *The Preservation of Antiquities.* London, The Museums Association, Chaucer House, 1934.

Pope, Arthur Upham and Ackerman, Phyllis. *A Survey of Persian Art.* New York, Oxford University Press, 1939.

Problems of Conservation in Museums. New York, International Council of Museums, 1969; distributed by Humanities Press, New York.

Robertson, Clement L. "The Visual and Optical Examination of Works of Art," *Museum News,* Vol. 46, no. 4 (December, 1967), Technical Supplement No. 20, pp. 47-52.

———. "A Museum Conservation Laboratory," *Museum News,* Vol. 45, no. 5 (January, 1965), pp. 15-21.

Rosegrant, Robert G. "Packing 'Problems' and Procedure," *Technical Studies in the Field of Fine Arts,* Vol. X, no. 3 (January, 1942), pp. 138-256.

Runes, D. D. and Schrickel, H. G. (Eds). *Encyclopedia of the Arts.* New York, Marlboro Books, 1969.

Savage, George. *The Art and Antique Restorers' Handbook—A Dictionary of Materials and Processes Used in the Restoration and Preservation of All Kinds of Works of Art.* New York, Frederick A. Praeger, 1967.

Silverfish. United States Department of Agriculture, Washington, D. C., U.S. Government Printing Office, 1957.

Snyder, Thomas E. *Control of Nonsubterranean Termites.* United States Department of Agriculture, Farmers' Bulletin No. 2018, Washington, D. C., U.S. Government Printing Office, June, 1969.

Sugden, Robert P. *Care and Handling of Art Objects.* New York, The Metropolitan Museum of Art, 1946.

Summer, W. *Ultra-Violet and Infra-Red Engineering.* London, Sir Isaac Pitman & Sons, 1962.

"Technical Recipes for Museum Work," *The Museums Journal,* October, 1930.

Thomson, Garry. "Impermanence: Some Chemical and Physical Aspects," *Museums Journal,* Vol. 64, no. 1 (June, 1964), pp. 16-36.

———. (Ed). *Recent Advances in Conservation: Contributions to the IIC Rome Conference,* 1961. London, Butterworth's, 1963.

UNESCO. *The Conservation of Cultural Property, Museums & Monuments XI.* Paris, UNESCO House, 1969.

———. *The Organization of Museums—Practical Advice.* Paris, UNESCO House, 1960.

Young, William J. (Ed.). *Application of Science in Examination of Works of Art—Proceedings of the Seminar: September 7-16, 1965* (Conducted by the Research Laboratory of the Museum of Fine Arts, Boston). Greenwich, Conn., New York Graphic Society, 1968.

———. (Ed.). *On the Scientific Examination of Works of Art.* (Proceedings of the Second Seminar at the Museum Of Fine Arts, Boston.) New York, October House, Inc., 1967.

TEMPERATURE AND HUMIDITY

Ahrens, Werner. "Controle et Réglage de la Température et de l'Humidité dans les Musées," *Mouseion* Vol. 25 (1934).

Bois, P. J. "Moisture Content in Homes" *Forest Products Journal*, Vol. 9 (1959).

Buck, Richard D. "A Specification for Museum Airconditioning," *Museum News*, Vol. 43, no. 4, Technical Supplement No. 6 (December, 1964), pp. 53-57.

Carson, F. T. *Effect of Humidity on Physical Properties of Paper.* National Bureau of Standards Circular No. C.445. Washington, D. C., United States Government Printing Office 1944.

Coremans, P. "Air Conditioning in Museums," *The Museums Journal*, Vol. XXXVI (1936), pp. 341-345.

Cursiter, Stanley. "Control of Air in Cases and Frames." *Technical Studies in the Field of Fine Arts.* Vol. V (1936), pp. 109-116.

Kennedy, Robert A. "Conservation in the Humid Tropical Zone," *Museum News*, Vol. 38, no. 7 (March, 1960), pp. 16-20.

Laurie, A. P. "Atmospheric Humidity and Works of Art" *The Museums Journal* (May, 1935), pp. 51-52.

MacIntyre, J. A. "Air Conditioning for Mantegna's Cartoons at Hampton Court Palace," *Technical Studies in the Field of Fine Arts* (April, 1934), pp. 171-184.

Mallette, F. S. (Ed.). *Problems and Control of Air-Pollution.* New York, Reinhold Publishing Corp., 1955.

Plenderleith, H. J. and Philippot, P. "Climatology and Conservation in Museums" *Museum*, Vol. 13, no. 4 (1960), pp. 201-289.

Rawlins, F. I. G. and Keeley, T. R. "Air Conditioning at the National Gallery, London," *Museum*, Vol. 7 (1951).

Ruskin, R. D. (Ed.). *Principles and Methods of Measuring Humidity in Cases*, Vol. I of a series, *Humidity and Moisture—Measurement and Control in Science and Industry*. New York, Reinhold Publishing Corp., 1965.

Saitch, H. "On Architecture and Moisture: Especially on the Moisture of the Storehouses of National Treasures," *Scientific Papers on Japanese Antiques and Art Crafts* (Tokyo), Association of Scientific Research of Antiques, Vol. I (January, 1951), pp. 49-54.

Sander, Harold J. and Colwell, Ralph E. "An Electric Heat Pump for All Year Heating and Cooling," *Library Journal*, Vol. 79, no. 22 (1954), pp. 2433-2434.

Solomon, M. E. "Control of Humidity with KOH, H_2SO_4 and Other Solutions," *Bulletin of Entomological Research*, Vol. 42 (1951).

Some Notes on Atmospheric Humidity in Relation to Works of Art.

London, Courtauld Institute of Art, University of London, 1934.

Stolow, Nathan. *Controlled Environment for Works of Art in Transit.* London, Butterworth's, 1966; published for the International Centre for the Study of the Conservation of Cultural Property.

Thomson, Garry. "Impermanence: Some Chemical and Physical Aspects," *The Museums Journal,* Vol. 64, no. 1 (June, 1964), pp. 16-36.

———. (Ed.). *1967 London Conference on Museum Climatology.* London, International Institute for Conservation of Historic and Artistic Works, 1968.

Thring, M. W. (Ed.). *Air Pollution.* London, Butterworth's, 1957.

MUSEUM LIGHTING

Balder, J. J. *The Discoloration of Colored Objects Under the Influence of Daylight, Incandescent Lamplight, and Flourescent Lamplight.* Leiden, The Netherlands Museum Association, 1956.

Bloch, Milton J. "Lighting," *Museum News,* Vol. 47, no. 5 (January, 1969), pp. 20-29.

Feller, Robert L. "Control of Deteriorating Effects of Light on Museum Objects," *Museum,* Vol. XVII, no. 2 (1964), pp. 57-98.

———. "The Deteriorating Effect of Light on Museum Objects," *Museum News,* Vol. 42, no. 10, Technical Supplement No. 3 (June, 1964), pp. i-viii.

Harrison, Laurence S. *Report on the Deteriorating Effects of Modern Light Sources.* New York, The Metropolitan Museum of Art; *Illuminating Engineer,* 48: 253, 1954.

Illuminating Engineering Society. *Lighting Handbook.* 4th ed. New York, 1966.

International Lighting Review. Vol. 15 (1964), published by Stichting Prometheus, Amsterdam; entire issue devoted to museum lighting.

Kelly, Richard, "Museum Lighting," *Museum News,* Vol. 37, no. 3 (May, 1959), pp. 16-19.

Richter, G. A. "Relative Permanence of Papers Exposed to Sunlight," *Industrial and Engineering Chemistry,* Vol. XXVII (1935), pp. 177-185.

Use of Fluorescent Lighting in Museums. Paris, International Council of Museums, UNESCO House, 1953.

Wall, Alexander J, Jr. "In Search of Light," *The New York Historical Society Quarterly Bulletin,* Vol. XXII, no. 4 (October, 1938), pp. 107-124.

307

LIST OF ILLUSTRATIONS

NOTE: Dates of ancient works given here and in the captions   309
have been supplied by the museums owning the works.

PHOTOGRAPHIC CREDITS

Colonial Williamsburg Foundation figs. 5, 80, 115, 124

Cooper-Hewitt Museum of Design, Smithsonian Institution figs. 111, 112, 120, 126, 127

Fine Arts Gallery of San Diego and The Conservation Center, Los Angeles County Museum of Art fig. 11

Fogg Art Museum, Harvard University figs. 32, 38
—Louise E. Bettans Fund fig. 20
—Samuel C. Davis Bequest fig. 58
—Gift of Charles E. Dunlap fig. 24
—Alpheus Hyatt Fund Purchase fig. 35
—Prichard Fund Purchase fig. 19
—Bequest of Belinda Randall fig. 30.2
—Gift of Mata and Paul J. Sachs figs. 16, 36, 39
—Gift of Mrs. J. Montgomery Sears fig. 23
—Bequest of Mrs. K.G.T. Webster fig. 41
—Grenville L. Winthrop Bequest figs. 13, 30.1, 78

Isabella Stewart Gardner Museum, Boston figs. 14, 55, 89, 141

Gemini G. E. L., Los Angeles fig. 25

John Woodman Higgins Armory, Inc., Worcester, Massachusetts fig. 73

Los Angeles County Museum of Art figs. 2, 7, 15, 18, 25, 52, 68, 69, 79, 88, 105, 123
—Anonymous Gifts figs. 50, 140, 145
—Los Angeles County Funds Donated by Anna Bing Arnold fig. 43
—The Mr. and Mrs. Allan C. Balch Collection figs. 45, 57, 61, 65, 67, 84
—Conservation Center figs. 1, 29
—Contemporary Art Council Purchase in Memory of Hans de Schulthess, Photography by Seymour Rosen fig. 81
—Purchase with Costume Council Funds fig. 116
—The Colonel and Mrs. George J. Denis Collection fig. 132
—The Mr. and Mrs. George Gard De Sylva Collection fig. 51
—Gift of Miss Mary M. Edmunds fig. 60
—Gift of Mr. and Mrs. John Jewett Garland fig. 114.1
—Gift of Mr. and Mrs. David Gensburg fig. 27
—Gift of J. Paul Getty fig. 122
—The William Randolph Hearst Collection figs. 12, 62, 77, 82, 86, 109, 110, 119, 121, 146
—Gift of Mr. and Mrs. Arthur Hornblow, Jr. fig. 131
—Gift of Marie Hughes fig. 70
—Gift of Miss Bella Mabury fig. 125

—Gift of Harry Masser fig. 102
—Museum Purchases figs. 48, 71, 113, 137
—Gift of Mrs. Josephine Bay Paul fig. 118
—Gift of Mrs. Aldrich Peck fig. 114.2
—The Pfaffinger Foundation fig. 66
—Gift of Winthrop Rockefeller fig. 49
—Gift of Mr. and Mrs. William T. Sesnon, Jr. fig. 64
—Gift of Walter Stein fig. 33

Priscilla Lucier, Boston fig. 37

The Metropolitan Museum of Art, New York figs. 117, 130
—Bequest of Benjamin Altman fig. 75
—Gift of George Blumenthal fig. 94
—Harris Brisbane Dick Fund figs. 26, 31
—Fletcher Fund figs. 74, 135
—Michael Friedsam Collection fig. 6
—Gift of J. Pierpont Morgan fig. 97
—Gift of Mr. and Mrs. Herbert N. Straus fig. 34

Pierpont Morgan Library, New York fig. 143

Museum of Fine Arts, Boston figs. 17, 21, 42, 56, 104, 129
—Research Laboratory figs. 3, 4, 8, 9, 10, 28, 44, 54, 128, 139
—Frederick Brown Fund and H. E. Bolles Fund fig. 92
—Centennial Purchase Fund fig. 93
—Helen and Alice Colburn Fund fig. 95
—Gift of Miss Martha Codman fig. 134
—Horatio G. Curtis Fund fig. 142
—Gift of Mrs. W. Scott Fitz fig. 91
—William Amory Gardner Fund fig. 40
—Gift of Miss Hope Gray in memory of Samuel S. Gray fig. 133
—Gift of Mrs. William Hewson fig. 144
—Gift of Jonathan Joseph fig. 103
—Arthur Mason Knapp Fund fig. 85
—Helena Woolworth McCann Collection fig. 63
—William E. Nickerson II Fund fig. 96
—Richard C. Paine Fund fig. 59
—C.P. Perkins Collection fig. 138
—H.L. Pierce Fund figs. 76, 87, 136
—Gift of Charles Cobb Walker fig. 101
—William Francis Warden Fund figs. 46, 53, 83
—Harvey Edward Wetzel Fund fig. 47
—Adelia Cotton Williams Fund fig. 72

Clements L. Robertson, Conservator, City Art Museum of St. Louis fig. 22

Steuben Glass, New York figs. 106, 107, 108

Collection of the Author figs. 90, 98, 99, 100

INDEX

ERRATA

page 36: Ruheman *should be* Ruhemann

page 61, Beck: Performance *should be* Permanence

page 63, line 7: gauges *should be* gouges

page 83: Auvil, Kenneth *should be* Auvil, Kenneth W.; Azechi, Umetara *should be* Azechi, Umetaro

page 118: Charleston, Rober J. *should be* Charleston, Robert J.

page 133, Carter: *title is* Four Thousand Years of China's Art

page 134: Willette *should be* Willetts

page 134, Yamasaki: Vol. XXX *should be* Vol. XXV

page 165, line 25: Malloran *should be* Mallowan

page 242, line 24: sheets or *should be* sheets of

page 244, Greene: pp. 11-16 *should be* pp. 1-16; Turkham *should be* Turkhan

page 266, Chippendale: Dictionary *should be* Directory (ital.)

page 266: Hayward, Helen *should be* Hayward, Helena; Prax *should be* Praz

page 302, Bredius: *title should be* "Les Dangers..."; *citation should be* Vol. 5, no. 3 (1931), pp. 75-76

page 305, Rosegrant: pp. 138-256 *should be* pp. 138-156

fig. 2, line 2: Tony Smith *should be* David Smith

fig. 7, lines 7-8: *should be* ...was secured in this frame by only four straps when it was shipped

fig. 13, line 8: scrumbles *should be* scumbles

fig. 14, lines 15-16 (rt. col.): *should be* Paolo Uccello's *A Young Lady of Fashion* (fig. 141)

fig. 17, line 1: Meseika *should be* Mesheika

fig. 25, line 2: Nicolas Krushenick *should be* Nicholas Krushenick

fig. 26, line 2: 1494 *should be* 1444

fig. 38: this is a drawing, not a print

fig. 48, lines 1-2: Gozanza *should be* Gazanze

fig. 51, line 1: *title is* Arabesque Ouverte sur la Jambe Droite, la Bras Gauche en Avant, Deuxième État

fig. 71: dating of this piece has been revised from Kamakura Period to Nanboko-cho Period

fig. 76, line 2: *should be* early 5th century B.C.

figs. 85, 86: numbers are reversed on the ills.; large plate at bottom is by Palissy

fig. 90, line 4: black outline does not show in the printed illustration

fig. 118, line 3: *should be* This photograph was made before permanent installation in a gallery.

fig. 127, line 2: Black printed *should be* Block printed

fig. 140, line 1: ca. 2000 B.C. *should be* ca. 3rd century B.C.